Julia Margaret Cameron

Lewis Carroll

Francis Bedford

Henry Holiday

Henry Peach Robinson

The Pre-Raphaelite Camera ❧ ASPECTS OF VICTORIAN PHOTOGRAPHY

The Pre-Raphaelite Camera ❧ ASPECTS OF VICTORIAN PHOTOGRAPHY

Michael Bartram

A New York Graphic Society Book

Little, Brown and Company   Boston

For Jessie

Author's Note

Abbreviations. The following abbreviations have been used in the captions and the notes:

AJ	*Art-Journal*
Ath	*Athenaeum*
BJ	*British Journal of Photography*
PJ	*Photographic Journal*
PN	*Photographic News*
QR	*Quarterly Review*

The years of volumes are only given where the volumes overlap calendar years.

Annotation. This has been partially limited so as to avoid cluttering the text. The reader will find that all photographic references, as well as other lesser known sources, have been given.

Dates. Photographs and paintings are dated according to their publication or exhibition, unless there is clear evidence that they were carried out in a different year.

Dimensions. These are given in inches and centimetres, height before width.

Photographic Processes. Leaving aside the daguerreotype, the most important technical distinction in early photography is between paper and glass (collodion) negatives. There were many variations on the paper and glass processes and in the paper used for printing. The entire process including negative and print is in many cases impossible to determine incontrovertibly. Rather than litter the photographic captions with question marks, I have decided with one or two exceptions, to limit the descriptions to the basic negative type: that is, to what can readily be ascertained and what (as the text makes clear) was most important aesthetically.

Retouching. Original spots and blemishes have been left unretouched. This is important since the refusal to retouch on the part of some photographers was an early manifestation of photographic purism.

Acknowledgments

I would like to thank the many people who have helped me since I began to investigate 'Pre-Raphaelite photography' some time ago. They fall into various groups. First there were those in the art and photographic world, and in various institutions who confounded the researcher's expectation of unanswered letters and hurried excuses by giving generously of their time and knowledge: Mary Bennett, Judith Bronkhurst, Julia Brown, Rupert Chapman, Philippe Garner, Arthur Gill, Howard Grey, Professor Margaret Harker, Mark Haworth-Booth, Robert Hershkowitz, Ken Jacobson, Bill Jay, Valerie Lloyd, Terry Pepper, Michael Rich, Pam Roberts, Helen Smailes, Mike Weaver and Christopher Wood. A second group of specialists allowed me to pluck threads from the tapestry of their knowledge and weave them into my own cloth: Carolyn Bloore on the early amateur photographers, David Cordingly on John Brett, James Dearden on Ruskin, Richard Morris on John Dillwyn Llewelyn, Roger Taylor on George Washington Wilson. Without the encouragement and random insights of friends the book would have been much the worse: Bill Feaver, Andrea Rose, Valerie Taylor, Diana Trainor, and in particular David Matthews who went over the text in the final stages. Finally, in a category of her own, my editor Caroline Zubaida who was an unfailing support and took on more than any author had the right to expect.

fig. 1
David Wilkie Wynfield
John Everett Millais (1862)
Collodion
$8\frac{3}{8} \times 6\frac{7}{16}$ in   21.3 × 16.3 cm
National Portrait Gallery, London

fig. 2
Ronald Leslie Melville, 11th Earl of Leven
Mrs Godfrey Clarke (1860s)
Collodion
$9\frac{3}{16} \times 6\frac{11}{16}$ in   23.4 × 17 cm
Scottish National Portrait Gallery

Library of Congress Catalogue Card Number: 85–40023
International Standard Book Number 0–8212–1595–7

First published in Great Britain by Weidenfeld & Nicolson

Designed by Simon Bell, assisted by Sheila Sherwen

First United States edition
New York Graphic Society books are published by Little, Brown and Company. Published simultaneously in Canada by Little, Brown and Company (Canada) Limited.

Printed and bound in Italy

Contents

Introduction

fig. 3
John Everett Millais
John Ruskin (1853–4)

Oil on canvas
31 × 26¾ in   78.7 × 68 cm
Private Collection

'Pre-Raphaelite Camera' – the phrase evokes mildly comical images: Dante Gabriel Rossetti's dogtooth check trousers protruding from beneath a black hood, or William Holman Hunt striding chin-forward across some barren tract, canvas and paintbox under one arm, camera and tripod under the other. These visions, in fact, coincided with events – more or less. Rossetti, at the height of his passion for Jane Morris, turned photographer for a day and posed her in his back garden in Chelsea; and, while Hunt never took photographs, a friend, living in Jerusalem at the time, used to go out to the hinterland with him and set up his camera alongside the artist's easel.

People have so often remarked that Pre-Raphaelite paintings look just like photographs that any proof of the painters' involvement with photography is bound to be interesting, especially since these photographic flirtations were often surreptitious. Those with the patience to hunt through the archives can find further evidence: that, for example, Ford Madox Brown had long conversations with the famous photographer of the Crimean War, Roger Fenton, and was employed for a time at Lowes Dickinson's portrait studio 'working up' photographs; that John Everett Millais from the mid-1850s onwards, relied more and more on photography for landscape backgrounds and portraits; that fringe Pre-Raphaelites were even more involved: John Brett was a keen photographer and Atkinson Grimshaw secretly painted over photographs. But anyone investigating the links between photography and the Pre-Raphaelites will sooner or later be distracted from this detective work by Victorian photography itself, and the remarkable influence flowing in the opposite direction – from Pre-Raphaelitism.

It is less intriguing that Millais, genius departed, used photography as an occasional crutch than that countless photographs of the time bear his imprint, so to speak: little patches of English ground culled from *Ophelia* or *Ferdinand Lured by Ariel*, where foxgloves and nettles, ivy and dockleaves, motionless, seem locked in secret combat. Looking further we find landscapes that recall Holman Hunt, where the bark of each tree and the rock fissure stand out like fretwork and where the air has been sucked dry so none can breathe; photographic Rossettis also, where the women have fashionable faraway eyes, flowing hair, and medieval gowns – even Mariana and the Lady of Shalott herself. This is the 'Pre-Raphaelite Camera': the infusion of photography itself with Pre-Raphaelite spirit.

Talk of a 'spirit', which might seem at first too vague, is justified since the Pre-Raphaelite Movement has defied all attempts to erect it as a cleanly cut art-historical edifice. It was a mood or an impulse which evolved, took on a variety of shapes, and of its very nature wafted into unlikely corners: the decorative arts, fashion – and photography. The facts are well known. The original Pre-Raphaelite Brotherhood was formed in 1848 by Hunt, Millais, the Rossetti brothers, and the obscurer James Collinson, Thomas Woolner and F. G. Stephens. There was a brief period of unanimity. The Brethren agreed that what was taught at the Academy was arid and what was annually exhibited there was trivial or vapid; the faults could be traced back to the tradition of Raphael; the new models should be the purer Italian 'Primitives' and above all nature itself. This 'truth to nature' was the great principle of their slightly elder contemporary, the critic John Ruskin, and this ambition above all cemented their purpose. Recognizing that he had been fortunate enough to find some disciples, Ruskin was before long complimenting the Brethren on their 'absolute, uncompromising truth'.

Meanwhile, Pre-Raphaelitism's rival, Photography, was dominated in its early days in Britain by top-hatted, frock-coated gentlemen amateurs who had little in common with the intense young Brotherhood. Fingers blackened by chemicals, though hardly dirtied by labour, they had more scientific than artistic pretentions. Yet they were equally obsessed by the truth, exultant at the literal accuracy that the medium seemed to guarantee them. 'Exactitude is the tendency of the age,' confirmed the photographic critic of the *Athenaeum* in 1856, and photography was the embodiment of that tendency. Every year it was better able to render 'the surface of objects, the frittered crumblyness of stone, the crisp wrinkles of tree-bark.'[1] Like the Pre-Raphaelites, particularly the new generation of Ruskin disciples who emerged after the original Brotherhood had disbanded, the photographers scoured nature for any scene that would show off their powers as conjurors of the intricate and the densely-textured: the wheatfield, the pebbled beach, the ivy-covered wall, the escarpment.

Pre-Raphaelitism itself was soon to evolve: by the 1860s, many art journalists were saying the Movement was a thing of the past – we go against contemporary perceptions by referring to the languid fantasies and looser technique of 'Rossetti-ism' (then in its heyday) as Pre-Raphaelitism. Nevertheless the label is now as securely attached to this later 'poetic' phase as to the 'prosaic' beginnings (this helpful but ultimately inaccurate distinction was Ruskin's). There was in any case a thread of continuity between the ideals of 1848 and the products of the Rossetti dream factory. Unlike the later Symbolists, Dante Gabriel Rossetti, Edward Burne-Jones, and their followers tempered their otherworldliness with passages of exceedingly lifelike detail: the stamens of honeysuckle, the strands of damask. Their poetic subjects were also an evolution of the romantic literary tastes of the young Brethren for medieval myth, for Dante, Shakespeare, and Keats.

At the point where Pre-Raphaelitism was merging from 'prosaic' to 'poetic', and was becoming, as it happened, more fashionable, photography began to harbour artistic aspirations and to look round for models in paintings. From then on its connection with Pre-Raphaelitism was less a matter of unconscious similarity of aim as of deliberate emulation. Socially, the photographic and Pre-Raphaelite worlds began to merge a little. The landed gentry still dominated establishment organizations like the Photographic Society and the Amateur Photographic Association, but there were now two other recognizable groups. There were quirky Dickensian entrepreneurs like Oscar Rejlander and Henry Peach Robinson who, without profound sensitivity to Pre-Raphaelitism courted success with photographs of soulful women and Tennysonian *tableaux*. (The *Athenaeum* critic had been

fig. 4

John Everett Millais
Ophelia (1851–2)

Oil on canvas
30 × 44 in   76.2 × 111.8 cm
The Tate Gallery, London

fig. 5

Henry Peach Robinson
The Lady of Shalott (1861)

Collodion, combination print
$12\frac{9}{16} \times 20\frac{5}{8}$ in   31.9 × 52.4 cm
From the collection of the Royal Photographic Society

Of all Victorian photographers, Robinson succumbed the most happily to the Pre-Raphaelite mood. Recalling the floating *Ophelia* of Millais, he selected another stricken heroine whose end was watery and fate emblematic. Later he came to feel that his composition (from two negatives) had been full of 'absurdities' though it had seemed necessary at the time to show that photographers could treat as well as painters the 'weird and wonderful'. [*The Practical Photographer*, 8, 1897, p. 358.]

right to predict that before long photography 'will copy mediaevally-dressed models better than the Pre-Raphaelite'. Rejlander and Robinson ran thriving studios stocked with exotic props and models whom the fastidious dismissed as 'prostitutes'. But their practical knowledge of the medium made them useful acquaintances of the second group: the cultivated, self-consciously artistic amateurs who often played host to Pre-Raphaelite painters. Julia Margaret Cameron, Lewis Carroll, Rejlander, the Rossettis, Arthur Hughes (to name a few) were part of a large social network permeated equally with a photographic and a Pre-Raphaelite enthusiasm.

'Pre-Raphaelitism,' wrote Roger Fry from an immediate post-Victorian standpoint, 'had leavened the cultivated society with an extraordinary passion for beauty.' Fry was writing with particular reference to Cameron (whom he admired more than any Victorian painter).[2] With her longing 'to arrest all the beauty that came before me'[3], she supremely infused the Pre-Raphaelite spirit into photography. She was not, indeed, Pre-Raphaelite if we are restricting the term to the hard edges and brilliant colours of the 'prosaic' phase of the Movement. But as she browbeat the famous into sitting for her ('You will have to do whatever she tells you', her friend Tennyson told Longfellow)[4] and exercised through photography her unusually sympathetic eye for female beauty, she followed the lead given by Rossetti. He had softened outlines and aimed at breadth and tonal consistency in the interests of inward vision. She softened focus to permit her inescapably realistic medium to penetrate, as she believed, to the inner person. She was not entirely alone. Other amateur photographers cultivated the creed of beauty with, as Fry said, 'all the energy and determination of a dominant class': the fancy-dress enthusiast, David Wilkie Wynfield, whom Cameron acknowledged as her only mentor; Lewis Carroll, for whom beauty was the face of innocence; and Lady Hawarden, whose images point to the claustrophobic passions of the closed circle.

Contemporary foreign photography also shared certain Pre-Raphaelite qualities. In landscape, for example, French photographers, like the British amateurs of the 1850s, clearly delighted in corners of woodland, while an American pioneer like Timothy O'Sullivan was as likely as a Briton to set up his equipment in front of a vertical rock face. But these parallels are at the same time immediately instructive. French photography had from the first a conscious grace and artistry lacking in Britain. Gustave Le Gray or Henri-Victor Regnault transformed a clearing in the woods into a delicate flickering web of light: what we would expect perhaps in the home of Impressionism, and very different from the hard textures and frozen organic patterns of the British photographers. O'Sullivan on the other hand chose his subjects for their remarkableness. The rock face would be huge or staggeringly novel in its striations. As the West opened up, revealing one fresh splendour after another, trees of vast girth, cataracts and chasms, the photographers, often employed in systematic surveys, recorded these wonders rather than reveal, as did the British, the strange qualities in the representative and the accessible. The British photographers' delight in the intrinsic qualities of ordinary trees, flowers and rocks was something they shared more with their intense countrymen the Pre-Raphaelites, than with foreign photographers.

There are, of course, pitfalls in comparing paintings and photographs. To look at a photograph and a painting of tree roots or of Jane Morris is not to compare like with like. Apart from the self-evident contrast between the often brilliant colour of Pre-Raphaelite paintings and the subtle tones of old photographs, it is important to remember that whatever the similarity of outcome, photograph and painting were the result of entirely dissimilar manipulations and that, above all, there is a fundamental difference between the two in their relation to time. A photograph is a slice, at right angles as it were, across the dimension of time, exposing the nerve ends of reality. A painting is the creation of the artist working in time and hence of a particular organizing capacity. For the painter there is total control if it is willed, for the photographer hardly ever.

Nevertheless, if carefully approached, the comparisons in this instance remain valid. Despite the differences, the mental traits called for by the painstaking procedures of early photography and Pre-Raphaelite painting were not at all dissimilar. In psychological terms there was little to distinguish a photographer, like Roger Fenton, and a Ruskin disciple, like Alfred William Hunt, braving the wind, rain, and stony tracks of Snowdonia. Must there not have been a competitive element in such dedication? As for the gulf between the two media in their relation to time, this was narrower in the era before the snapshot, when exposures could last as long as fifteen minutes (though half a minute was average). Early photographs generally lack that talismanic quality which has intrigued some of the most perceptive writers on photography like Roland Barthes and Susan Sontag: the capacity to capture what is gone in an instant, to fix what lacks all fixity, to mediate between the temporal and the eternal. Early photography draws nearer to painting. Whether the subject was an ivy-covered wall, someone dressed as Dante, or a Tennyson *tableau*, the photographer of the time organized it, caressed it, stood it statue-like before the lens, and then of course worked on it in the developing and printing process. These were no Cartier-Bressons waiting in the wings of reality for the revealing gesture or accident. They were indeed like painters creating monuments to their handiwork.

No less than the work of Cartier-Bresson these photographs are, however, an open book in which may be read the features of their time – the Pre-Raphaelite time.

1 *Rivals*

fig. 6

Charles Allston Collins
Convent Thoughts (1850–1)

Oil on canvas
$33\frac{1}{8} \times 23\frac{1}{4}$ in   84 × 59 cm
Ashmolean Museum, Oxford

The Eyes of a Fly

'What would it be if I had the eyes of a fly!' – by the mid-nineteenth century Coleridge's question demanded an answer. Nose an inch from the ground, the young and curious lay consorting with beetles and blades of grass. A few, still, instinctively searched the sky for answers to imponderables rather than study the world at their feet or, exhausted with the quest, looked to the sea for consolation. 'What sort of men prefer the monotony of the sea?' asks Thomas Buddenbrook in Mann's novel. His answer recalls one perplexed Victorian: Matthew Arnold, who heard the 'eternal note of sadness' in the waves lapping on the pebbled strand: 'Those, I think, who have looked so long and deeply into the complexities of the spirit, that they ask of outward things merely that they should possess one quality above all: simplicity.'

Arnold sought simplicity, but he was not typical. For many of his generation 'complexities of the spirit' were assuaged by probing the complexities of matter. Ruminating in Kensington Gardens, Arnold was stirred by the 'endless, active life' of the minute creatures at his feet – but only momentarily. He must avoid being 'prevailed over by multitudinousness'. By contrast, Ruskin spent several days in the summer of 1847 acquiring an insect's-eye view of a patch of Perthshire. He drew 'the blades as they grew'. Every square foot of grass, buttercup, hawkweed and moss became 'an infinite picture and possession'. His *Modern Painters* began as a defence of Turner, but another compulsion lay behind the five volumes he was to spend nearly two decades completing: the desire to follow Coleridge in marking nature's most minuscule variations. The almost manic, compellingly-written first volume of 1843 in particular turned painters into meteorologists, and geologists. It inspired aesthetes to attend sometimes less to art than to that which could 'laugh' at art – 'the detail of a single weedy bank'.

William Michael Rossetti was among those who would turn a day in the country into a Brobdingnagian quest. In September 1849 he took a long walk on the Isle of Wight. He ferreted out beetles. He lay 'in the midst of long yellow grass'. Holding his hand to his face, he carried out minute optical experiments, 'opening and shutting either eye', noticing changes in the surrounding colours. His brother, Dante Gabriel, was more mystical in his investigations of nature's minutiae: a natural consequence of his sloth, he self-mockingly implied. He loved to lie on the cliffs since he felt them to be as 'lazy' as he himself was. With his head buried in the grass, he would 'symbolize' the daylight hours away. Sometimes he drew a metaphysical blank. The woodspurge resisted Wordsworthian infusion, the heart failed to leap up, the flower was merely itself: 'three cups in one'. Only, perhaps, in mid-nineteenth-century England would a poet have looked for serious enlightenment among 'some ten weeds'.

We get a flavour of the Rossetti brothers' activities by turning to a contemporary novel, Charles Kingsley's *Alton Locke* (1848). In his town upbringing and weekend enthusiasm for minuscule nature, if in nothing

fig. 7

Microscopic Study: Base of the Wing of the Common Fly from *The Wonders of the Microscope*, London, 1861

$7\frac{1}{16}$ in   18 cm   diameter
The British Library

The photographic pioneer, Henry Fox Talbot, had taken photographs through the microscope in the early 1840s. *The Wonders of the Microscope* was the first attempt to introduce micro-photography to the public in book form. Reflecting the search for spiritual certainty through minute particulars, the publication boasted '*perfect transcripts of nature* ... exquisite and surprising manifestations of divine contrivance'. [*The Wonders of the Microscope* (London 1861), pp. i–ii.]

else, the proletarian hero of the book was a reasonable fictional counterpart to the Rossettis. Alton knew every leaf and flower in his little front garden, 'every cabbage and rhubarb-plant in Battersea field'. When for the first time he escaped to the countryside, he did not waste much time before lying face down on the ground. He fingered over 'the delicately cut leaves of the weeds'. He turned on his back and watched 'a thousand insects, like specks of fire, that poised themselves motionless on thrilling wings'.

The insects aroused in Alton an altruistic curiosity. He wondered whether they 'thought about anything, and whether they enjoyed the sunlight'. But he also saw them as symbols. The wild flowers, chance beetles, and butterflies which he brought home to pore over 'were to me God's angels, shining in coats of mail and fairy masquerading dresses'. He longed for the day when priests would 'go forth into the highways and the hedges' and preach to the ploughman and the gypsy the message that God was to be found 'in every thicket and fallow field'. The Gate of Heaven was no longer a great arch in the sky, but the eye of a needle. To merge with essential processes and discover the Answer, when all around had lost it, one had to *shrink*.

Microscopes stimulated the imagination of the 1850s to journey through uncharted territories. The top of a mountain was where, traditionally, the spiritual aspirant felt closest to God, but when the eminent geologist, John Tyndall, stood on the summit of Monte Rosa in the 1850s, he was moved, not by Alpine Sublimity or the firmament to which he was now so close, but by a passing snowflake. Taking an imaginary microscope, he allowed himself to enter a magical world. The molecules and atoms floated and arranged themselves in a kind of stately concrete music: 'brute matter' was redeemed. G.H.Lewes, literary man, and owner of a microscope, confirmed that his instrument increased his 'reverence'. Each particle of earth was revealed as a microcosm, a 'world within world'. The imagination was borne into 'the very homes and haunts of Life itself'. A scientific agnostic could be as reassured by minute probings as a Christian like Kingsley.[1]

Nevertheless, these activities are often thought to indicate a spiritual malaise, a desperate search for the tangible as religious certainties ebbed away. Certainly science was destroying biblical beliefs in the earth's youthfulness and the immutability of each species that were basic to humanity's view of its place in the cosmos. Browning's progress, for instance, from *Pauline* (1832), an early exercise in Shelleyan generalities, to the atomizing of reality as found in his mature verse, marked the shift from a unified to a fragmented vision of life. There were also peculiar psychological factors operating at this time, like the obscure guilt felt by those brought up under harsh religious creeds. Ruskin is the obvious example. From the earliest distracted tracings of patterns in his nursery carpet, he would seek relief in trivia. The same tensions are embodied in Tennyson's *Maud* (1855). There, the hero, a murderer, sexually obsessed and alienated from self, society and the woman he loved, could do nothing (until resolving finally to join the army) but focus on rose petals or the configurations on a shell: the 'overwrought' mind, suddenly striking 'on a sharper sense/For a shell, or a flower . . .'

fig. 8
John Brett
Ash Profile (1857)

ink
Private Collection

fig. 9
William Henry Fox Talbot
Leaf of a Plant (1845)

Photogenic drawing
10 × 8 in   25.4 × 20.3 cm
The Science Museum, London

Talbot's photogenic drawing was published in *The Pencil of Nature* (1844–6). The photographer was proud of his invention's capacity to record minutiae. He believed that no painter would bother with counting ears of corn or tracing leaf veins. He failed, however, to anticipate the Pre-Raphaelites, who eagerly answered Ruskin's call to 'descend to the lowest details'. Brett's sketches express, like Talbot's image but by more laborious means, the era's fascination with particular forms.

fig. 10

Ernest Edwards
Cleft in the Rock. Anchor Church. Derby
(1860s)

Collodion
$9\frac{7}{16} \times 7\frac{5}{16}$ *in*   *24 × 18.6 cm*
From the collection of the Royal Photographic Society

fig. 11

James Campbell
The Dragon's Den (c.1860)

Oil on canvas
$15\frac{13}{16} \times 15\frac{3}{4}$ *in*   *40.1 × 40.1 cm*
*Merseyside County Council, Walker Art Gallery,
Liverpool*

'I hate the dreadful hollow behind the
little wood,' declares the morbid narrator
in the first line of Tennyson's *Maud*.
Fascination if not abhorrence is suggested
by photographic and Pre-Raphaelite
investigation of dreadful hollows. The
sinister feeling in Edward's photograph is
objectified (albeit minutely) in Campbell's
painting: a dragon stands on the ledge
above the cave. Campbell was one of many
Liverpool artists influenced by Pre-
Raphaelitism in the later 1850s.

    This vision of life could be taken to pathological extremes, but its artistic
manifestations should not necessarily be written off as the mere febrile
excesses of a depleted culture. The most enduring nineteenth-century art –
German music, French painting, the Russian novel – lacked this obsessive
'particularity' (or absorbed it into something larger).[2] But in Britain, at least
for a decade or two, the accumulation or scrutiny of detail was *the* energizing
impulse. Victorian writers who continued to ride on the clouds of generality
no longer waylay us, while rumbustious masters of the particular, like
Thackeray or Browning, still buttonhole us and demand we give them a
hearing. In painting, the heirs of 'Sir Sloshua' performed their flaccid
routines. Those who conjured with nature's most intricate forms moved to
the centre of the stage.

fig. 12

John Atkinson Grimshaw
Thrush's Nest (early 1860s)

Oil on board
12 × 16 in   30.5 × 40.6 cm
Sotheby's, London

fig. 13

Alfred Rosling
Young Emeus (sic) and Eggs, bred at Brackham
Lodge (late 1850s)

Collodion
$5\frac{15}{16} \times 5\frac{11}{16}$ in   15.1 × 14.5 cm
Colnaghi

The inspiration for both Grimshaw and
Rosling was William Henry ('Birds Nest')
Hunt. Hunt had been painting his
delicately crowded watercolours of nests
and flowers long before Pre-Raphaelitism,
but they commanded a new respect with
the microscopic enthusiasms of the 1850s.
Ruskin himself took lessons from Hunt.
George Eliot equated the artist's vision
with the desire 'to escape from all
vagueness into the daylight of distinct,
vivid ideas'.

Beating Them Hollow

Particularity in painting triumphed during the period between the formation of the Pre-Raphaelite Brotherhood in 1848 and the waning of Ruskin's influence on the practice of painting in the early- to mid-1860s. In the later 1850s it became a kind of rage and the 'Pre-Raphaelite measles' affected countless artists who are not generally thought of as Pre-Raphaelite in any other sense at all. 'It will be the duty ... of the landscape painter,' Ruskin urged in 1855, 'to descend to the lowest details with undiminished attention.' Every flower, rock, and cloud had a distinct character which must be studied conscientiously and rendered precisely.

A mania for minute transcription had not been the only motive force behind either Ruskin's theories, or the youthful alliance of Rossetti, Holman Hunt, Millais, and the other Pre-Raphaelites. Attentive reading of Ruskin soon shows that he believed too fervently in the transforming power of the imagination to recommend 'duckpond delineation' for any but the beginner. As for the Brethren, their perfunctory knowledge of early Italian art, reflected in the pristine angularity of some of their early works, was as important as their literary taste which produced a distinctive narrative pathos in their paintings. But, though significant, these features were not especially shocking. Taste for the Italian 'Primitives' had been growing since the 1830s, when Alexis-François Rio's *De la Poësie chrétienne* had enjoyed a vogue. Ruskin had contributed to this revival with his paean to Fra Angelico in the second volume of *Modern Painters* (1846) and while the Pre-Raphaelites were among the first to illustrate Malory, Keats, and Browning, their other most frequent sources, the Bible, Shakespeare, and Walter Scott, had frequently inspired other literary-minded painters.

It was the violence the Pre-Raphaelites did to appearances that was at first shocking. In fact it can still seem so. In classic Pre-Raphaelite masterpieces like Millais's *Ophelia* (1851–2; fig. 4) or Hunt's *The Hireling Shepherd*, (1851–2) the details stand out as in a mosaic of precious stones, glistening and intensely alive. But the final effect is oddly claustrophobic, even hallucinatory. To the Victorians this was even more disconcerting than the 'ugliness' of the models which, in a famous outburst, Dickens compared to that of 'a monster in the vilest cabaret in France or in the lowest gin-shop in England'.

Diaries and letters confirm that the painters' energies went into recording nature's minutest details: days spent wrestling with dandelion puffs and blossoms, a reed warbler's nest built between three reeds, a bumble bee, a small feather on a patch of ground, diverse pebbles. This devotion to minutiae had a monastic quality. A day painting the ivy for *A Huguenot* (1851–2; fig. 118) ended for Millais with readings from the Thirty-nine Articles and a religious discussion with Hunt and Charles Collins. No doubt he saw angels in the ivy leaves just as Alton Locke had found them in the wild flowers, beetles and buttercups. Certainly, if Millais had read his Emerson (most people *were* reading Emerson at this time), he would have learned that 'every

fig. 14
William Holman Hunt
The Haunted Manor (1849–c.1856)

Oil on millboard stuck on panel
$9\frac{3}{16} \times 13\frac{5}{16}$ in   23.25 × 33.75 cm
The Tate Gallery, London

fig. 15
John Dillwyn Llewelyn
Botanical Study with Bird (early to mid-1850s)

Paper negative
$7\frac{7}{8} \times 9\frac{13}{16}$ in   20 × 25 cm
From the collection of the Royal Photographic Society

The sunlit background and evocative title of Hunt's painting were added later to make the work more popular with the public. To the artist himself, a patch of sodden ground, slippery slabs of stone and dank vegetation were enough of a subject. Llewelyn also liked these unpropitious retreats, though with him embellishment took the form of a stuffed animal or bird. Llewelyn was both a naturalist and creator of symbols for the darker corners of the Victorian psyche.

natural fact' was 'a symbol of some spiritual fact'. F.G.Stephens writing in the Pre-Raphaelite magazine, *The Germ*, confirmed that, 'A single leaf earnestly studied ... may do its share in the great labour of the world.' Sir Joshua Reynolds's instructions to imitate nature's general forms were being swept away. A medieval typology of the natural world was re-emerging through the 'visionary vanities of half-a-dozen boys'.

Lurking, however, in an as yet obscure recess of the visual culture was Pre-Raphaelitism's unacknowledged relative. This cousin apparently excelled where its newborn rival could only aspire:

We have ... boughs on which you may count the leaves; leaves, on which you may number the veins ... shores, whose froth and surface you can follow with microscopic truth; grass is no longer a green smear, but a world of netted beauty, teeming with flowers, and susceptible of magical wonders of light and shade; rock ... given with geological truth and an accuracy you may swear to in a court of justice ...[3]

Photography, the product of the cumulative endeavours of Niépce, Daguerre, and Henry Fox Talbot, was achieving new wonders of fidelity to nature at the very time Pre-Raphaelitism was setting out on the same course.

Within three years of the Brotherhood's formation there were three important technical innovations in the new medium. Two of these came from France: Gustave Le Gray's Waxed Paper negatives, a variant of Talbot's calotype process and L.D.Blanquart-Evrard's albumen paper. With Le Gray's process, the paper for the negatives was waxed before being sensitized and, though this could mean lengthier exposure times of up to fifteen minutes, the paper could be kept longer and recorded finer detail. Albumen paper improved detail at the printing end of the process. This simple evolution of the earlier, rougher, salted printing paper, involving a coating of egg white, remained the principal medium for photographic printing until the end of the century when it was superseded by gelatine-based papers. Shorter lived, but equally significant for the evolving aesthetics of photography, was Frederick Scott Archer's wet collodion process, the first practicable process for negatives on glass. Practicable, but only just so: it required exceedingly delicate manipulations and was cumbrous to a degree. This only deterred the casual amateurs and faint-hearts, however, as the process had the advantage of shorter exposures and high resolution of detail. The triumph of these inventions involved the demise of the daguerreotype which, while it too was sensitive to detail, lacked the benefit of a repeatable image.

Photographers naturally went in search of subjects that showed off the new process's strong point. They were urged on by magazines like the *Athenaeum* and the *Art-Journal*, which were now sitting up and taking note of photography, and by the specialist periodicals such as the *Photographic Journal*, *Photographic News*, and the Liverpool-based *British Journal of Photography*. The names of the tangled, rough-textured objects the camera now caught so well were chanted by the critics with onomatopoeic enthusiasm: 'entanglements of twig and spray' exulted one writer typically, '... thorny, trailing, spiny,

fig. 16

John Spiller and John Percy
The New Mill, Near Lynton, North Devon
(1856)

Collodion
12 × 9 7/16 in   30.3 × 23.9 cm
From the collection of the Royal Photographic Society

A millwheel is a perennially picturesque subject: Constable loved 'The sound of water escaping from Mill dams'; in George Eliot's *The Mill on the Floss*, Maggie Tulliver felt 'awe as at the presence of an uncontrollable force'. With the Pre-Raphaelite and photographic sensibility all sound and movement ceased. Romantic awe crystallized into love of intrinsic qualities. The churning millwheel and gently-waving ferns are frozen. The uncontrollable force is arrested and each component in the scene held up for minutest scrutiny.

bristling . . . broken thatch and crumbly loose tiling . . . labyrinthine boughs . . . a roof black with moss . . . pebbly banks'.[4] Nor did the photographic critics hesitate to claim for this kind of subject matter a significance which the Pre-Raphaelites attached to it in their own field. Ruskin's arguments and rhetoric were purloined to establish photography as the successor to an obsolete visual language.

He had made the phrase, 'go . . . to nature' his own; 'What it is,' echoed the *Athenaeum* on photography, 'to go direct and humbly to Nature.' Ruskin had helped Pre-Raphaelitism by condemning both the 'inaccuracies' and the classical trappings of the Old Masters: the *Athenaeum* praised photography for its absence of 'brown trees . . . gingerbread rocks . . . barley sugar temples . . . nymphs and satyrs'. Ruskin had exhorted painters to 'descend to the lowest details'. 'In this detail,' confirmed the reviewer, on behalf of photography, 'lies all the glory and divinity of nature'.[5] A writer in the *Photographic Journal* summarized the case with a yet fiercer iconoclasm. Photography had come to supplant 'wearisome' Madonnas, Nymphs, and Venuses – 'dead Christianity and . . . deader Paganism'. It washed the world clean, revealing 'fresh pastures, virgin earth'.[6]

fig. 17

Albert Moore

Trunk of an Ash Tree with Ivy (1857)

Watercolour

12 × 9 in 30.48 × 22.86 cm

Ashmolean Museum, Oxford

fig. 18

Francis Edmond Currey

Foxglove (1869)

Collodion

$7\frac{7}{8} \times 5\frac{7}{8}$ in 20 × 15 cm

University Art Museum, University of New Mexico, Albuquerque

Moore's drawing is a typical Ruskinian study of the later 1850s. For artists like Moore or Frederick Leighton, hedgerows and tree stumps were an irresistible but temporary compulsion. Photographers could pursue such subjects at less cost to their sanity and eyesight. Pin-sharp studies of patches of rank vegetation could still be found some time after the fashion for them had passed in painting.

As with children resorting to opposing methods of rebellion against overbearing parents, photographers and Pre-Raphaelites watched each other's activities jealously. There was much feigned indifference and mutual disparagement. Among the Pre-Raphaelites, figures as diverse as Rossetti, Ruskin, Madox Brown, Millais, William Dyce, John Brett, Atkinson Grimshaw and Frederic Shields became involved with photography at one time or another. Another Pre-Raphaelite associate, William Bell Scott, later asserted that photography was 'the seed of the flower of Pre-Raphaelism'.[7] This was an exaggeration. In the early days of Pre-Raphaelitism there was far too much to be got out of 'going to nature' for the young visionaries to be content with sitting at home, copying photographs – if that is what Bell Scott was implying, but the facts lend at least some credence to claims made by the *Photographic News* in the early 1860s that the Pre-Raphaelites had shown 'strict and judicious attention to the productions of photography'.[8]

There was, for example, a suspicious sensitivity on the subject of photography among the painters. When Shields was arranging the terms of partnership for a photographic publishing venture in which Madox Brown was to be involved, the godfather of Pre-Raphaelitism cautioned him conspiratorially: 'one thing that must be a *sine qua non* is secrecy. *Our* names will not appear – nor be hinted at even.'[9] Since the main business of the company was to be photographic reproductions of paintings, the tinge of paranoia seems at first surprising, but there was a fear that association with any kind of photographic enterprise would confirm the public suspicion that Pre-Raphaelites indulged in the shocking practice of painting over photographs.

Occasionally, they did. Rossetti in 1862 painted over a photograph of his recently dead wife, Lizzie (née Siddal). Three years later he varied the practice by painting over a photograph of one of his own works, *The Beloved* (1865–6), commissioned by his solicitor, J. Anderson Rose. When in 1867 Rossetti discovered that the painted photograph was about to be sold at Christie's without an accurate description of its hybrid nature, he panicked. He wrote a confession, albeit an incomplete one, stating that it was the only time he had painted over a photograph and would remain so. (This did not prevent him from copying photographs for backgrounds till the end of his life.)

Ruskin had had to defend the Pre-Raphaelites, in his 1853 Edinburgh lectures, against the charge (then probably false) that they copied photographs. But, aside from this issue, the ramifications of photography were troubling to adherents of the strict fidelity principle. (It should in passing be recalled that Rossetti, moving in the mid-1850s into medieval fantasy and into a new medium, watercolour, was only briefly among the devotees of strict fidelity.) Photography, faithful servant of reality, mocked their every effort. That which set them apart from their profane predecessors in art – the capacity to transcribe every vein and tissue of a divinely-charged Nature – was called into question by the existence of a machine which could do the same, sometimes in a matter of seconds.

For a time it was possible to ward off a sense of futility by drawing attention to the *un*truth of photography. 'What you say of Calotypes is quite true –'

fig. 19

John William Inchbold
The Chapel, Bolton (1853)

Oil on canvas
$25\frac{1}{2} \times 33$ in 65×83.8 cm
Northampton Museum and Art Gallery

fig. 20

Frederick Scott Archer
*Kenilworth: Caesar's Tower from the Inner
Court* (1851)

Collodion
$8\frac{1}{16} \times 6\frac{15}{16}$ in 20.5×17.7 cm
From the collection of the Royal Photographic Society

The chief advantage of Scott Archer's collodion process was sensitivity to detail. This was not immediately apparent. The first photographs Scott Archer took with the new process, at Kenilworth, were no sharper than many images from paper negatives. Yet the Pre-Raphaelite sensibility in photography was already at work, as the similarity with Inchbold's work at Bolton Priory shows. In both cases, the subject stands boldly before the spectator, the sky all but excluded. The patterns formed by vegetation and crumbling stone take priority over atmospheric evocation.

Ruskin wrote to the painter George Price Boyce in 1854, 'you know they not only misrepresent colour – but violently exaggerate shadow & thereby lose all truth.'[10] But the calotype was superseded, and photography rendered light and shade with increasing precision. Moreover it became obvious that one day colour photography would come as well. By the early 1860s only the most convinced exponents of hard-edge Pre-Raphaelitism, such as Holman Hunt and John Brett, could see the sense in continuing to compete. Millais was the most celebrated example of a painter who changed to a broader style. The journals of the time were full of references to the 'now defunct' style of Pre-Raphaelitism and to a 'reaction' against the school.

None were more eager to accuse the Pre-Raphaelites of mere mechanism in their art than the photographers themselves. The photographic critic of the *Athenaeum* expressed the hope that, as a consequence of photography, 'the Pre-Raphaelite will in despair give up mere imitation and aim at higher principles of art.'[11] This was a traditional line of argument and leads us to an important feature of photography's early history in Britain: its conservatism. Photography was an expensive pastime. Enthusiasts came mainly from the higher social classes. The sedate couplets they appended to their photographs tell us as much about their attitudes as their choice of subject matter, which shows a myopic disregard of social realities. Many of them had had a traditional artistic training. William Lake Price, a well-known photographer in the 1850s, had been exhibiting regularly at the Academy since 1828. Another important figure, Roger Fenton, had studied painting under the orthodox Delaroche in Paris.

Giving artistic advice to photographers in the *Photographic News*, Price put his Academic training to good use. He might just as well have been addressing painters for all the notice he took of the conditions and limitations of the new medium. He stressed unity and simplicity. He advocated classical composition: the balance of forms, contrast of detail and general effect, non-repetition of objects, the principle of leading into the picture. He illustrated his points with Old Master engravings. He quoted the French authority, Dufresnoy and Reynolds. His strictures on the 'sharp' school of photographers for failing to allow '*mind* and sentiment' to 'spread over the whole', were a paraphrase of Reynolds's criticism of the Dutch school of painting.[12] These traditional arguments, used here by one photographer to cajole other photographers, could, if necessary, be deployed by photographers against rival painters, especially since the arguments derived in the first place from theories of painting. An instinctive rivalry made it necessary to direct them against the Pre-Raphaelites. Despite the propaganda from people like Price to render nature 'artistic' in photography, the impetus behind the new invention came from the quest for truth. This was clear from the onset – both Daguerre and Fox Talbot were artists frustrated with their inability to fix nature's elusive beauties. And now, just at the moment of triumph, a school of painters emerged whose priority was identical (even if the end result, a brilliantly coloured painting, bore little superficial resemblance to a monochrome photographic print). Pre-Raphaelites may have felt that photography demeaned their unique achievements, but photographers felt exactly the same about Pre-Raphaelitism. If conservative arguments about harmony, balance and taste were required to rout the usurpers, then most photographers knew how to employ them.

The battle was really over the rival claims to truth. Ruskin and George Price Boyce were convinced of photography's deceptions. Photographic critics went to great lengths to draw attention to the errors of the Pre-Raphaelites. The competitive venom, which some photographers had cultivated by the end of the 1850s, is exemplified by a paper read to the South London Photographic Society on 20 October 1859 by H. L. Keens, Senior, entitled: 'Truth in Art illustrated by Photography'. He argued that photography had a historic role: to lead art out of the dark age of Pre-Raphaelite distortion. This rescue mission had already been performed once in art, when the Renaissance had extinguished the ineptitudes of the first Pre-Raphaelites and ushered in an era of 'truth in art'. Renaissance artists had 'delighted to study nature ... in a mirror': they would have rejoiced in photography. Now the invention had come 'like an angel from heaven to the benighted traveller'. Ignoring the discrepancies between the vision of the camera lens and the eye, Keens recommended artists to copy the outlines of photographs. This way, the 'stiff and mannered' forms of the Pre-Raphaelites 'must be driven from the walls of our exhibitions, like horrid witches flying at the approach of innocence and truthfulness'.

Owing to changes of taste in painting, and to photography's destruction of the miniature-portrait business, more and more conventionally trained painters were taking to photography as a means of securing a living. Keens's audience in South London probably contained a proportion of out-of-work painters. They no doubt nodded sympathetically when Keens hinted at personal motives for his tirade: the minds of patrons had, he believed, become so unhinged by the Pre-Raphaelite fever, 'that (as I know from my own experience) many artists lost their commissions or employment.' But beyond that the issue remained the simple one of truth versus distortion: on the one side, the Old Masters and their allies, the photographers, able to unite foreground detail with convincing atmospheric perspective; on the other, the Pre-Raphaelites. In the latter's claustrophobic, 'morbid' productions, objects seemed 'cut out of pasteboard and pasted on the canvas'; a distant hill or cloud was seen 'attaching itself to the head of some miserable figure in the foreground'. Keens's paper struck a chord. He sat down with 'expressions of applause' from the audience.[13] Until Pre-Raphaelitism changed in the course of the following decade and became less centrally concerned with fidelity to nature, his was the party line followed by photographers. The annual round of exhibitions was regarded by photographic critics as a gladiatorial contest. Millais could be 'beat . . . hollow' by photography.[14] Francis Bedford's studies of plants 'would set a Pre-Raphaelite crazy'.[15]

The interest photographers and Pre-Raphaelites took in each other's activities has been little noticed by historians of the period. Few photographic historians follow up connections outside photography itself. Art historians, on the other hand, have not, at least until recently, concerned themselves with photography. They have doubted whether comparisons between painting and this artistically questionable (and disconcertingly popular) medium were valid. These doubts are fuelled in the present case by the fact that colour was absent in early photography. The contrast with the Pre-Raphaelites is indeed stronger than it might be with other schools of painting. The Pre-Raphaelites used particularly dazzling colours and they did not employ the traditional chiaroscuro that in some ways resembles the tonal system of monochromatic photography. But perhaps the most important reason why the subject has remained unexplored is the way the story of early photography in Britain has until recently been told.

Earlier historians of the subject concentrated on a particular lineage. This led from Fox Talbot to the calotypists, Hill and Adamson in Scotland, and then, with a twenty-year leap, to Julia Margaret Cameron. Fox Talbot, though obviously important as the inventor of the calotype, was for a long time discounted as a photographic artist. Artistry was equated with the chiaroscurist portraiture of the two Scotsmen and Cameron. The long gap between these artistic peaks was filled with accounts of travel photography and of the vast commercial exploitation of photography – evident in the stereo, photography's incursion into three dimensions, which soon became a popular diversion after the introduction of the first stereoscopic camera in 1853, and the *carte-de-visite*, the little portrait of a loved-one or celebrity which it became a craze in the 1860s to collect in special albums. Missing, or misrepresented, was the 'sharp' school of domestic landscape photography:

the names who dominated the exhibition lists of the 1850s and 1860s – Roger Fenton, Francis Bedford, Henry White, John Dillwyn Llewelyn, John H. Morgan, John W.G.Gutch, Alfred Rosling, to name a few – the very photographers whose work often rivalled (and richly complemented) Pre-Raphaelite landscape painting. Much of this work had lain forgotten in family attics. With the upsurge of interest in early photography in the 1970s, a missing generation of photographers came to light. Roger Fenton was found to be no longer just the photographer of the Royal Family and the Crimean War, but a master recorder of the forms and textures of the British landscape. Amateurs like John Dillwyn Llewelyn and Henry White were revealed as true celebrants of the tangible, initiates in the potent mysteries of physical 'presence'.

fig. 21

Francis Bedford
Rock on the Seashore (1862)

Collodion
$9\frac{1}{8} \times 11\frac{1}{2}$ *in*   23.1 × 29.4 *cm*
Victoria and Albert Museum, London

Bedford's work, it was said, could 'set a Pre-Raphaelite crazy' [*PJ*, 7 (1860–1), 15 February 1861, p. 112]. This photograph from the 1862 International Exhibition shows how far the collodion process had improved the precision of the medium. Selecting a Ruskinian subject, Bedford adopted the 'Pre-Raphaelite' high vantage point, thus avoiding vertiginous, Romantic effects. The photograph serves well as an objective record, yet the barely discernible man leaning on the rock (the conventional 'marker figure' of early photography) seems about to be engulfed. The spiritual fears provoked by the revelations of geology are powerfully suggested.

T. Bedford

2   *Presences*

fig. 22
Edmund George Warren
Lost in the Woods (1859)

Gouache
28 × 18½ in   68.5 × 47 cm
Christopher Wood Gallery

The Dark Guilty Mass

'Pre-Raphaelite' photographers were inevitably drawn to the close-up, as naturally as 'Impressionist' photographers were later attracted to distance. Ferns and brackens, trailing ivy, branch patterns, tree trunks, corn stooks, and striated rocks: any subject interested them as long as it was natural enough to appease prevailing Wordsworthian sentiment, static enough to permit long exposure, and detailed enough to 'beat hollow' the painter. Each image was a plain statement of the facts, while at the same time powerfully conveying a state of mind. But, what was the state of mind? The photographers were maddeningly reticent about their work, but their counterparts', the Pre-Raphaelites', openness enables us to speculate much more fruitfully about their intentions. The young painters were also scrupulously recording facts, but, for their part, they, their adherents, and critics, were talking and writing a great deal about what their creations meant to them.

Ruskin's exhortations made it clear that their *first* duty was to the facts. In this he was merely – though eloquently and emphatically – re-stating a doctrine advocated by early Renaissance theorists like Alberti and Leonardo (it was the Mannerists and the Academicians who had relinquished it for the 'Ideal'). To him, although a primrose might symbolize the sun, a fairy's shield, or a forsaken maiden, this should never be allowed to detract from the 'plain and leafy fact' of the flower and he readily saluted the Pre-Raphaelites' exertions as they crowded their works with as many plain and leafy facts as they had patience for.

The Scottish painter and friend of Millais, Joseph Noel Paton, had heard Ruskin's orations in Edinburgh in 1853 on the virtues of leaf-by-leaf discrimination and, as a result, had produced a painting quintessentially Pre-Raphaelite in its combination of history and natural history, *The Bluidie Tryst* (1855). Ruskin thought the subject gloomy and the colour unsubtle, but he had nothing but praise for the botany: the 'little pinguicula alpina', the oxalis leaves, the red ferns, were all 'exquisitely articulated'. Paton produced other minutely detailed studies during this period (figs. 23, 57). With no fancy-dress antics, they are perhaps more appealing, though less ambitious than *The Bluidie Tryst*. These and similar works by other artists gripped by Pre-Raphaelite fervour, corroborate James Smetham's later conclusion that 'peeping and botanising' – in his mature view an intrusion of amateur science into art – amounted for a short time to a mania among painters.

But the facts were never intended merely to speak for themselves. Walter Scott, in *Marmion*, looked at an ancient thorn stem in Ettrick Forest and the pageant of Scottish history appeared before his eyes. His devoted admirers, the Pre-Raphaelites, saw hardly less in moss-covered tree roots or slabs of stone. In the early days of the Movement, natural objects were copied directly onto the canvas where they took their place in a literary-symbolic jigsaw. The Death's Head Hawk Moth in Holman Hunt's *The Hireling Shepherd* is a study 'in itself': it was also recognizable as the 'forebodings of evil', just as wandering sheep inevitably represented errant Christians. Millais's *Ophelia* is both a botany lesson and a glossary of the Victorian language of flowers. There are dozens of varieties, some with obvious connotations like the poppy for death, others only the cognizant would recognize, such as the meadowsweet for 'uselessness'.

As the Movement progressed, Pre-Raphaelite followers broke with this piecemeal symbolism. They started to carry out preliminary studies rather than always painting direct from nature, and also depicted landscapes with no overt narrative additions. Despite this, a vague symbolism often surrounds their work. Brett's stark Alpine study, *The Glacier of Rosenlaui* (1856; fig. 60) is not a mere transcription of three kinds of rock: the painter had been reading the fourth volume of *Modern Painters* and had adopted Ruskinian typology, so that the lumps represent nothing less than the three orders of Creation. Atkinson Grimshaw painted a mountain pass and called it *The Seal of the Covenant* (1868). Without narrative, the work was 'a kind of Key, commitment and pledge of his life'. John Inchbold's painstaking, 'subject-less', tree, wall, and mountainside studies have a similar air of religious and personal affirmation.

Such affirmations, such loading of meanings, are inevitably less obvious in photography. It may aspire to art, but its origins lay in science. A practitioner was of necessity a chemist, able to juggle test tubes of potassium iodide and understand the arcane mysteries of chemical reaction. And chemistry was often merely one of many scientific interests pursued in a spirit of curiosity ranging from the intense to the merely gentlemanly. J. D. Llewelyn, the son of an eminent natural historian, was himself a man of wide scientific

fig. 23

Joseph Noel Paton
Study from Nature, Inverglas (1857)

Watercolour
$14\frac{1}{2} \times 20\frac{1}{2}$ in 37×52 cm
Sotheby's, London

fig. 24

John Dillwyn Llewelyn
Lastrea Filix Mas (c.1854)

Collodion
$8\frac{1}{8} \times 6\frac{1}{16}$ in 20.6×15.4 cm
Richard Morris

To many photographers Pre-Raphaelites were tiresome rivals. Why, it was asked, could the painters not realize that what in photography was an 'inexhaustible delight' was in painting 'a tiresome pedantry of observation' [PJ, 3 (1856–7) 21 January 1857, p. 192]. The question was particularly asked of works such as Paton's study, which was actually less pedantic than any number of Victorian narrative pictures. Like comparable photographs of the time the work speaks of an intense involvement with the processes of growth and decay in nature; Paton with his rotten, moss-covered log and Llewelyn, focussing on an embattled fern — both hover between being delighted and menaced by their subject.

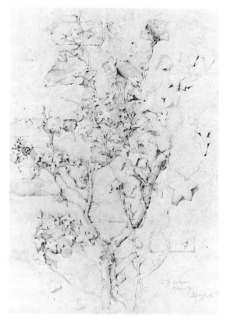

interests. His private papers chronicle a family life given over to scientific pursuits: seeking out wild lilies on the cliffs and photographing hornblende by day, watching the heavens from the observatory by night. Photography is seen here as one way – along with the pencil sketch or watercolour – of recording objects of diverse interest. It was thus through a general scientific concern that Llewelyn became the early master of the close-up.

Of all the sciences pursued in tandem with photography, botany was the most popular. 'Botanising' was in any case at the height of favour at this time. George Eliot, neither a photographer nor a botanist but a writer to whom one can always turn to catch the intellectual flavour of the period, was clear about the invigorating effects of identifying plants. She went for a walk with her companion, G. H. Lewes, in the lanes near Ilfracombe. Every yard was 'a "Hunt" picture – a delicious crowding of mosses and delicate trefoil and wild

fig. 25

Thomas Keith

Foliage on a tombstone, Greyfriars (Tomb of John Byres of Coates) (c.1852)

Paper negative
9⅞ × 11 in   25.1 × 27.9 cm
By courtesy of Edinburgh City Libraries

fig. 26

Frederick Sandys

Study of Ivy on an old Wall (1863)

Pencil and white chalk on grey paper
14⅛ × 10 1/16 in   35.6 × 26.6 cm
Courtauld Institute of Art

Ivy crept across innumerable Pre-Raphaelite backgrounds, offsetting doomed lovers, girls with sheaves of corn and (as in the case of Sandys's painting for which this is a study) clergymen. Photographers allowed the motif to speak for itself, which it was well able to do since it stood for memory, fidelity and dependent womanhood. As a master of chiaroscuro, Keith, unlike the Pre-Raphaelites, obscured the particular form of the plant.

strawberries, and ferns great and small'.[1] Her impulse to name every flower was, she realized, part of the desire 'to escape from all vagueness into the daylight of distinct, vivid ideas'. To botanize was to experience the world's multitudinousness without succumbing to it. How much greater the mastery if one could trap the plant world in the camera lens.

Henry Fox Talbot's first photographic patent was 'photogenic drawing' (e.g. fig. 9) – an image made by placing plants in contact with sensitized paper and letting the light pass through the leaves. Hill and Adamson had photographed bracken and trees. An image of ivy trailing across a tomb in Greyfriars Cemetery in Edinburgh (fig. 25) was one of the most original achievements of Thomas Keith, their successor with the calotype in Scotland. The subject was evocative. The grainy imprecision of the paper process added to the mystery. Photographers struggled to overcome this 'fault', which can now seem a virtue, and in plant photography often created new problems for themselves, alluded to by a perceptive critic of photography, Lady Eastlake, in a lengthy 1857 *Quarterly Review* article. With the wet collodion process, there was a new precision. But with foreground weeds and herbage, and in particular, she argued, with holly, laurel, ivy and other smooth-leaved evergreens prevalent in England, the images were barely true to the facts. The dark green registered black, the shine on the leaves white. Trees and plants looked as if 'strewn with tiny bits of tin, or studded with patches of snow'.[2] But as photographers gained increasing control over intermediate tones such criticisms became redundant. Numerous images from the 1860s with titles like *A Bit in the Glen* (fig. 27) and especially F. E. Currey's *Foxglove* (1869; fig. 18), a full-toned study of botanical fecundity, confirm this.

Even Ruskin was forced to admit the uses of plant photography: *even* Ruskin because, by this time, the critic had become disillusioned with photography. As a young man in the early 1840s, he was enchanted with the new invention. He had borne daguerreotypes away from Venice like miniature trophies. He had pursued photography to help him with his architectural studies (the employment of his manservants being conditional on their being able to operate a camera). It was a 'noble' and 'blessed' invention, a 'glorious thing'. Anyone, he wrote, 'who has blundered and stammered as I have done for four days, and then sees the thing he has been trying to do so long in vain, done perfectly and faultlessly in half a minute, won't abuse it afterwards'. This was an inaccurate prediction since, within a few years, he was himself abusing photography as being untrue to nature: 'it either exaggerates shadows, or loses detail in the lights' – or, if true, only 'in the sense in which an echo is true to a conversation'. It certainly had 'nothing to do with Art properly so called' and was at root expressive of the soulless mechanism of the age. In a typical later outburst, Ruskin urged his 'chemical friends' to throw their 'vials and washes down the gutter-trap' and apply their energies 'to draw a skilful line or two, for once or twice in your life'.[3]

Nevertheless, even at this later stage, the practicalities of Ruskin's role as the nation's drawing master demanded photography's assistance. He could

not personally supervise the gathering of primroses and ivy leaves for every artist in need of them. If he saw a plant whose form perfectly illustrated the principle of growth in the species, and there was no time to draw it, he would photograph it. In 1858 he photographed a medieval courtyard in Abbeville (fig. 29). There was an insignificant sprig of leafage growing up the carved porch. Twelve years later this sprig appears in the *Rudimentary Series* for Ruskin's drawing school in Oxford as a sepia drawing (fig. 28). On this occasion it was not the form of the plant which had intrigued Ruskin, but the impression of mystery deriving from its distance from the lens. If photographs (or drawings from them) were needed to show people how to render leaves from a distance, then Ruskin was ready to overcome his

fig. 27

Anon.

A Bit in the Glen (1867)

Collodion
$8\frac{3}{4} \times 10\frac{1}{16}$ in   *22.2 × 27.2 cm*
From the collection of the Royal Photographic Society
This Amateur Photographic Association prizewinner is relatively restrained, but concentrated plant studies could suggest the chaotic struggle between species; the nightmare of uncontrolled procreative urges.

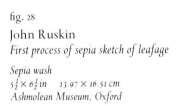

fig. 28

John Ruskin

First process of sepia sketch of leafage

Sepia wash
$5\frac{1}{2} \times 6\frac{1}{2}$ in   13.97 × 16.51 cm
Ashmolean Museum, Oxford

fig. 29

John Ruskin

A Courtyard in Abbeville (1858)

Collodion

fig. 30

Detail from A Courtyard in Abbeville
*Collection of the Guild of St George, on long term
loan to Sheffield City Art Galleries*

Objects at a distance from the lens, like the
spray of leaves in this Abbeville courtyard,
could register indistinctly and help impart
the lesson of 'Turnerian' mystery
according to Ruskin; it was necessary to
learn to draw these leaves as the
photograph represents them'. [*The Works of
John Ruskin* (London 1903–12), XXI, p. 294].

distaste. He clearly sensed, though he could not at this late stage acknowledge, that this mere machine could help the eye see the world in a fresh or mysterious way.

Ruskin was perhaps not unaware that the best photographs of plant life contained an inherent 'mystery'. With all their 'botanizing' associations, the plant images of this period have qualities transcending any scientific purpose. Frequently, as in Llewelyn's *Snowdrops* (1852), they convey the photographer's fascination with the random abstract patterns formed by the accidents of vegetable life. This interest would have quite cut across any intention of using the photograph for botanical classification. The photographs also set up further associations. There is a sinister impression of abundance conveyed by myriad details emerging from the depth of shadow. Passages from Keats, or perhaps the 'dreadful hollow behind the little wood' in *Maud*, stocked with the lush ferns and strangulating brambles that can so ably conceal a murder victim, suggest themselves. Did these connections occur to the photographers? Did they, like the Pre-Raphaelites, see plant life as symbolic? An 1858 *Athenaeum* review, suggests they did:

It is like reading Keats and Tennyson to look at the soft, white, velvet hair of the poisonous, veined nettle-leaves, green and rank, huddling up in a dark guilty mass to hide where the murdered child was buried, while the bee sings round the white diadems of their beguiling flowers as if nothing was wrong and earth was still a Paradise. How the wild hops, vine-like, cling and twine, – how the hooked bramble, with its square red stalk, trails and spreads . . .[4]

That perennially arresting fantasy, the tainted Paradise, could it seems be evoked by images of the commonest plants, created by the impassive machine and its scientifically-minded operator. The South London Photographic Society's strictures on Pre-Raphaelite 'morbidity' might be turned against the photographers themselves. Apart from the technical challenge offered to the new medium and the new kind of painting by intricate plant studies, the photographers' and Pre-Raphaelites' interest in the subject reveals underlying tensions. Rank vegetation evoked ideas which many Victorians were not anxious to contemplate. One of these was Evolution. The spectacle of voluminous vegetable growth encouraged the vision of life as a mindless, eternal struggle for existence among the species. This haunted the literature of the period, giving rise to descriptions of wastelands of devouring plants: the 'starved ignoble nature' in Browning's 'Childe Roland to the Dark Tower Came' (1855) where cockle and spurge have consumed all but ragged thistle-storks and torn, perforated dock leaves; the 'ruinous and deathful riot' of brushwood in *Proserpina* (1875), Ruskin's idiosyncratic study of flowers. In Ruskin's vision, as in Browning's and that of the *Athenaeum* photography critic, nature is tainted. Thorns strangle each other, holly collects in 'choked stragglings'; the bramble and the rose are dead, 'untouchable, almost unhewable . . . laid over rotten ground'.

Plants could also suggest sexuality. Shelley had expressed the idea of *feeling* flowers in 1811: 'Perhaps,' he wrote, 'the flowers think like this . . . have their attachments ... adore, despond, hope, despise.' Ruskin, for his part, was unwilling to investigate the sex life of plants: 'with these obscene and prurient apparitions,' he concluded in *Proserpina*, 'the gentle and happy scholar of flowers has nothing whatever to do.' Perhaps the procreative images which appeared on their collodion plates provided some photographers with sublimated erotic satisfaction. It is better to tread carefully here and merely draw discreet attention to the sexually redolent vocabulary – 'vein', 'guilt', 'Paradise', 'cling', 'twine' – in the passage of photographic criticism quoted above.

Nature did not always run riot when the photographers and painters depicted botanical abundance. J. D. Llewelyn lent an aura of orderliness to woodland scenes by including neatly dressed children. Thoughts of the slow thrusting and entwining that is going on around them are banished. Vegetable chaos recedes; primal innocence is restored. Paintings like Arthur Hughes's *The Woodman's Child* (1860; fig. 153) showed that, to the Pre-Raphaelites also a 'Babe in the Wood' deflected attention from nature's blind impersonal forces. The parallel between the photographic and Pre-Raphaelite interest in this theme is even more apparent with a work like George Edmund Warren's *Lost in the Woods* (1859; fig. 22) where, as Ruskin pointed out, the trees surrounding the child were 'skilfully correspondent with photographic effect'.[5]

Another idea was to substitute animals for the children. William J. Webbe, a disciple of Holman Hunt's, painted in *After Sunset* (1855; fig. 32) a rabbit against a beguiling background of primroses, ferns, and grasses. The animal is alert but protected by his surroundings. The painting is similar in feeling to Llewelyn's *Rabbit* (early to mid-1850s; fig. 31). 'Mr Llewelyn has been very busy lately,' wrote his wife Emma in 1859 to her relative, Constance Talbot (wife of the photographic pioneer, Henry), making pictures of stuffed animals and birds with an artificial landscape, in real trees, shrubs, flowers and rocks and even shallow pools of water.'[6] Without this evidence of taxidermy we might wonder how Llewelyn persuaded the rabbit to 'freeze' as convincingly as his brother in Webbe's painting.

Llewelyn's *Rabbit* and the dark, intensely still *Piscator No. 2* (1856; fig. 33) (a stuffed heron in one of the 'shallow pools') prompt a mixed response. They are inventive, but superfluously so perhaps. The surroundings have a life of their own and require no faked animal embellishment. Whether with Fenton's architectural façades, Cameron's monumental portrait heads, or Llewelyn's own rock studies (fig. 43), Victorian photography is most impressive when most direct, least reliant on extraneous devices and picturesque formulae. Llewelyn's botanical studies are more evocative than his animal pictures for the same reason that Paton's unembellished Inverglas *Study from Nature* (1857) can seem more interesting than his costumed fancy, *The Bluidie Tryst*. Intending to say less they actually say more: we are less distracted by the creator's conscious foibles.

Yet Llewelyn's creatures point to a state of mind prevalent at the time, the desire to create intense little havens from a world perceived as harsh, and a

fig. 31
John Dillwyn Llewelyn
Rabbit (early to mid-1850s)

Paper negative
$8\frac{1}{2} \times 6\frac{5}{16}$ *in*   *21 × 16 cm*
From the collection of the Royal Photographic Society

fig. 32
William J. Webbe
After Sunset (1855)

Oil on canvas
Diameter 14 in   *35.6 cm*
Mrs Crawford J. Campbell

Webbe was an obscure disciple of Holman Hunt. It is in the work of such 'humble' yet intense devotees of nature that Pre-Raphaelitism moves closest to the vision of men like Llewelyn. The photographer's rabbit is stuffed: no live rabbit could have endured the exposure time.

fig. 33
John Dillwyn Llewelyn
Piscator No. 2 (1856)

Collodion
$9\frac{1}{2} \times 7\frac{1}{2}$ *in*   *24.1 × 19 cm*
From the collection of the Royal Photographic Society

A stuffed heron stands in an artificially created pool, but the darkness banishes a sense of contrivance. A mysterious stillness – a potent feature of much early photography – is emphasized.

universe understood to be limitless. The eighteenth-century gentleman liked rationally ordered vistas; the Victorian, retreats where every little thing could be seen close to and could provide emotional security. Llewelyn, like his contemporary the novelist George Borrow, was a 'lover of nooks and retired corners'. Perhaps to him, as to Lucy Snowe in Charlotte Brontë's *Villette*, or to Arnold in his Kensington Gardens meditation, such places were symbols of the inner life. He felt strongly enough the attractions of a haven, anyway, to do what no one else thought of doing: build one himself and capture images of it for future generations to ponder.

The Good Harvest

Not all the highly detailed images from this period point to the chaos and riches of the 'buried life' (in Arnold's phrase). Some photographs celebrate order and pattern in the natural world: sheaves of corn gathered in rows under an open sky, or the silhouettes of tree branches on a still winter's day. There were practical reasons for the choice of both these subjects. The gathering of the harvest was of necessity a time of settled weather – August – when, in any case, photographers were out on their 'summer campaign' (as many liked to call it). The harvest also provided a rare example of rapid transformation in the appearance of the landscape. Photographers were able

fig. 34

Henry White
Wheat (1856)

Collodion
$7\frac{11}{16} \times 9\frac{5}{8}$ *in*   *19.5 × 24.4 cm*
Sotheby's, London

fig. 35

Charles Allston Collins
The Good Harvest of 1854

Oil on canvas
$17\frac{1}{4} \times 13\frac{3}{4}$ *43.8 × 34.9 cm*
Victoria and Albert Museum, London

Ripe corn was an appealing subject to Pre-Raphaelites for its biblical and nostalgic associations and for the chance it gave them to advertize their dedication: Collins was driven by his exertions to give up painting soon after finishing *The Good Harvest*.

The photographer could prove with this of all subjects the magical precision of his medium. Interest in the intrinsic qualities of objects led photographers to abandon those rules of composition derived from painting which critics urged them to conform to: the foreground looms unnaturally in White's image, an early masterpiece of 'photographic seeing'.

to record an interesting variety of images without having to move their elaborate equipment. The choice of leafless trees was determined by exposure length. Even with the faster collodion negatives this could be as long as a minute or two – time for a tree in fluttering leaf to register on the negative as a massive blur.

With a subject such as a haystack or a cornfield there was another imperative. In his photographic publication *The Pencil of Nature* (1844–6), Talbot had explained his reasons (now familiar to us) for photographing an uninterestingly shaped haystack. 'It will enable us to introduce into our picture a multitude of minute details which will add to the truth and reality of the representation, but which no artist would take the trouble to copy from nature.'[7] One aim as always was to triumph over the painter.

This might have remained a dead issue had not the Pre-Raphaelites picked up the gauntlet. The counting of strands of hay and ears of corn advertized their dedication: the fact that with this type of subject every item is laboriously identical made it indeed the very index of their sacrifice. But the vivid yellow cornfield in Holman Hunt's *Hireling Shepherd*, the numbered sheaf in the child's arms in Collins's *The Good Harvest of 1854* (fig. 35), register more than a belief in the virtues of tireless enumeration: there is a fondness for the myth of harvest safely gathered in; nostalgia for a fast vanishing rural England; renewed faith through the biblical associations, not least with Ruth, given more recent lustre amid Keats's 'alien corn'. Above all, there is the love of the mere look of the ripe corn, the image of abundance. The diary Madox Brown was keeping at the time of his landscapes, *Carrying Corn* (1854–5) and *The Hayfield* (1855–6), is poignant in its sensitivity to such beauties. Poignant also is the painter's rage at the futility of trying to capture them:

About 3 out to a field ... found it of surpassing loveliness, Corn shocks in long perspective, farm, hayricks ... By the time I had drawn in the outline they had carted half my wheat ... How despairing it is to view the loveliness of nature towards sunset & know the impossibility of imitating it ... What wonderful effects I have seen this eveng (*sic*) in the hay fields ... with lovely violet shadows & long shades of the trees thrown athwart all & melting away one tint into another imperceptibly, & one moment more & cloud passes & all the magic is gone ...[8]

Remarkable among photographers for his interest in harvested corn – certainly for its look and, for all we know, also for its associations – was Henry White. White is an elusive figure. In his authoritative *History of Photography* (1955), Helmut Gernsheim singled him out as a precursor of the New Objectivity school in Weimar Germany. Ever since, researchers have been trying to uncover facts or statements which would explain the presence of a photographer of such rigorous avant-garde vision in Victorian England. It is known only that he was active in the 1850s and early 1860s, and that he was a solicitor by profession, living probably in Surrey.

This anonymity is all the stranger in view of White's spectacular reputation with his contemporaries. 'White's works,' wrote one reviewer, 'are so well known, that it is almost superfluous to mention them.'[9] He won a first class medal at the 1855 Paris Universal Exhibition. He dominated the 1856 Manchester exhibition. 'The finest works there,' wrote 'Theta' in the *Photographic Journal*, 'are undoubtedly those by Henry White; there is not a single picture in the gallery which can be compared to them.'[10]

The Victorians did not admire White in quite the same way as Gernsheim. They liked his photographs not so much because corn stook or hedge stood in bold close-up and declared simply, *I am here*, in the manner of a Renger-Patzsch tree-stump or an Ansel Adams fence, but because clear foreground was often combined with unusually sensitive atmosphere and distance. White overcame technical limitations and aligned photography at last with traditional pictorial values. 'They are more artistic,' wrote 'Theta' of White's exhibits, 'and more like *pictures*, than anything else in the rooms.' The critics also made the type of literary associations we have anticipated. One was reminded of Thomson's *The Seasons*[11]; for another White's cornfields were 'the whole book of Ruth in miniature'.[12]

All the same, White's contemporaries probably realized that he had got 'inside' his subjects in an unusual way. It is instructive to compare him here with Madox Brown. Brown, burdened with financial cares and self-doubt, ill-equipped technically to paint a fluent, conventional harvest scene, seemed all the more able to lose himself in intrinsic qualities. He arranged the components of the scene into patterns, yet allowed them to speak for themselves, highly textured so that our feet feel the uneven tread of the ground and we long to reach out and touch the ears of corn.

White also combined ordering with 'entering' and 'possessing'. He arrived at his field like Gerard Manley Hopkins hurrahing at harvest time: 'these things were here and but the beholder/Wanting'. Beset with practical problems like all the photographers of his day, he positioned himself to achieve exquisite arrangements of corn stocks 'in long perspective', or standing against the remainder of the uncut field (figs. 34, 37). But the look and feel of the corn itself predominates: 'nature itself,' as the *Art-Journal* declared, '... depicted with such fidelity, minuteness of detail, and accuracy of drawing, as the graver can never hope to equal'.[13] We can never know what White really thought when he set up his camera in the Surrey fields at harvest time. What we sense is a personal obsession that is at the same time paradoxically impersonal. The self-effacement of the passionately involved landscape photographer was described by a later master, Edward Weston, with whom it is perhaps not too indulgent to associate the elusive Victorian solicitor.

I am no longer trying to 'express myself,' to impose my own personality on nature, but without prejudice, without falsification, to become identified with nature, sublimating things seen into things known – their very essence – so that what I record is not an interpretation, my idea of what nature *should* be, but a revelation – an absolute, impersonal recognition of the significance of facts.[14]

Certainly Weston's phrase, 'the significance of facts', is redolent of the mental atmosphere breathed by Henry White's generation.

fig. 36
Ford Madox Brown
Walton-on-the-Naze (1869–60)

Oil on canvas
$12\frac{1}{2} \times 16\frac{1}{2}$ *in*   *31.7 × 42 cm*
By courtesy of Birmingham Museums and Art Gallery

fig. 37
Henry White
Oats (1856)

Collodion
$7\frac{1}{2} \times 9\frac{5}{8}$ *in*   *19 × 24.5 cm*
Michael Rich

In painting and photograph the gathered sheaves are wonderfully 'present'. At the same time the rows draw the eye into the distance – unnaturally clear in Brown's vision, hazy with late-summer heat in White's photograph. White's skill in combining the mysteries of distance with sharp foreground qualifies the view of him as a 'Pre-Raphaelite' photographer. For the true Pre-Raphaelite landscapist detail was razor-sharp on every plane and, as with *Walton-on-the-Naze*, two-dimensional patterning was at war with perspective.

Dark Rivers

Edward Weston's desire to become 'identified with nature' recalls Ruskin. In his manual, *The Elements of Drawing* (1857), Ruskin recommended the student of art to begin drawing from nature by tracing a 'map' of branches across the sky. 'Consider them as so many dark rivers,' he advised. This laborious but no doubt rewarding exercise had its origin in personal revelation. As a young man Ruskin had lain on a bank near Fontainebleau. Casually sketching the outline of an aspen tree nearby, he became gradually aware that the branch patterns were 'tracing themselves'. To act as cipher for the principle of organic form embodied in the tree was, Ruskin realized, the true function of the artist. Altering the form of a particular tree to comply with conventions of good taste was an affront to God's laws. The humble aspen was far lovelier than man's loveliest creations, even Gothic tracery or oriental embroidery. To allow the tree to trace itself on to one's paper was to receive a Divine dictation. The laws of creation determining its shape also 'guided the cloud, divided the light, and balanced the wave'. Branch patterns were now to Ruskin a code for 'the bond between the human mind and all visible things'.

There is no record of such exalted interpretations among photographers, but, for twenty years after Talbot's invention, Ruskin's dark rivers flowed across innumerable photographic skies – a pleasingly intricate silhouette which, the earlier the photographs and the less able the photographer to register details of tree texture, the more it recalled Ruskin's metaphor of creation. Talbot's calotypes of trees from the early 1840s are true silhouettes. More tonal variation is visible in Sir William Newton's well-known calotypes from the 1850s of Burnham Beeches, but since Newton was at this time advocating an 'artistic' blurring of the image, textures are sacrificed to allow the trees to merge with woodland atmosphere.

Another fine calotypist, Benjamin Brecknell Turner, effectively incorporated lower textures with upper silhouette, but it is only the collodion photographers, such as J. H. Morgan, who really exploited both facets of the tree image together. A Bristol photographer who was linked with J. D. Llewelyn and gained a reputation for his tree studies around 1860, Morgan liked to concentrate on single objects, as did other photographers with a recognizable Pre-Raphaelite sensibility. But, whereas a Pre-Raphaelite could fill up his composition piecemeal, detail by detail, a photographer would lose everything if he brought one object into particularly sharp focus. *The Photographic News* criticized Morgan for this: he sought 'the most perfect image possible of the principal objects, without any consideration for those which occupy a less prominent position'.[15] But this fault (if fault it is) is not apparent in Morgan's forceful study *Trees* (late 1850s; fig. 39). The receding line of trunks is well articulated. This line, and the texture of the main trunk, provide a foil to the two-dimensional patterning above. Compositionally, the image resembles, as it happens, one of the purest of Pre-Raphaelite landscapes, Inchbold's *A Study, in March* (1855; fig. 38).

fig. 38
John William Inchbold
A Study, in March (1855)

Oil on canvas
21 × 14 in   53 × 35 cm
Ashmolean Museum, Oxford

fig. 39
John H. Morgan
Trees (late 1850s)

Collodion
10 × 7 15/16   25.5 × 20.2 cm
From the collection of the Royal Photographic Society

Long exposure reduced trees in leaf to a blurred mass. Hence the popularity of winter trees in early photography. Like Inchbold in his beautifully observed *Study*, Morgan offset the confused branch silhouette with an ordered arrangement beneath. The principal tree in each case is chosen for its knotted, grainy qualities.

fig. 40

Thomas Lukis Mansell
Lane Guernsey (1855)

Collodion
$9\frac{3}{4} \times 8\frac{3}{16}$ *in*   *24.7 × 20.8 cm*
From the collection of the Royal Photographic Society

In another image echoing Inchbold's *Study*, Mansell has achieved the hallucinatory clarity throughout that is the hallmark of the Pre-Raphaelite sensibility. The differentiation of tree forms was to Ruskin a moral quality. 'The man who can best feel the difference between the rudeness and tenderness of humanity,' he wrote, 'perceives also more difference between the branches of an oak and a willow.'

There is perhaps an even stronger affinity between Inchbold's picture (much praised by Ruskin) and a photograph taken in the same year by T. L. Mansell, *Lane Guernsey* (fig. 40). Mansell, whose 'Pre-Raphaelite' qualities were remarked on by Gernsheim, selected a scene where the trees, themselves intricate in growth and texture, stood on banks studded with varieties of plant life. Detail spreads across the image, but the effect is not like those French photographs of this period that transform woodland into a shimmering 'Impressionist' mass of lights and darks. As with Inchbold, detail in Mansell's photograph is particularized down to each twig and leaf strewn on the path. The branches form a hieroglyph of variegated nature below.

By the 1860s, winter trees had become *passé* among photographers. Atmospheric studies of trees in leaf were now more feasible. But the graininess of wood still fascinated some. Indeed, for photographers who maintained the Pre-Raphaelite interest in texture through the 1860s, there were greater rewards to be had from the ever-increasing sensitivity of the camera. No one was keener than Frank Mason Good to position his camera unconventionally to highlight the feel of objects. In his woodland study (fig. 41), he was probably as intrigued as Millais in his *Winter Fuel* (1873; fig. 42), by the way wood could form itself into an 'aimless mess or minglemangle ... in under-your-nose-foreground' – this was how Gerard Manley Hopkins described the Millais work. Perhaps Good, like the Jesuit priest, located Christ in these unpropitious corners of the natural world. As a later photographic pilgrim to the Holy Land, he could possibly have been one of those for whom faith and photography were intermingled. Certainly the focus on intrinsic qualities at the expense of woodland 'atmosphere' imply once again Weston's passionate self-effacement. Gernsheim isolated Henry White as the precursor of the twentieth-century avant-garde but one begins to suspect that this was for lack of other evidence. If a greater range of images had been available to him when he wrote his *History*, he would have concluded that there was virtually a school of pre-Modernist photographers tramping the lanes of mid-Victorian England.

Mountains in Miniature

fig. 41

Frank Mason Good
A Study of Trees (1870)

Collodion
$9\frac{1}{16} \times 11\frac{1}{3}$ *in*   23.5 × 29 *cm*
Michael Rich

fig. 42

John Everett Millais
Winter Fuel (1873)

Oil on canvas
$76\frac{1}{2} \times 59$ *in*   194.3 × 149.3 *cm*
City of Manchester Art Galleries

The foreground of this later Millais work marks a momentarily zestful return to his Pre-Raphaelite principles. It is one of his most tactile works in which he applied himself to the kind of granulated clutter photographers imagined to be their exclusive preserve. Good, an early master of texture in photography, precipitates us, like Millais, into confrontation with a tangly foreground.

Boulder, cliff face, quarry. Many early Victorian photographers found these stark subjects yet more of a challenge than hedgerows and cornfields. Cathy in *Wuthering Heights* (1847), contrasted foliage and rocks. Time, she said, would change her love for the insignificant Linton, 'as winter changes the trees'. But her love for Heathcliff 'resembles the eternal rocks beneath – a source of little visible delight, but necessary'. Emily Brontë's contemporaries were attuned to the 'necessity' of rocks. Protruding from the earth's surface in their arresting configurations, they were still for many a symbol of endurance to be set beside more transient enchantments, while for others the 'necessity' lay in the duty to confront the appalling, nullifying secrets they contained.

The famous 'geological stanzas' in Tennyson's *In Memoriam* (1850) reveal nightmare thoughts. It is from the 'scarped cliff and quarried stone' that the poet learns of Nature's supreme indifference to individual human destiny. Geology challenged the literal truth of the Bible on the question of the earth's age, but this was not so shocking – the idea that the earth was only a few thousand years old had long seemed a preposterous fairytale to many. It was the encouragement that geological findings gave to materialism that disturbed the Victorians deeply: countless defunct species embedded in rock; nothing enduring the relentless ravages of time but particles of matter forming and reforming into eternity. Generations which had loved, suffered ills, and fought their battles now lay, in Tennyson's chilling metaphor, 'sealed within the iron hills'. G. H. Lewes had a further grim message: rocks were 'mutinous with change'. If human eyes could attune themselves to the slow pace of geological change, they would see that the rocks, too, 'grow, and change, and die'.[16] The old symbols of endurance were disintegrating.

Not everyone was discouraged, however: geology could be a diverting pastime. Like botanizing it could, with propriety, be pursued in mixed company. A geological expedition could turn into an idyll:

> . . . Many a little hand
> Glanced like a touch of sunshine on the rocks,
> Many a light foot shone like a jewel set
> In the dark crag: and then we turn'd, we wound
> About the cliffs, the copses, out and in,
> Hammering and clinking, chattering stoney names
> Of shale and hornblende, rag and trap and tuff,
> Amygdaloid and trachyte . . .

Tennyson's *The Princess* (1847) associated geology with the pleasures of flirtation and semi-knowledgeable badinage. 'Mute unfathomable conversations' with rocks of the kind that Goethe had written about in *Wilhelm Meister* were often as incongruous in real-life geology as on Princess Ida's excursion.

Many pursued the science for the satisfaction of contributing to a vast accumulation of facts. Like everything else at the time, geology was becoming more 'particular'. The great geologists of the past had had to deal with the subject in mass. Now, as John Tyndall pointed out, 'facts are flowing in, which ... are gradually supplanting ... uncertain speculations'. But, to some at least, these facts were not *mere* facts, rather as Tyndall said, 'so many telescopes to our spiritual vision'.[17] Belonging to the generation which saw geology come of age as a science, he confirmed its deeper ramifications.

J. D. Llewelyn was the first to recognize how well equipped photography was to record geological facts. As early as 1852, he was writing from Cornwall that he had hopes of getting 'an interesting series of illustrations of the various geological formations of the country'. He had already photographed slate, granite and greenstone, and was 'looking forward to the Serpentine at the Lizard'. When he arrived at this southern promontory with his wife and children, they set to with usual zest, observing intently, collecting plants, sketching. Geology, married with photography, was predominant. 'John made some fine photographs of the Serpentine rocks and of the hornblende,' wrote Emma to her mother; '... we saw more caves and arched rocks, pillar rocks and variety of formations in the small compass than we have seen anywhere else ... The Serpentine rocks [here she alluded to delights photography was unable to capture] are of a fine colour and when wet with the waves appear scarlet, green and purple with white veins ...'[18]

For obvious reasons, the lack of colour was least felt by photographers with this of all subjects. The *Times* photographic critic observed that a photograph of a rock could for some purposes be more useful than a specimen in a museum case. Together with palpable detail, it gave 'the larger geological characters' of the rock,[19] but, judging from the critical effusiveness, it was the detail in the photographs that excited the Victorians most. 'Here,' wrote another critic of J. W. G. Gutch's rock studies, 'we have the very split and cleavage of stone, its crumbles, hollows, frets, angles, mammocks, ledges and multitude.'[20] Gutch was among a number of photographers in the 1850s who followed Llewelyn in his systematic geological surveys. Another was Joseph James Forrester who took 220 photographs in 1855 of the margins of the River Douro in the Port-wine district of Portugal, 'to exhibit the bed and margin of that river at all seasons'.[21] But with most photographers there was no overt scientific purpose. Rock studies took their place alongside equally 'speaking' images of trees and undergrowth. The rock – a single boulder, a striking formation – stood face to the camera, an easy victory, apparently, for photography over rival forms of representation.

Photographers, however, had to reckon with the geological fervour of Ruskin. Few of the more compelling photographs of rocks do not resemble, in detail and composition, work done by Ruskin himself or his disciples. The saga of Ruskin's relationship with geology started in youth when he began confident that geology, along with the other sciences, deciphered 'God's universal laws'. The study of rocks merely increased a sense of wonder in Nature. Into a single stone, he exulted, Nature 'can compress as many

fig. 43
John Dillwyn Llewelyn
View of Rocks (c.1854)

Paper negative
Sotheby's, London

It is tempting to read much into such stark geological studies: the spiritual crisis engendered by fossils; the desire to cling to rocks as symbols of endurance when science was revealing that they, like everything else in nature, disintegrated with time; perhaps, too, an answer to a certain harshness in the age. It is unlikely, however, that Llewelyn was conscious of any of this. Everything we know about him suggests that he would have viewed the rockface with the scientific detachment of the photographer-geologist.

changes of form and structure, on a small scale, as she needs for her mountains on a large one'. A stone was in fact 'a mountain in miniature'. But by the 1850s, geology was chipping away at Faith. It would not 'let him alone'. He heard the clink of 'dreadful Hammers ... at the end of every cadence of the Bible verses'. Like the sceptical G. H. Lewes, Ruskin realized that the hills 'which as living beings, seem "everlasting" are, in truth, as perishing as they': it was now mere 'cunning deception' to see 'only beneficence in the natural creation'.

The often-told story of the Scottish holiday in 1853 when Millais fell in love with Ruskin's wife, Effie, confirms Emily Brontë's idea that rocks could be personally 'necessary'. While the rain and wind in the Trossachs subjected the party to an uncharitable buffeting, and the chief protagonists entered an emotional vortex, everybody involved set about painting rocks. Even though he had gone there for a rest, Millais was, within a short time of arrival, 'painting a little among the rocks'. He drew a small but detailed picture of Effie sitting on them and then moved on to a larger full-length study of his loved-one's husband posed against those elements of which he was so much the High Priest (fig. 3). The rocks here were delineated with unprecedented crispness and were to cause months of trouble to the painter. Ruskin meanwhile completed his own painstaking drawing of *Gneiss Rock, Glenfinlas* (fig. 45). Even Effie, it is believed, painted a waterfall study, while William Millais, the painter's brother, sought refuge from the surrounding entanglements by painting another.

It is useless to speculate whether such emotions also infused the rocks that littered Pre-Raphaelite canvases in the decade that followed this central episode in the movement's history. The Millais-Ruskin drama has always aroused curiosity and there is enough information for us to infer how, for example, Millais felt as he transcribed every fissure, curve, and shadow of Glenfinlas gneiss. Less is known about what motivated Henry Wallis when he painted *The Stonebreaker* (1856–8); Frederic Shields with *The Wild Sea's Engulfing Maw* (c.1860; fig. 46); or William Lindsay Windus with *The Stray Lamb* (1864) (of which rocks, rather than the lamb, are the subject). Certainly, these painters were under Ruskin's general sway. Turner was 'as much of a geologist as he is of a painter'; the challenge offered by observations like this in *Modern Painters* was difficult to resist. With those artists like Brett, who knew Ruskin personally, there was the additional leverage of his supervision. Only an artist of Dante Gabriel Rossetti's independence and indolence could resist if asked by Ruskin to go to Wales and 'make me a sketch of some rocks in the bed of a stream'.

References to the Pre-Raphaelites are so frequent in the photographic journals of the late 1850s and early 1860s, that photographers were undoubtedly aware of the geological efforts of their rivals – while continuing to maintain that 'your sun is your only bearable pre-Raphaelite'.[22] Conversely, the painters were aware of photographic rock studies. Ruskin himself took daguerreotypes of rocks in the 1850s (fig. 44). Other painters may have used such studies to aid them with larger works, but this seems out of

fig. 44

Rock Study (late 1840s to mid-1850s)

Daguerreotype
$5\frac{3}{4} \times 8\frac{1}{16}$ in   15 × 20.5 cm
The Ruskin Galleries, Bembridge School, Isle of Wight

fig. 45

John Ruskin
Study of Gneiss Rock, Glenfinlas (1853)

Pen, wash and bodycolour
$38\frac{1}{2} \times 12\frac{6}{16}$ in   97.6 × 31.5 cm
Ashmolean Museum, Oxford

Rocks were for Ruskin the part of landscape in which nature 'most clearly develops her principles of light and shade.' He drew them frequently but photography was in a sense a more suitable medium for one who salivated over the 'most delicious distinctness' of 'every crack and fissure'.

keeping with the intense gratification so many artists clearly derived from 'going to nature' direct. In the end, however, the link between painters and photographers lies less in what one can discover about their mutual awareness than in that they both aimed to supplant obsolete visual conventions by having recourse to the facts. *The Germ*, following Ruskin, discoursed upon 'murky old masters' with their 'rocks that make geologists wonder'. The photographic critic of the *Athenaeum* could give no higher praise to Gutch's rock photographs than that they improved on 'the mud-heaps of Ruysdael or the little blue hillocks of Perugino'.[23]

But was it legitimate to compare photographs with the works of Perugino and Ruisdael? There was a heated debate about this. Some – even certain modest photographers – denied that photography could ever be an art: it was predominantly mechanical; the nobility of art depended on culling nature's best parts. Their opponents argued that painting, drawing, and engraving also involved mechanical skills; that the patience and dexterity needed in these arts and in photography were equal; above all, that the photographer had to exercise as much pictorial taste in choosing the right position for his camera as the painter in making his selections from nature.

Ruskin, as we have seen, was among those who regarded photography as no more than a mechanical medium, but he worded the argument in such a way as to reinforce a connection between photography and painting – as it was developing under his influence. Just as a photograph was not a work of art, though it required 'delicate manipulations of paper and acid, and subtle calculations of time . . . so neither would a drawing like a photograph, made directly from nature, be a work of art although it would imply many delicate manipulations'. Whatever the photographer's skill with the glass vial or the painter's with the camel's hair brush, the production of neither photograph nor painting was true art unless the 'inner part of man' had stood forth and declared, '"Behold, it is I".'[24]

Writing this in 1851, Ruskin was anticipating his own later, fully-fledged impatience with his followers, like Brett, who could only aspire to 'mirror's work, not man's' and with photographs – 'for geographical and geological purposes . . . worth anything; for art purposes – a good deal less than zero'.[25] But, negatively and without intending praise, Ruskin had pointed to the very strength of the works we have been considering in this chapter. It is not in any obvious sense the 'inner man' that stands forth from Inchbold's and Morgan's tree studies, or Brett's and Llewelyn's rocks – it is the trees and rocks themselves. It is certainly rewarding to investigate the associations of these images: what Roland Barthes might have called their 'polysemic' character – the 'floating chain of significance underlying the signifier'.[26] We know that Inchbold was thinking about Wordsworth when he painted *A Study, in March*, that Llewelyn was involved in a quasi-scientific enterprise; we have learned that trees meant one thing to the Victorians and rocks another; we could discourse further upon the fact that photographers were often rich men and painters poor ones; we could even investigate our own generation's responses – are not some of these pictures particularly pleasing to us because they combine directness (valued by our Modernist heritage), literalism (no longer disparaged) and the nostalgic appeal of all things Victorian? This done, we might conclude that these works deliver an unchanging message on behalf of their creators. Let us, as Weston put it, sublimate 'things seen into things known'. Let us lose ourselves in the quest for the 'very essence'.

Disturbing the conventional balance of self and object, these men created new visual languages in their respective fields that had much in common: both, simultaneously, sought to represent the truth — an eternally elusive goal, as elusive as the perfect projection of the globe on to the page of an atlas. Those who pursue it merely create new conventions of two-dimensional representation. The critics were right to point to the 'distortions' of those who set such store by their own veracity: the photographers with their vertical convergence, defective scale of light, and false representation of colour; the Pre-Raphaelites with their 'flatness' and failure to suggest movement and atmosphere. But the critics could not have it both ways. These very limitations were the back door by which something more personal (we might call it art) could enter. Unable to produce the perfect counterfeit to reality, photographers and Pre-Raphaelites were obliged, like any other artists, to exploit the limitations of their medium. Photographic vision and Pre-Raphaelite hyper-realism were pictorial modes to which artist-photographers and artist-painters could harness whatever talent they possessed.

fig. 46
Frederic James Shields
The Wild Sea's Engulfing Maw (The Gouliot caves, Sark) (c.1860)

Oil on canvas
$25\frac{3}{16} \times 30\frac{3}{4}$ in   64 × 78.1 cm
City of Manchester Art Galleries

fig. 47
George Washington Wilson
Fingal's Cave, Staffa (1856–8)

Collodion
$3\frac{7}{8} \times 3\frac{1}{16}$ in   9.9 × 7.8 cm
Roger Taylor

Myopic fascination with 'humble' nature was a feature of the sensibility of the 1850s, but painters and photographers were sometimes drawn to more spectacular scenes, especially if they were challengingly inaccessible or hitherto unrecorded. Contrasting and somehow rather Victorian responses to these strange miracles of nature — fear and staunch curiosity — are suggested by the figures here.

Wider Patterns

fig. 48

John Brett
Val d'Aosta (1858)

Oil on canvas
$34\frac{1}{2} \times 26\frac{3}{4}$ in   87.6 × 68 cm
Sir Frank Cooper, Bt

The Schizoid Soul

The Sunbeam: a Book of Photographs from Nature is an oddity of Victorian publishing. Appearing in 1859, it contained twenty photographs, accompanied by prose descriptions and bland lines from now-forgotten versifiers. The photographers included the editor, Philip H. Delamotte, and other specialists in landscape, such as J. D. Llewelyn, Francis Bedford, and the Scottish professional photographer, George Washington Wilson.

To say that the book has period charm is true and yet it leads one straight to the contradictions of the photographic period in question. *The Sunbeam* is a characteristic, awkward product, evoking not one age but two. The writing invites us to meander in a standard pre-industrial idyll of sunny vales, sylvan groves, and swelling uplands. Claudian late-afternoon balm brushes the cheek. Scenic detail is submerged in authorial intimations of 'deep repose'.

The photographs wrench us from this blandly harmonious world. The balance between creator and his surroundings is reversed: apart from a stilted, though touching, study of a courting couple by a painter turned photographer, F. R. Pickersgill, there is little sense of authorial attitude. Everything is hard; there is no balm. In Wilson's striking composition, *A Highland Water-Mill*, rocks form a jagged crisscross; an anonymous fisherman dangles a rod in a milky river. The image proclaims itself a *photograph*, a brittle industrial artefact, unable to embody coherence between humanity and nature. Robert Patterson's accompanying verse would have us believe that distant mist-shrouded hills

> ... permit the mind to dream
> Of more aspiring summits than the truth
> Might offer to our gaze ...

But Wilson's photographic hills are as inspiring as theatrical stage flats. The mind does not dream nor is the eye distracted from the lively rhythms operating in the rest of the image.

The Sunbeam was an unpropitious beginning to the marriage of photographic image and word. The partners to the union inhabited a different universe. But it presented an accurate reflection of the schizoid soul of photography two decades after its birth: what it was, and what it wanted to be. It was what photography must always be: more servant than master of reality. What it wished to be was embodied by the seemingly ill-thought-out, but in this sense apt, literary accompaniment to the photographs: a blend of the Picturesque and the Wordsworthian.

The Picturesque aspirations of photographers are well represented by Wilson. He was never happier than when the landscape arranged itself according to the traditional formulae. Like Gilpin, the authority on the Picturesque, he favoured dark foregrounds to set off distance. He frequently employed the diagonal composition of classical painters. He defined pictorial space in a way that would have satisfied Poussin. Objects should compose

58 / The Pre-Raphaelite Camera

themselves 'in such a manner that the eye ... shall be led insensibly round the picture, and at last find rest upon the most interesting spot'. The final effect should be of such poise that the 'desire to know what the neighbouring scenery looks like is extinguished'.[1] This is certainly one way of organizing a landscape photograph, but Wilson's output alone shows a landscape image can 'work' without at all conforming to pictorial conventions.

Wordsworthian aspirations, on the other hand, encouraged photographers to look askance at detail. The poet had never allowed an eye for the particular in nature to intrude on thoughts of something more deeply interfused. Photographers were reminded that sharp detail was for the 'uneducated eye'. One commentator even suggested avoiding clear, brilliant days and photographing only in more atmospheric conditions, recording those 'tender gradations of love by which the sky and landscape are so sweetly united'. At all times a mass of distracting details should be avoided and breadth, the quality that stimulated uplifting rumination, should be cultivated: 'the simple grandeur of that all-important quality, breadth – the power of relief, and the poetic influence of harmony or keeping'.[2]

As Wilson's *A Highland Water-Mill* shows, photographers were at the time of *The Sunbeam* technically hampered in their pursuit of the 'tender gradations' of atmosphere. But Wilson was then actually engineering a breakthrough. Like many others, he had been stunned into a sense of British photography's inadequacies by Gustave Le Gray's *Seascape with Sailing Vessel*, exhibited in 1856. This showed shimmering sky and Turnerian sky in dramatic juxtaposition (whether Le Gray managed this with a single negative has still not been established). *Photographic Notes* now urged that the essence of landscape lay 'in the sky and distances, and in atmospheric effects'. From now on, photographers should 'aim at a higher class of subjects than field gates, stiff trees, and stuck up country mansions'.[3]

Wilson was determined to take up this challenge. He persuaded a boatman to row his family tranquilly around on the Loch of Park, near Aberdeen. Using a relatively instantaneous exposure time of a quarter of a second, he took a series of evocative photographs that made his reputation. By 1862, three years after *The Sunbeam*, the *Photographic News* was asserting that artistic standards in photography were higher than 'a few years ago'. It was now reasonable to expect an image that was 'soft and properly graduated, as well as sharp and brilliant ... made out, and properly defined in all its parts as well as atmosphere ... harmonious in tones and balanced in forms'.[4] A revolution, which would cultimate in the delicate atmospheric effects of P. H. Emerson's 'naturalistic' photography, was under way.

But it is to the earlier landscape of 'gates, stiff trees and stuck up mansions' that we revert. Here, we find an individuality born of the artists' very failing to fulfil the traditional pictorial ideals. Sensitivity to atmosphere eluded the photographers. Ignoring the derision of the critics for 'sharpness in every part' fit only for 'maps, micro-photographs, and geometrical designs',[5] the photographers compensated for this lack with intricate linear patterns spreading across the entire image. The same applied to problems of distance.

In the period before the revolution of Le Gray's and Wilson's Loch of Park pictures, distances (an essential, ethereal component of the traditional pictorial mode) did not resonate properly in photography. Fenton recommended to members of the Photographic Society that 'There should be a certain limit for distance within which every object might be rendered comparatively distinct.'[6] Since the far-flung shoulders of the universe registered patchily, or as molehills, photographers pointed their lens at escarpments, steep banks across rivers, four-square ruins, and produced strong and original images. But it was above all the problem posed by the sky that brought about a fruitful abandonment of the Picturesque aesthetic. So disproportionate is the light coming from the sky and the land that, in those early days, the attempt to capture one meant the loss of the other. A photograph of clouds would leave the landscape black. A properly adjusted landscape always had a blank white sheet for sky, whatever the weather. There were various solutions: the white sheet could be broken up with a series of verticles, such as trees; a photographer could shift the horizon near to the top of the image by photographing from a high vantage point; in woodland or mountain scenes, the sky could of course be excluded altogether. The first landscapes to include clouds either involved combination printing or substituted water (transmitting a light comparable to the sky's) for terrain. Alternatively, the sky was simply painted on to the negative – this appealed to the photographers who were worried about having wasted their artistic training.

These ruses gave offence to some. Mr Finlay Anderson told the Scottish Photographic Society that 'undue elevation of the horizon' spoiled his pleasure in photographic landscape. It should not surprise us that the complaint was made in the name of the long-acknowledged master of the ideal landscape: 'in the landscapes of Claude,' he pointed out, '. . . the true horizon . . . is almost invariably below the middle of the picture.'[7] Most photographers would have preferred to produce photographic Claudes: darkish foregrounds, clumps of trees to one side, leading to a middle ground dominated by a ruin or other picturesque object; gently shrouded hills in the distance. Technical limitations forced them into the creation of a new, short-lived pictorial mode: two-dimensional patterning took precedence over the atmospheric illusionism which had held sway for centuries.

Until technical advances enabling the more sensitive rendering of atmosphere banished this new mode, those who found it offensive combated it by blurring the entire image and creating Corot-like effects. The early days of the Photographic Society were enlivened by the strife between these 'artistic' photographers led by Sir William Newton, and the 'sharp' school. The terminology used by the editor of the *Photographic Journal*, George Shadbolt, to describe the debate is interesting. The exponents of the blur he called the 'Modern School', perhaps because he knew of Corot's work, but more likely because their emphasis on the general could be equated with current academic practice; their 'sharp' opponents, the vociferous majority he dubbed 'pre-Raphaelites'.[8]

This was apt. As in plenty of 'stuck up' photographs of the 1850s atmosphere in the Pre-Raphaelite landscape evaporated. Critics complained of this in Millais's *A Huguenot*. In reply, Ruskin assaulted the 'conventional and ridiculous' aerial perspective of conventional artists: 'pretendedly well-informed but really ignorant', they wreathed their distances in mist to conceal their inability to draw. For even at a distance of ten miles, objects are 'completely visible', Ruskin argued, and should be rendered with strict fidelity. Whatever the validity of the argument, its practical effects were soon apparent. Painters dispensed with the paraphernalia of landscapes on several planes shrouded in differing degrees of mist. Distant hillside and foreground daisy were rendered with equal precision: everything gathered on the same plane. As Ford Madox Brown remarked when he first saw Holman Hunt's *The Scapegoat* (1854–5, fig. 102): the background, hard in colour, 'eats up the foreground'. The effect was most disconcerting.

Like the photographer, the painter could escape from the problems of aerial perspective by choosing a near subject. The west front of St Mark's, Venice, Ruskin wrote to George Price Boyce in 1854, 'answers precisely to your wishes . . . *near* subject, good architecture . . .' Boyce was a minor artist on the fringes of Pre-Raphaelitism, but he had absorbed the same message in *Modern Painters* as had the major Brethren: that the *true* mysteries of atmospheric distance were attainable only by an artist of Turner's genius and experience, a beginner should start with a subject that stood squarely before him in broad daylight. Pre-Raphaelite works which followed this rubric – Millais's *A Huguenot, Ferdinand Lured by Ariel* (1849–50), and *The Woodman's Daughter*; Charles Collins's *Convent Thoughts* (1850–1; fig. 6); Holman Hunt's *Valentine Rescuing Sylvia from Proteus* (1850–1) – can only have confirmed the message for Boyce.

As for the sky, that too was conspicuous by its absence or insignificance in Pre-Raphaelite work. In his *Handbook of Painting* (1855), C. R. Leslie, friend of that master of clouds, Constable, gave voice to the traditional view that expression in landscape came 'from above'. It was, he claimed, no mere metaphor to say 'Nature smiles, or weeps, and is tranquil, sad or disturbed with rage, as the atmosphere affects her.' Yet, he complained, modern landscapists seem 'as if they had never raised their eyes above the horizon'. This was not unjust. Even in Pre-Raphaelite works, such as Hunt's *The Hireling Shepherd* or Millais's *The Blind Girl* (1854–6), where the painter had incorporated distance, the horizon was pitched high.

Leslie also noted the parallel with landscape photographers. Why, he asked, had photographers ignored the sky when 'the composition, and light, and shade of clouds are as much within the reach of the photographic art as any of the other great things of Nature'?[9] It was not easy for Leslie to accept that what is of intense interest to one generation invariably bores the next. The sky, with whose splendours Turner and Constable were so familiar, was no longer fascinating. Pre-Raphaelites banished it or reduced it to a thin blue strip. Photographers, who would perhaps have liked to represent it, were not prepared in the process to reduce the landscape beneath to a relatively unmeaning silhouette.

fig. 49
Alfred William Hunt
Welsh Scene: A Runlet Babbling down the Glen (1858)

Watercolour
$9\frac{7}{8} \times 14\frac{1}{4}$ in   *25.1 × 36.2 cm*
Ashmolean Museum, Oxford

fig. 50
Roger Fenton
North Wales: Hillside Study (1858)

Collodion
$9\frac{3}{4} \times 11\frac{3}{4}$ in   *24.8 × 29.8 cm*
Christie's South Kensington

Carried out more or less simultaneously in the same rugged vicinity these two works illustrate the eclipse of the Picturesque ideal. The facts of the terrain are confronted head-on. Crisp patterns replace illusionistic effects of atmosphere and recession. The sky is all but banished. Of incidental interest is Fenton's photographic van at the bottom of his picture.

The peep-hole vision of the Pre-Raphaelites also linked them to photography. It is because we have two eyes and not one that we can focus on objects and gauge distances. The effect in painting of bringing each object into focus is to destroy a sense of intervening space, to remove an eye. While photographers subjected the landscape to the flat gaze of their instrument, Pre-Raphaelites also peered through tiny holes. Advising his sister on rendering the true colours of nature, John Brett suggested she might do what Ruskin was telling working men to do: look through a hole in a card (so as not to be tempted, one might say, into normal, coherent perception). The assembly by such methods of separate ocular impressions again recalled optical instruments. Charles Collins's *May in the Regent's Park* (1851), wrote the critic of the *British Quarterly Review*, made one feel 'as if one were looking at a piece of the park through an eyeglass from the window of one of the neighbouring houses'. It was part of the barely-intended radicalism of the Pre-Raphaelite vision that the role of the spectator in painting changed. He or she was no longer encouraged to become enveloped in the atmosphere of the picture, to explore the receding spaces. There was neither atmosphere, nor recession. The spectator stood apart, the scene transmuted, as through a glass lens.

There was finally an undeniable temperamental bond between the Pre-Raphaelite and photographic landscapist. The Pre-Raphaelites, with Holman Hunt at their head, are always cited in any survey of the Victorian gospel of work. Ruskin, himself no slouch, worried about his young protégés. In some of their pictures, he felt, sight had 'failed from weariness' and 'the hand refused any more to obey the heart'. The melancholic James Smetham felt similarly oppressed. 'Surely few persons have any idea,' he wrote, 'what it is to be a painter': a poet like Southey could spend fourteen hours in his library and take an inspiring mountain walk whenever he pleased; a painter, for his material, had to go in all directions: to Kew Gardens to paint a gourd, to the East End for a sailor's head. He had to 'haggle . . . with a Jew' or hunt through a library for costumes. For primroses, anemones and hyacinths, he had to travel to Kent: and then 'The golden day arrives when he could go to the woods, but the primroses are dead, the hyacinths drooping.'[10] Authenticity in painting caught on partly because it demanded qualities of endurance the age valued highly. Landscape photography demanded hardly less. On any serious expedition, the wet-plate photographer had to arrange for the transport of mahogany cameras, brass-bound lenses, sheets of glass, bottles of chemicals, and a darkroom tent. Once a site was selected, the tent had to be erected, a bucket of water fetched from the nearest village, and the camera focused. All this was nothing compared with the difficulty of preparing the plates for exposure in a small, dark, airless tent, full of ether fumes, frequently buffeted by the wind. Once prepared, the plate had to be loaded into the camera while still wet. After exposure, the photographer had to rush back to the tent to develop the plate immediately. While it was drying, lingering dust and debris had to be kept scrupulously at bay. Once all these operations had been completed, the plate could be stacked away for printing on returning home. The chemicals could then at last be loaded up, the darkroom dismantled, and everything transported to a new location. Aesthetically, the chief importance of these laborious procedures was that they bred an intense watchfulness – a Ruskinian virtue that, had Ruskin himself known more about serious photography, might have disarmed his criticism. For a photographer it was hardly worth going to the trouble of unpacking the equipment on a mere suspicion that one had a good subject. One had to be sure. Fenton's or Wilson's choice of subject was little less conscientious than Hunt's in Surrey or Inchbold's on the Isle of Skye.

The fate of an artist who was more at home with the old pictorial mode but had to adapt to the new trends is well illustrated by Smetham. A biographical note by his friend, William Davies, commented sadly after Smetham's death that his style had essentially been that of the 'old broad school' of Wilkie's time. He had failed ultimately as an artist because he had compromised with new trends. Davies had no doubt about what had led Smetham to forego his ample touch and harmonious colour: 'Photography, Pre-Raphaelism, and Ruskinism. He had not the power to resist these . . .'[11]

Hillside Calligraphy

On 17 September 1854, Ford Madox Brown, with his wife, child and maid, took a rural stroll from their home in Finchley to Mill Hill. His notebook records as much as his small oils, *Carrying Corn* and *The Hayfield*, the gentle enchantments of standing across a valley a few miles from the heart of London in the mid-nineteenth century.[12]

For the sterner spirits of the time, there was something missing in such scenes. Church, farmsteads, crops, and hedges spoke of human intervention. It was perhaps too easy for an artist to treat them merely conventionally. To many who, perhaps unconsciously, sought symbols of alienation, the barren shoreline or rockface was a more rewarding subject. Untamed nature could also provide keen visual delights of its own: crisp detail that transformed itself on canvas into an intricate calligraphy.

Painters and photographers turned their backs on the rural south and advanced towards the Celtic fringes of Britain. In Snowdonia or the Isle of Skye, densely-figured verticals predominated: mountainsides crisscrossed with foaming white streams, strewn with lichenous rock, furze and heather; ancient tracks and bridges hewn out of the landscape. 'O the dreary, dreary moorland! O the barren, barren shore!' – dreaming of Tennyson's *Locksley Hall* (1842), Inchbold, for one, abandoned the sunlit felicities of such works as *A Study, in March* and turned to Dartmoor and to Skye. Ruskin praised his 'exquisite painting of heather and rock' in *The Cuillin Ridge Skye* (fig. 51), exhibited in 1856. But Inchbold's true reward probably came from knowing that where he had gone, none could go further. He had confronted the most inhospitable terrain the country had to offer and depicted it with a fidelity few would ever be in a position to challenge.

His frozen vision was, however, emulated by others. The Liverpool painter, Alfred William Hunt, was influenced by Ruskin and Pre-Raphaelitism in the 1850s. The asperities of North Wales particularly appealed to him. Previous painters of this landscape such as the Birmingham artist, David Cox, romantically in love with bad weather, had lifted Snowdon from its foundations and swept it into a vortex. Hunt on the other hand portrayed the mountains as ramparts, firm in mass, fine in surface detail (fig. 49).

William Dyce, who shared the mountain temperament and (despite being Scottish) a love of Wales, pointed out what his generation got from this landscape. The explanation was geological: unlike the mountains of Scotland, which are granite and rounded through the action of the weather, Welsh mountains are made of slate rock. This material, Dyce noted, 'does not crumble like granite dust or sand but splits and tumbles down in huge flakes'. The peaks are thus 'as sharp and angular as if they had never been acted upon by the atmosphere at all'. Pre-Raphaelites were so indifferent to atmosphere, it seems, as to prefer rock that showed no hint of its workings through the centuries. In his paintings Dyce set off the terrain with figures: unlikely historical or biblical characters, peasant women knitting enigmatically in *Welsh Landscape with Figures* (1860). But his attention to the uniquely 'rugged, stoney ... precipitous ... awful and terrible looking' background shows where his chief interest lay at this time.[13]

North Wales had long been a haunt of artists in search of picturesque scenery. When George Price Boyce visited Bettws-y-Coed in 1849, he received advice from the ageing David Cox. For Cox and his generation, this charming village was both a shrine in its own right and a centre for mountain excursions. Photographers were led automatically to such places. Once they had developed ambitions beyond the trees at the bottom of the garden, rivalry with painters and the challenge of an arduous journey rewarded by a plethora of 'bits', propelled them where so many had been before. Besides his photographs of his native Surrey, some of Henry White's most successful images came out of a trip to Bettws-y-Coed (fig. 58).

Of all the photographers who trundled their equipment through the passes of North Wales, none had a finer feeling for the cragginess of the landscape than Roger Fenton. Fenton toured North Wales in 1858 and exhibited the results the following winter. It may seem strange to regard him as in any sense a 'Pre-Raphaelite' photographer. Though he was acquainted with Ford Madox Brown through a mutual friend, the painter Charles Lucy, his moneyed background, traditional artistic training under Delaroche in Paris, connections with the Royal Family and photography of the Crimean War, placed him far from the current Pre-Raphaelite ambience of obscure, unrewarded endeavour. He was strongly motivated by commerce through his involvement with the Photo-Galvanographic Company (a photo-engraving business) and Lovell Reeve's stereoscopic publications. Like most photographers, he saw himself as a traditionalist, ever 'in search of the

fig. 51

John William Inchbold
The Cuillin Ridge, Skye (The Burn, November – The Cucullen Hills) (1856)

Oil on canvas
20⅛ × 27⅛ in   51.1 × 68.9 cm
Ashmolean Museum, Oxford

fig. 52

Roger Fenton
Falls of the Ogwen: North Wales (1858)

Collodion
13⁷⁄₁₆ × 16¼ in   34.2 × 41.3 cm
From the collection of the Royal Photographic Society

From stark landscape, painter and photographer create visually energetic images, assisted by the patterns of gushing streams. Fenton supplied a hint of human presence by including a bridge. Yet it is absorbed into the terrain, 'flattened' in the Pre-Raphaelite manner by the slightly raised vantage point.

picturesque'.[14] As with George Washington Wilson, if the landscape arranged itself before the lens according to the formulae, he was delighted to record it. But this was not often the case, and he became, as it were, Pre-Raphaelite *malgré lui*. The pressure to produce images forced him to look for alternatives to traditional composition. He had a strong feeling, some would say a genius, for nature's geometry. He would reduce everything to juxtaposed or interlocking geometrical forms or place a sharp diagonal for maximum effect, but bounding across the whole are part-sinuous, part-jagged interweavings of linear detail. Unable to render atmosphere, Fenton focused on this combination of geometry and patterning. His *North Wales: Hillside Study* (1858; fig. 50) echoes in its directness the works of Inchbold and A. W. Hunt. Fenton deprives himself of any variation that would come from including the winding road just visible at the bottom of the image. He highlights the patterns formed by the expanse of striated, lichenous rock. The subject in *Falls of the Ogwen: North Wales* (1858; fig. 52) is closer: ground rising sharply in massed but uncluttered profusion of detail; the bridge, a natural part of the barren terrain, lending both formal and thematic balance. With these stark subjects, Fenton demonstrated the purely visual delights that compensated in photography for the absence of sky, atmosphere, and recession.

In this type of landscape, a more tangible link between Pre-Raphaelitism and photography is provided by Atkinson Grimshaw. The Leeds painter began his career in the 1850s under the influence of his fellow-citizen, Inchbold, and, hence, of Ruskin. His early work includes Ruskinian studies of grasses, moss, and rocks. Before turning to the nocturnal dockland scenes and townscapes with which he is mainly associated, he produced figure compositions influenced by Millais and Arthur Hughes and a group of highly elaborated Pre-Raphaelite landscape paintings. At the same time, he was interested in photography. This interest is unusually well-attested for landscape painters of this period. He lectured to the Leeds Photographic Society and is known to have made use of a magic lantern for photographic enlargement onto canvas. He indulged occasionally in the roguish practice of overpainting photographs and selling them as his own paintings. Internal evidence from many of his paintings suggests frequent assistance of landscape and architecture photographs. More important, photography played a part in the evolution of his style – detailed and descriptive, with the intricate silhouetting and hard shadows that are rarely a part of ocular perception but correspond with the way the camera often transposes reality.

In the 1860s Grimshaw was particularly interested in the Lake District. He owned an album containing photographs of the area by local photographers such as Thomas Ogle of Penrith. Indeed the suspicion with *Nab Scar*, (1864; fig. 54) is that it was painted mainly from Ogle's photograph (fig. 53) with little, if any, reference to the actual scene. The detailed foliate foreground, absent in the photograph, was possibly painted from nature locally – or from another photograph. The suspicion is strengthened by certain qualities in the work itself. Embodying, in a sense, the bond between photography and Pre-Raphaelitism in the sphere of landscape, the painting is nevertheless, despite

fig. 53
Thomas Ogle
Nab Scar Rydal Water – Hartley Coleridge's Cottage Home (c.1860)

Collodion
$2\frac{5}{16} \times 3\frac{3}{8}$ in   *5.8 × 8.6 cm*
In the collection of Leeds Art Galleries

fig. 54
John Atkinson Grimshaw
Nab Scar (1864)

Oil on board
25×30 in   *63.5 × 76.2 cm*
Private Collection

Grimshaw painted the scene both meticulously and directly. In this respect he was Pre-Raphaelite. However the painting lacks a sense of immediate contact with nature since it was painted mainly from Ogle's photograph. *Nab Scar* embodies a shift from an era when painters unconsciously mirrored photographic effects to one where these effects were copied from actual photographs.

its brilliant colour, more photographic than Pre-Raphaelite. Foreground and background, instead of adhering too closely to one another as in much Pre-Raphaelite work, inhabit two rigidly separate planes. Nab Scar itself, rising from across the lake, has a certain flatness but not the kind we associate with a painter like Inchbold. The true Pre-Raphaelite flatness results from the rush towards the picture-plane of each detail, however distant. It has a stippled quality and creates a sense of abnormally immediate contact between painter and subject. Grimshaw's details, on the other hand, are curiously amorphous, as if he did not really know what, in any accurate sense, he was painting.

An impression of detachment is further emphasized by a faint suggestion of mist hanging over the mountain. This, too, has a photographic look. Probably barely perceptible in the reality, it is the kind of vaporousness left out by orthodox Pre-Raphaelites in their quest for accuracy of form. Photographers, like Ogle or Fenton in some of his Welsh work, would have preferred such vapour to vanish entirely and reveal the precise geological formations, but, in photography, this rarely happened with so distant a subject. It is this very vapour, which the eye of the pure Pre-Raphaelite obliterates but which the camera takes note of, that finds itself subtly reproduced in Grimshaw's painting.

Nab Scar was, then, a pivotal work for Grimshaw. He was no longer a painter who, being Pre-Raphaelite, happened to share certain preoccupations with photographers but rather, was beginning to copy effects which belonged to photography itself. The direction of his later work confirms this. Grimshaw seemed to follow in the wake of photography. Effects such as a mottled sky hanging over a twilit city, which were beyond photography at the time of *Nab Scar*, intruded in his work as they came within photography's grasp and helped to forge his mature style.

There are certain photographs that testify directly to the shared interest of painters and photographers in the mountainous regions of Britain: images of artists perched, brush in hand, on a rock in the middle of a torrent – for all the world like one of the Millais-Ruskin party on the ill-fated Trossachs expedition. Ruskin excitedly described the setting for Millais's portrait of him in a letter to his father: 'a lovely piece of worn rock with foaming water and weeds and moss, and a noble overhanging dark crag'. This type of subject has a perennial fascination. The immobile rock and swirling water suggest fundamental oppositions. To Coleridge, the eddying torrent beneath a waterfall, 'obstinate in resurrection', blossoming up by fits and starts to form a constant shape, was nothing less than 'the life that we lead'. In *Easter 1916*, Yeats saw the stone as the 'hearts with one purpose alone': the determined political consciousness eternally present to 'trouble the living stream' of daily existence. But to the artists of the 1850s this subject was all the more fascinating because it presented them, in particular, with technical challenges that have seemed less pressing to other generations: the duty to transcribe faithfully a rich conjunction of rocks and plants. There was also the problem of water – how to do justice to that sparkling, foaming cascade

fig. 55

Joseph Paul Pettit
The Torrent-sculptured Bed of the Conway, North Wales (1858)

Oil on canvas
$43\frac{3}{4} \times 52\frac{1}{8}$ in   110.3 × 132.4 cm
The Trustees, The Cecil Higgins Art Gallery, Bedford, England

fig. 56

Francis Bedford
Bettws-y-Coed. Ffos Noddyn (The Fairy Glen), No. 1 (c.1860)

Collodion, one of a stereographic pair
$3\frac{1}{8} \times 3$ in   8 × 7.8 cm
Philippe Garner

The year 1858, when Pettit, as well as Fenton and A. W. Hunt, made excursions to North Wales, was the *annus mirabilis* of artistic achievement in the region. Ruskin's influence was then at its height. Pettit's work shows the extent to which even conventional artists succumbed. His tunnel composition, and his handling of distance and vegetation are orthodox, but the rocks are given a reverently exact treatment inconceivable before the advent of Ruskin. Bedford's stereo demonstrates that painters and photographers were almost falling over each other in their enthusiasm for mountain streams.

when its very movement did violence to prevailing static conceptions of art? The work of Millais in the Trossachs and of artists like Paton, or the Birmingham painter Joseph Paul Pettit (fig. 55), show the difficulties in depicting these waters without an aesthetic (such as Turner's or the Impressionists') that assimilates movement as an essential ingredient of reality. For a decade the artists were entranced – and the photographers recorded their efforts, though they, with their long exposures, were equally doomed to falsify ripples and cascades. In Bedford's (fig. 56) and White's photographs, the artists sit decorously, intent on a rock-face above glutinous white pools. The images are a fetching record of an era when Shakespeare's 'sermons in stones, books in running brooks' were an urgent reality.

Alpine Facts

For true mountain splendour, however, it was necessary to quit the shores of Britain altogether. Alpine landscape had, since the Romantic Movement, emerged from the indifference with which European culture had long treated it. Wordsworth had crossed the Simplon, Shelley had apostrophized Mont Blanc. Painters from J. R. Cozens to Turner had registered their awe. Nevertheless, it was only in the mid-nineteenth century that the British became properly acquainted with the Alps. The 1850s saw the foundation of the Alpine Club. It was a typical gentlemen's association of the time, composed chiefly of clergymen and dons. Like John Tyndall, they evidently held that there was 'assuredly morality in the oxygen of the mountains', although there was also a hint of neurotic escapism. A Yale man who met some Club members in Zermatt found them to be 'a set of Englishmen so peculiar as to be well worth knowing'. Murray's *Handbook* was harsher. It pointed out that many who had ascended Mont Blanc were 'of unsound mind'.

'Troubled' might have been a fairer word. Leslie Stephen's essay, 'A Bad Five Minutes in the Alps', written at a slightly later period, is indicative. Literary man, agnostic, and Alpinist, Stephen retired to the mountains to escape the transient and to make sense of the entirety of human history: 'to find some breath from the dead centuries lingering amongst the eternal hills'. Like Tyndall with his snowflake, Stephen, surrounded with sublimity, fixed on the minute: half-a-dozen ants he had inadvertently dispatched with the tip of his walking-stick on his ascent. Would his own death be 'of any more significance than theirs?' If he fell from a precipice, was there any comfort in the fact that in time the components of his body would merge with the glacier or mountain deposits? Without consciousness, matter – even one's own body – was 'supremely uninteresting'. God, even could one believe in him, was no comfort: 'in the presence of Infinity, what is the difference between a man and a flea?'

fig. 57

Joseph Noel Paton
A Study from Nature, Inverglas (1857)

Watercolour, 15 × 21½ in   38.1 × 54.6 cm
Sotheby's, London

fig. 58

Henry White
The Lledr Bridge, near Bettws-y-Coed
(1855–60)

Collodion
7¹¹⁄₁₆ × 10¼ in   19.6 × 26 cm
Victoria and Albert Museum, London

Paton's watercolour is intended as a self-effacing record of the scene, but like all the best work carried out at the apex of Ruskin's influence, it is infused with energy, transmuting the scene into a pattern of writhing forms. In the manner of photographs of the time the work contains a 'marker figure' (wearing a kilt to provide a hint for the location). White's typically lucid composition is further testimony to a current artistic obsession.

fig. 59
William England
Study of a Waterfall (mid-1860s)

Collodion
$8\frac{1}{4} \times 6\frac{5}{16}$ *in*   *21.1 × 16 cm*
Victoria and Albert Museum, London, on long loan
from Mr R. Mitchell

Denied Sublimity by their incapacity with
atmosphere and distance, early Alpine
photographers rejoiced in vertical patterns.

fig. 60
John Brett
The Glacier of Rosenlaui (1856)

Oil on canvas
$17\frac{1}{2} \times 16\frac{1}{2}$ *in*   *44.5 × 41.9 cm*
The Tate Gallery, London

fig. 61
Ernest Edwards
Upper Ice-fall of the Ober Grindelwald Glacier
(1866)

Collodion
$6\frac{11}{16} \times 5\frac{1}{4}$ *in*   *17.1 × 13.4*
The British Library

Edward's distance only just registers. Brett
is able to make a feature of his though his
main concern is the foreground, even
down to the smallest stones.

Stephen's lugubrious musings were rooted in what he saw, typically for
one who came of age in the early 1850s. The climate had changed since the
'Dizzy Ravine' had prompted Shelley 'To muse on my own separate fantasy'.
Stephen sought illumination from 'hard, tangible, unmistakeable facts' –
although he had 'A Bad Five Minutes' because, suspended from a precipice,
he was forced to confront the apparent comfortlessness of a materialist creed.
Stephen in fact had made up the precipice episode, but the piece was clearly a
true record of thoughts engendered by mountain 'facts'.[15]

The factual also dominated the ineffable in early mountain photography.
The first serious British mountain photographers worked not in the Alps but

in the Pyrenees. Two important figures in the early history of photography, Maxwell Lyte and John Stewart (brother-in-law of the eminent scientist and photographic enthusiast, Sir John Herschel), lived in Pau, in the French Pyrenees. Stewart showed his calotypes at the earliest exhibition of photography in London in 1852. Herschel referred in the catalogue to the 'exquisite ... finish' of Stewart's 'representations of superb combination of rock, mountain, forest, and water'.[16] The concentration on finish and hard detail was inevitable. Unable to echo the ethereal effects of previous generations of painters, photographers of the 1850s and 1860s recorded the mountains as massive material presences. Exhibition photographs, stereos, and illustrated books gave the photographers' stay-at-home compatriots the facts about mountain geology, vegetation, and glacier.

William England (fig. 59) and Ernest Edwards (fig. 61), in Switzerland in the 1860s, were interested, like Stewart before them, in the two-dimensional patterning that presents itself with the choice of a high horizon: a white cascade frozen between minutely figured banks of firs, a glacier, vertical before the lens, every line sharp in the hard mountain light. The comparative absence of colour in this landscape made it a particularly suitable subject for photography at this period. Occasionally, contemporary fascination with mountains is underlined by a dwarfed Alpinist, pick in hand, or a crinolined figure, pensive, intrigued.

Among those who took a camera to the Alps was Ruskin. After the buildings that he loved, mountains were what he most liked to subject to that 'heartless', but in some ways reliable, instrument. In 1849, after finishing *The Seven Lamps of Architecture*, he travelled to Switzerland to resume his mountain studies for the later volumes of *Modern Painters*. In Volume I, which he realized had not been scientific enough, he had merely treated the stones, hills, and peaks of mountain terrain as pictorial features – the foreground, middleground, and background in paintings by Turner and the Old Masters. His new studies, continued intermittently through the 1850s, were intended to unravel the secret principles of mountain formation. Painstaking drawings must be backed up with daguerreotype studies (fig. 62), leaving no detail to chance.

Ruskin had a further bout of mountain photography in the 1870s, when he became involved in controversy over glacier formation. Moving against Tyndall and other scorned authorities, Ruskin was at pains to demonstrate that a glacier had much in common with a dollop of ice-cream. A glacier was fluid: 'one great accumulation of ice-cream, poured upon the tops, and *flowing* to the bottoms, of the mountains'. The exhibits at the Ruskin Museum at Bembridge, Isle of Wight, give an idea of the extent to which Ruskin harnessed every means of visual representation to enforce his views on such matters. The 'Mer de Glace', central to his argument, appears drawn in watercolour, engraved, and photographed. Ruskin, the conscientious pedagogue, is touchingly brought to life by one exhibit: a small piece of card inscribed in his own hand (fig. 63). On it he has pasted an engraving of the 'Mer de Glace', detached from his own copy of Tyndall's *Glaciers of the Alps*

fig. 62

John Ruskin
Mountain Study (1854)

Daguerreotype
$4\frac{3}{4} \times 6\frac{1}{8}$ 12×15.5 cm
The Ruskin Galleries, Bembridge School, Isle of Wight

This is a rare Ruskin daguerreotype of a distant mountain scene – 'the fiery peaks' which in the euphoria of his youth Ruskin saw 'lift up their Titan heads to heaven, saying "I live forever!"' By the time this photograph was taken (with the help of his servant, Crawley), Ruskin was less sanguine about mountain durability. Everything in nature perishes, he realized: the 'veins of flowing fountain weary the mountain heart, as the crimson pulse does ours.'

State of Mer de Glace in 1874.

fig. 63

John Ruskin
Card showing
State of the Mer de Glace in 1874

Collodion
$6\frac{3}{16} \times 7\frac{1}{2}$ in   15.8 × 19 cm
Frontispiece to Tyndall's 'Glaciers of the Alps' (1860)
Engraving from drawing by P. Justyne
3 × 5 in   9 × 14 cm
The Ruskin Galleries. Bembridge School, Isle of Wight

In 1874 Ruskin travelled to the Alps to
gather material for his lectures on glacier
formation (published in *Deucalion*, 1875–83).
This card is related to these lectures and to
his contempt for the glacier authority,
John Tyndall. The photograph may have
been commercially available, or possibly he
arranged to have it taken while in the
vicinity.

Frontispiece to Tyndall's "Glaciers of the Alps"

(1860), and a photograph showing the state of the glacier in 1874. To Ruskin, upstaging erroneous 'experts' was a legitimate use of photography: ultimately one of the few reasons he had to be thankful for its invention.

He was so omniverous in relation to certain phenomena, that at times he could not forbear to use the camera – as if it were a necessary extension to his over-stretched sense of sight. But besides his more general reservations about photography, he was on the whole disappointed with the results where mountains were concerned. His early daguerreotypes are often little more than silhouettes of mountain crests; the later photographs, dull scientific records, giving no sense of mountain scale. Ruskin equated the photographic image with the mere glance of the 'careless observer', or the mundane perceptions of the 'ordinary artist'. Only the true artist, he who, for example, had looked long and hard at the structure of *aiguilles*, could perceive the profound truth that they were 'welded' together, 'like the bones of the jaw of the saurian'. Photography and second-rate art picked up only the 'cragginess and granulation' of mountains, missing the 'make and growth'.[17]

Where his beloved Alps were concerned, Ruskin could not abide superficiality of any kind. He derided the members of the Alpine Club – unfairly, considering their earnestness and sometimes fatal courage: 'You look upon (the Alps) as soaped poles in a bear garden, which you set yourselves to climb, and slide down again with "shrieks of delight".' The artists whom he persuaded, directly or indirectly to go to the inconvenience of painting the Alps, fared little better in his estimation. Inchbold, painting at Chamonix, 'got entirely off the rails', Ruskin believed. In his *Academy Notes* for 1857, Ruskin ignored (apart from a passing mention) the artist's *Jungfrau from the Wengern Alp*, which he himself had commissioned. The saga of John Brett's *Val d'Aosta* (1858; fig. 48) is no less sobering. 'What would he not make of the chestnut groves of the Val d'Aosta!' Ruskin declared after seeing the artist's *The Stonebreaker*, set in the more modest sublimities of the Dorking region of Surrey. Obediently, Brett set off. He spent the summer of 1858 perched across a twelve-mile stretch of valley, visited occasionally by his mentor who would drop by to give him a 'hammering'.

When the painting was exhibited, Millais gave vent to his contempt and continuing relief at being free from Ruskin's tutelage. 'There is a wretched little work like a photograph,' he wrote to Effie, 'evidently painted under his influence'.[18] Ruskin, disappointed with a work which purported to follow his principles, but which, in his view, failed to depict the mountain essence, also resorted to the comparison with the camera: Brett had taken 'to mere photography'.[19] Indeed, Brett's picture, brilliant-hued *tour-de-force* that it is, has a cartographic accuracy and a carefully organized avoidance of sublimity that make it comparable with Alpine photography of the period.

Although, as Millais's remark makes clear, Ruskin was seen as the man who was making artists paint photographically, Ruskin himself was ready to dismiss a painter, as he dismissed Brett, if that was what he thought he was doing. He had a guilty conscience about it (which led him dutifully to buy *Val d'Aosta*). He knew that his eulogies of the imagination of artists like Tintoretto were barely reflected in his practical advice to painters. This advice, backed up by his personal 'hammering', had only stressed the facts, and he realized that if impressionable young artists took him at his word he himself was partly responsible. He had, of course, said little about how a young artist should imaginatively transform reality or get to the heart of it, because, like Reynolds and all the great art teachers before and since, he knew that this was a mystery that could not be taught. If in future he recommended artists to paint like 'mere photographers' he was careful to link this with the preservation of records of threatened landscapes and architecture, and not to involve himself in the suggestion that this was a royal road to art. Meanwhile the idea that photography itself, in the hands of an artist-photographer, could imaginatively transform reality was neither considered by Ruskin nor by hardly anyone else at this time.

Consanguinity with Molluscs

The statement that Brett had taken to photography was truer than Ruskin knew. It is not clear precisely when he took it up, but it was probably after he had stopped worrying about what Ruskin thought of him and had begun to consider how to combine earning a living as a painter with leading an agreeable life. He started a family, took up sailing and decided that, England being England, there was always a market for seascapes and coastal scenes. His Pre-Raphaelitism would remain uncompromised in that he would continue to aim as far as was possible for absolute truth of representation. To help carry out this intention with this most capricious of subjects (as well as to record moments from the new and better life that beckoned) he would use a camera.

We get some idea of how photography fitted in with Brett's work as a painter from an 1883 entry in the diary of Beatrix Potter. On the first of what was to become many meetings, the creator of Squirrel Nutkin missed the touchiness noted by others in Brett, responding instead to his bonhomie and his red whiskers.

He was such a hearty little man, stout with dark red whiskers. He was very kind and told us a great deal of interest. He goes sailing about the west coast of Scotland in his sailing yacht in the summer, making small oil sketches which he uses for the colour in his pictures which he paints in the winter months, chiefly from memory, though also assisted by photographs, for he is a successful photographer.

The entry concludes with a statement that will not surprise anyone familiar with the realities of Academic art at this time: 'Mr Millais says all the artists use photographs now.'[20]

If the large Academy vehicles, which emerged from Brett's annual round, have a routine quality, they at least brought him success and compensated

fig. 64

The Lion Rock from Asparagus Island
(1870)

Pencil
$5\frac{9}{16} \times 9\frac{1}{4}$ in   14.2 × 23.5 cm
J. D. B. Watson

fig. 65

Lizard (1889)

Oil on canvas
10 × 19 in   25.4 × 48.3 cm
N. R. Omell

fig. 66

The Lion, the Lizard, and the Stags (1889)

Oil on canvas
42 × 84 in   106 × 213 cm
Courtesy of Christie's

fig. 67

John Brett
The Lion Rock from Asparagus Island
(1870)

Collodion
$6\frac{7}{8} \times 9\frac{1}{8}$ in   17.5 × 23.2 cm
J. D. B. Watson

These four items show how
photography fitted into the
procedures of a successful Academic
painter instilled in youth with the
Pre-Raphaelite regard for accuracy.
Photograph and pencil sketch were
inserted opposite each other in
Brett's notebook for July–October
1870. On the decision to work the
subject up into a large Academy
piece, the small oil sketch was carried
out on the spot for colour notes.
Taken in the service of another
medium Brett's image shows how
photography, extracting colour and
movement, was well suited to
express sombre Victorian perceptions
of the seashore.

for earlier humiliations. Photography did not, as in the case of Atkinson Grimshaw, foster an alternative vision; it just made his life easier. It was, as for 'all the artists', a useful resource. In 1889 he exhibited *The Lion, the Lizard and the Stags* (fig. 66), a large oil painting of that same Lizard coast on which the Llewelyn family had diverted itself some thirty-five years previously. This painting seems to have been worked up from at least three sources: an oil sketch of the type mentioned by Beatrix Potter bearing the inscription *Lizard 1889* (fig. 65), a pencil sketch from 1870 and a photograph apparently taken at the same time as the latter (figs. 64, 67). The only variation in Brett's normal practice here is the nineteen-year gap between the beginning and the culmination of the procedure. He had clearly used the sketch and photograph to make a mental note of a subject that might be worth taking up at a later stage.

Brett's attitude to photography was casual and workaday. He delighted in photographing his family on board his yacht or painting pictures of each other. Yet photography remained a serious index of his basic Pre-Raphaelite creed, which survived long after Pre-Raphaelitism itself had become *passé*, and after he had restricted himself to a limited subject-range, eschewing the overt literary-moral emphasis of the original movement.

For Brett, accuracy remained a prime goal. Indeed, this led him, some might think woefully, to misjudge other artists. As late as 1895, he was lauding J. F. Lewis as the greatest master of modern art at the expense of the 'superficial' Constable. He scorned the Impressionists, but this was not surprising in one who still condemned a seventeenth-century painter like Ruisdael in the language of *Modern Painters*: 'No such trees, no such watercourses, much less any such rocks or clouds as he shows . . . ever could have any counterpart in the real world.'[21] If Brett made any retreat from 'mirror's work' in his later years and relied to some extent (as Beatrix Potter indicates) on memory, this was not from conviction, but convenience – and the reaction of his contemporaries. In a paper read at the Camera Club in 1889, Brett was rueful on the subject of accuracy: 'it is disheartening to know that the taste for accuracy is not a plentiful endowment of human nature. People are rarely thankful for it and in some cases they are offended at and resent it.'[22] So speaks, decades after the humiliations of *Val d'Aosta*, the faithful and embattled spirit of the 1850s.

Brett's coastal paintings might impress more if Victorian interest in the subject had not found consummate expression in William Dyce's *Pegwell Bay, Kent – a Recollection of October 5th, 1858* (fig. 70). Dyce's family is on the sea-shore at low tide in the waning light. They are collecting shells, but the activity is desultory, overshadowed by private worlds. The geologically-rendered cliffs and Donati's comet, a thin line, evoke the brevity of life and the passing of time. The mournful work has accredited Pre-Raphaelite and photographic associations. (Dyce, an older man, was never a part of the Pre-Raphaelite Movement proper.) *Pegwell Bay* lacks the bright colour of mainstream Pre-Raphaelitism and, being a 'Recollection' worked up from sketches and memory, did not obey the letter of the Movement's doctrine. But with its geology and astronomy, precise location and minute handling, the painting has an air of insistent accuracy which marks it as a central product of the Pre-Raphaelite era. Its photographic character comes partly from the artist's vantage point. Dyce positioned himself as if he were having to take account of a photographic problem: that of foreground distortion. If photographers of the time wanted to avoid an expanse of foreground, they would raise the camera angle, or crop the print: either way, the image began, as it were, at some distance from the camera. *Pegwell Bay*, too, is set at a distance. The effect is not to make us lose interest in the protagonists. On the contrary, we scrutinize them with enhanced curiosity. We become alert to every nuance in their relation to the surroundings. The photographic impression is further strengthened, meanwhile, by the predominant monotone and, of course, the detail.

fig. 68
William Dyce
The Ferryman (c.1857)

Oil on canvas
$19\frac{1}{2} \times 23\frac{1}{2}$ in   49.5 × 59.6 cm
Aberdeen Art Gallery and Museums

fig. 69
John Dillwyn Llewelyn
Thereza with a Telescope (c.1854)

Collodion
Sotheby's, London

fig. 70
William Dyce
Pegwell Bay, Kent — a Recollection of October 5th, 1858 (1858–60)

Oil on canvas
25 × 35 in   63.5 × 88.9 cm
The Tate Gallery

The photographer George Washington Wilson claimed to know for a fact that Dyce's *The Ferryman* was painted from a photograph. The detail and predominant monochrome of *Pegwell Bay* led to similar accusations. One thing is certain: the enigmatic mood of Dyce's masterpiece is also found in the photography of the period. Llewelyn's protagonists, like Dyce's, wander on the shore, gaze distractedly at their feet or ponder the horizon. Llewelyn's aim here was to capture the breaking wave and billowing dress with his 'instantaneous' exposure, but as in *Pegwell Bay* Tennyson's 'terrible muses', astronomy and geology, are at hand.

Comparisons with photography were made from the first, no doubt further fuelled by Dyce's longstanding association with that photographic pioneer, David Octavius Hill. The defensiveness of an article by James Dafforne in the *Art-Journal* suggests that accusations were rife. The 'supposition' that the work was based on photography had been encouraged, Dafforne admitted, by the 'wonderful elaborate detail'. But, he claimed confidingly, 'we happen to know that it was done from memory, aided by a slight and hasty sketch, in pencil, of the locality'.[23]

Whatever the truth about *Pegwell Bay*, defenders of Dyce had no right to be outraged at the 'supposition' that he was capable of copying a photograph. The following bears witness:

Some years ago, I was photographing in the country, and was struck with the picturesque appearance of an old boatman on the river Dee. I arranged him to my mind, and took a photograph of him whilst sitting beside his boat on the banks of the river. A copy of this photograph I presented to a celebrated Royal Academician, since dead, and he painted a picture from it, which was exhibited at the Royal Academy.

The photographer who wrote this was George Washington Wilson. The 'celebrated Royal Academician' was Dyce. The painting in question was *The Ferryman* (c.1857; fig. 68). Unfortunately, Wilson's photograph has not been traced so we are not in a position to verify the photographer's claim that Dyce copied it 'literally, even to the threadbare knees of the boatman's corduroys' – still less to adjudicate on whether, as Wilson felt, it had as much claim to art as a painting 'acknowledged to be . . . an embodiment of all that was precious in pre-Raffaeleism'.[24] There is no reason to doubt Wilson's evidence – nor, perhaps, that of Dafforne. Probably Dyce was capable of copying a photograph straight; probably also, despite the photographic features of *Pegwell Bay*, he had not done so with that picture. In any case, with a work of such calibre, it is of little more than documentary interest.

Photography may also lie behind Charles Napier Hemy's *Among the Shingle at Clovelly* (1864; fig. 71) with its near-monochrome sharpness. The work does not evoke the same unease as *Pegwell Bay*, however. For this we must look to photography itself. A number of photographic images confirm a sense of the centrality of Dyce's picture. The key to their success lies, as it does in *Pegwell Bay*, with the aura surrounding the figures. A convention had arisen in photography of depositing members of the better-dressed classes before ruin or rock-face, where (as one critic noted) they adopted a genteel air of 'waiting for the operation to be finished'.[25] In photographs of beaches and rocky coasts by Llewelyn and one or two others, this ineptitude in the treatment of figures is overcome. They seem not so much temporarily discomfited as, like Dyce's distracted protagonists, provoked into uneasy meditation.

One reason for the power of these images was the response the sea and the coastline evoked in most Victorians. There was no need for the figures to pose. Their interest and their awe communicated themselves naturally. It has often been said that the Victorians discovered the seaside. It was not just that

fig. 71
Charles Napier Hemy
Among the Shingle at Clovelly (1864)

Oil on canvas
$17\frac{1}{8} \times 28\frac{3}{8}$ in   43.5 × 72.1 cm
Laing Art Gallery, Newcastle upon Tyne

fig. 72
Francis Frith
Hastings from the Beach (Low Tide) (1864)

Collodion
$4\frac{3}{8} \times 5\frac{15}{16}$ in   11.1 × 15.1 cm
Victoria and Albert Museum, London

Hemy's painting is indebted to Pre-Raphaelitism: to his teacher, William Bell Scott, to Ruskin, and to Brett's *The Stonebreaker* (1857–8). But Hemy was also, like Atkinson Grimshaw at this time, beginning to copy photographic effects: even tonality, and receding, misty distances. Beyond that, the picture confirms the message of Frith's photograph taken in the same year: the shore was a place for desultory activity and wan communion with self.

they learned to transpose cockney pleasures to the sands of Ramsgate, and to potter in rock-pools and caves; they found a new symbolic suggestiveness in the very meeting of the sea and the land. In *Dover Beach* (1867), Arnold entreated his companion

> Come to the window, sweet is the night-air!
> Only, from the long line of spray
> Where the sea meets the moon-blanch'd land,
> Listen!

The ceaseless action of the waves sounded for the poet the tragic facts of human existence which religion could no longer ameliorate.

With the consolation of science, if not of religion, G. H. Lewes was more sanguine. There was mystery and beauty in the way the soft waters worked at transforming the rugged shore. It was like the action of love itself, 'the sterner asperities of life . . . moulded finally by tenderness and love'. But for Lewes, too, the essential message remained that of human insignificance. When he and his companion at Ilfracombe, George Eliot, saw clusters of houses on the cliffs, they perceived that man was no more than a 'parasitic animal living on a grander creature', his dwelling-place mere barnacles. 'In vain,' Lewes concluded, 'does our pride rebel at the thought of consanguinity with a mollusc.'[26]

It is absurd to speculate whether the figures in photographs dwelt on human destiny as they sat on rocks and gazed at the sea. More likely they, and the photographers, had their minds on practical problems: Llewelyn's letters refer to the actinic rather than the spiritual vibrations emitted by rocks. Nevertheless, the photographs, consciously or otherwise, convey states of mind through compositional and thematic choices. The figures are invariably dwarfed by the rocks, almost swallowed up in Bedford's *Rock on the Seashore* (1862; fig. 21), for example – as if the geological facts, because of the pressure to deny them, required all the more massive assertion. In Llewelyn's pictures, that other background component of *Pegwell Bay*, astronomy, appears in the form of a telescope wielded by his daughter, Thereza.

In *Thereza with a Telescope* (c.1854; fig. 69), Llewelyn no doubt intended first to record his pride in his favourite daughter's scientific pursuits and secondly (since he was at the time pioneering instantaneous photography) to record the action of the wave and the billowing of her dress in the wind. But if we do not know this, the image is of one who desperately scrutinizes the horizon – stranded, we might feel, on the barren shores of rationalism, searching for a sign from the Infinite. It is, above all, the authentic air of distraction, combined occasionally with suggestions of desultory activity, that cements the link between these images and Dyce's *Pegwell Bay*. There are no convivial groups in these photographs. Even at a resort like Hastings, as recorded by Francis Frith (fig. 72), each figure is bent on solitary communion. With their constricting clothes, these pensive beachcombers are unmistakably of their time. But as they string themselves out along the rocky strand and stare out to the eternal sea, they appear emblems of a universal humanity.

fig. 73

John Dillwyn Llewelyn
Two Girls on the rocks at Dunraven (c.1854)

Collodion
$6\frac{1}{2} \times 8\frac{1}{2}$ *in*   *16.5 × 21.6 cm*
Richard Morris

This image portrays Llewelyn's daughters, Thereza and Emma Charlotte. Though one of the girls is casually sketching, the unease of Dyce's *Pegwell Bay* is present. Rocks, the focus at that time of anxiety and religious controversy, loom over the figures, whose solitude and displacement is curiously emphasized.

Literalism in Walls

The shore was a particularly effective image of desolation, since it registered few marks of activity. Ancient ruins, another subject popular with both Pre-Raphaelites and photographers, also delivered a bleak message on transience. In early Pre-Raphaelite works – such as Millais's *A Huguenot*, Collins's *The Good Harvest of 1854*, Hughes's *Home from Sea* (1856–62) – crumbling, ivy-covered walls, though in the background, attracted attention through their meticulous treatment. In the hands of Pre-Raphaelite followers walls relinquished their background status and became more or less the true subject of the painting.

It was remarked of Brett, when he exhibited his *Warwick Castle* (1861), that he seemed 'unable to bear up against the paralysing influence of an overmastering literalism in stone walls'. This might more fairly have been said of Inchbold, who twice applied himself meticulously to the irregular stonework of Bolton Priory (figs. 19, 74). Boyce, meanwhile, cultivated a more orderly, if not even more minutely-textured vision. His speciality was the old manor-house or working farm, which he painted brick-by-brick in delicate-hued watercolour (fig. 77). Old buildings, central to the Picturesque, had long been a popular subject for British painters. Inchbold and Boyce re-orientated the tradition. For poetic atmosphere, emphasized by the inclusion of surrounding country, they substituted the Pre-Raphaelite interest in the tangible.

Inchbold appended lines from Wordsworth's 'The White Doe of Rylstone' (set at Bolton) to his pictures of the Priory. But it was Scott, the other of the two most widely-read writers of the time, who chiefly fed enthusiasm for ruins. Such places invariably provided the setting for his work. Standing in gaping nave or on tottering rampart, the romantic Victorian tourist became enveloped in the aura of Scott's half-bogus but persuasive fictions. One sighed for the education of Marmion. As a child, the part-noble, part-villainous hero of this 'Tale of Flodden Field' discovered the charms of the obscurest recesses of these buildings:

> . . . well the lonely infant knew
> Recesses where the wall-flower grew,
> And honey-suckle loved to crawl
> Up the low crag and ruin'd wall

Long before, quoting a passage like this from Scott, William Pitt had remarked that this was 'the sort of thing which I might have expected in painting but would never have fancied being capable of being given in poetry'. This admiration for Scott's word-painting was widely shared. It was for this, as much as for his medievalism, that Rossetti was inspired to become his frequent illustrator and William Morris to yield 'to no-one, not even Ruskin, in my love and admiration for Scott'. In *The Germ*, William Michael Rossetti's 'To the Castle Ramparts' evoked mildewed walls, rusty-hinged doors, winding towers and battlements. The ineptitude of the verse makes it kinder to forego quotation.

Ruins became the most popular of all photographic subjects. As William and Mary Howitt remarked of Kenilworth in their photographic publication, *Ruined Abbeys and Castles of Great Britain and Ireland* (fig. 76): 'had not Sir Walter Scott made it the theme of one of his most thrilling romances, its ivied ruins would now have stood little regarded'[27] – little regarded, and little photographed. The formidable Quaker pair, the Howitts, added to their modern causes (civil liberties, animal protection, mesmerism) both Pre-Raphaelitism and photography. Their ruined buildings publication included the work of the masters of the collodion era, Fenton, Wilson, Bedford, and many others.

Interest in this subject stretched back to Talbot himself. He had photographed Melrose Abbey, made famous by Scott's moonlight evocation in *The Lay of the Last Minstrel*. Another innovator, Frederick Scott Archer, tried out his new wet collodion process in a series of views of Kenilworth (e.g. fig. 20). Fenton, wishing to test his photographic van (a converted Canterbury wine merchant's carriage) for his planned visit to the Crimea, toured the Yorkshire Abbeys in 1854. Philip Delamotte and Joseph Cundall followed him

fig. 74

John William Inchbold
At Bolton (The White Doe of Rylstone) (1855)
Oil on canvas
27 × 20 in   68.6 × 50.8 cm
In the collection of Leeds Art Galleries

fig. 75

Joseph Cundall and Philip Henry Delamotte
Bolton Priory (1856)
Collodion
$11\frac{1}{4} \times 8\frac{9}{16}$ in   *28.5 × 21.8 cm*
From the collection of the Royal Photographic Society

Pre-Raphaelites and photographers feasted on the textures of stones, ivy and lichens. *The White Doe of Rylstone* is a prolix narrative by Wordsworth.

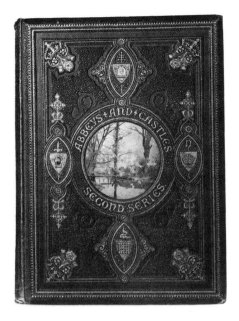

fig. 76

Front cover of William and Mary Howitt's *Ruined Abbeys and Castles of Great Britain and Ireland*. Second Series, 1864, including part of Stephen Thompson's 'General View of Kenilworth'.

8 × 6 in   22.7 × 16.4 cm
The British Library

The Howitts' work was the best-known of numerous photographic publications surveying the ancient ruins of Britain. The subject had been popular since the eighteenth century, but the camera's capacity to register each evocative scar convinced photographers that they had outclassed their rivals with the brush. They did not reckon with the Pre-Raphaelites whose 'overmastering literalism in stone walls' presented an equal challenge to the Sublime or Picturesque approaches of the past. Thompson's photograph of Kenilworth looks incongruous in the middle of a mock-medieval cover design: as was perhaps the entire enterprise of harnessing nineteenth century literalism to nostalgic ends.

there and produced *A Photographic Tour among the Abbeys of Yorkshire* in 1856. The very popular Howitt work appeared in two volumes in 1862 and 1864, sandwiching yet another such publication, Dr Hemphill's *Photographic Illustrations . . . of Clonmell* of 1863.

There was a curiously Victorian blend of romance and realism about all this. The images nourished reverie and fantasy. The *Art-Journal* reviewer of the 1856 Photographic Society exhibition, surveying the 'many examples of "Ruined fanes, relics of hood and cowl devotion", of crumbling castles and tottering mansions', discoursed upon the workings of 'Time's effacing fingers'.[28] Another photographic critic saw, Scott-like, the windows of Kenilworth as 'panes through which bright eyes have gazed and angry looks passed – where, as in a cage, pied, yellow, and red jesters have gambolled and ladies sighed and laughed'.[29] But the photographers were also responding to a market. Scott-based literary tourism (encouraged further by the railways and Queen Victoria's promotion of all things Scottish) and the lapse in the 1850s of the writer's copyright created a Scott industry in publishing. The photographers were naturally eager to exploit this. Pandering to fantasy, they contrived to exalt fact: stressing photography's superiority over its rivals in reproducing each scar on the weather-worn building, 'every channel which the rain drops and the wind has worn': not 'pleasant fictions', boasted the Howitts, but 'realities'.

'The reader,' they declared, 'is no longer left to suppose himself at the mercy of the imaginations, the caprices, or the deficiencies of artists, but to have before him the genuine presentment of the object under consideration.'[30] The same critic who had seen Scott's jesters and sighing ladies at Kenilworth was contradictory enough to affect a disdain for the fictionalizing painting of the past, such was his urge to exalt photography. His regard for the truth-giving qualities of the new medium produced a paean to the modern age. Few people who had seen such photographs, he argued, would any longer believe that 'exactitude is unpoetic or fidelity unimaginative'. Photography's capacity to 'carry off this affidant of the transitory' exemplified 'the wealth and science of the nineteenth century'.

We have already seen that this enthusiasm among photographers for 'exactitude' and 'fidelity', though it sometimes induced ribaldry at the expense of the art of the past, did not lead the photographers to respect the Pre-Raphaelites. It nevertheless brought about inevitable similarities in the treatment of this, as of other subjects. Frank Mason Good (whom we met earlier as an enthusiast for tree texture) tackled a manor-house (fig. 78) in the same way as Boyce. He avoided recessional emphasis and arranged façade, roof, and wall into a pattern of flat planes varying minutely in texture. Inchbold's Bolton pictures, with their close view of the interplay of foliage of worn stone, were echoed by Delamotte and Cundall when they visited the same Abbey (fig. 75); Inchbold was also anticipated by Scott Archer at Kenilworth. Nor were these photographers alone in this concentrated approach to the subject. The *Photographic News* complained of 'a fault very common amongst many young, and some old, photographers, that of

making the building fill the picture, so as to exclude entirely its surroundings'.[31] Once again, lured by their mastery of concrete detail into 'Pre-Raphaelite' composition, photographers had offended pictorial conventions according to which a ruin should be seen set back, in harmonious surroundings. The only concession to the surroundings made by Delamotte and Cundall, was that allowed by Inchbold in *At Bolton* (1855; fig. 74): a 'hole' in the composition, through which they could be cursorily glimpsed.

No ruin photographs were more remarkable for detail than Fenton's *Raglan Castle* series. It was clearly because of this that *The Watergate* (fig. 79) was chosen to be among the first of Paul Pretsch's photo-galvanographic prints, issued in October 1856. The ivy, smothering the ancient walls, joins with the myriad leaves of the adjacent trees to encrust the greater part of the image. The victory of nature over the works of humanity is announced. This encrustation, together with the stillness of the reflecting moat, makes the image unnaturally static – a quality further emphasized by the photo-galvanographic form in which the image has survived (the process involved weeks of hand retouching).

Is this not the landscape of Tennyson's 'Mariana' (1830) – the mosses which 'crept' and the waters which 'slept' around the 'lonely moated grange'?

> About a stone-cast from the wall
> A sluice with blacken'd waters slept,
> And o'er it many, round and small,
> The cluster'd marish-mosses crept.

Millais, in treating the poem, depicted Mariana in her chamber, and used her restless pose and warm colour to suggest the fervour of her suppressed emotions. He relinquished an important element in the poem, the deathly calm of the surrounding landscape and its colourlessness – 'grey' and 'silver-green'. Calm and colourlessness (inevitably) are captured in *The Watergate*: a dream-like clarity and bloodless quiescence evoke the desolation which lies at the heart of the poem, though we cannot know whether Fenton had Tennyson in mind.

The beautiful stagnation of *The Watergate* is marginally alleviated by the stairway leading up from the moat. It beckons us to climb and enter. Painters and photographers often add a hint of mystery in works of this type with half-open doorways and dark, receding hallways or corridors. Surface patterns are broken up with areas of darkness. The Liverpool Pre-Raphaelite, William Davis, does this with his *Mary's Well near St Asaph* (1859; fig. 80). A study by a member of the Amateur Photographic Association portrays a woman reading a book in front of a particularly ghostly ruin (fig. 81). We are likewise prompted to 'read' the ruin. Like Davis's well, it evokes the idea of ruin as labyrinth – appropriate considering the intricate web of literary and historical associations these buildings possessed at this time. As the *Photographic News* confirmed: 'The landscape photograph is beautiful, but we look at it and pass it by having no associations . . . But think of our ancient buildings. How easily . . . can we make the dry bones live.'[32]

fig. 77

George Price Boyce
Farm Buildings, Dorchester (c.1860)

Watercolour over pencil on paper
$14\frac{9}{16} \times 21\frac{1}{8}$ in   37 × 53.5 mm
Fitzwilliam Museum, Cambridge

fig. 78

Frank Mason Good
A Cotswold Farm (late 1850s)

Collodion
$6\frac{11}{16} \times 8\frac{5}{8}$ 17 × 22 cm
Michael Rich

Like the watercolourist, George Price Boyce, in his Pre-Raphaelite phase, Good here provided an ordered and intimate vision of English rural architecture. Space is limited and the foreground emphasized. Minutely varying textures are organized to form a simple overall pattern.

fig. 79

Roger Fenton
Raglan Castle, the Watergate (1856)

Photo-galvanographic print
$8\frac{15}{16} \times 7\frac{3}{16}$ *in*   22.7 × 18.4 *cm*
From the collection of the Royal Photographic Society

A perfect image for the display of Paul Pretsch's photo-galvanographic process; this method of photo-engraving involved extensive hand-retouching. Harnessing the Pre-Raphaelite era's mania for encrusted detail to long popular Picturesque subject matter, the image is weirdly static and unreal. The claustrophobia of Tennyson's 'Mariana' comes to mind: the 'moated grange' where 'the blacken'd waters slept' and the 'cluster'd marish-mosses crept'.

fig. 80

William Davis
Mary's Well near St Asaph (1859)

Oil on board
$12\frac{3}{4} \times 18$ *in*   32.5 × 46
Sotheby's, London

fig. 81

Anon.
Goodrich Castle (1860s)

Collodion
$9\frac{1}{2} \times 11\frac{5}{8}$ *in*   24.1 × 29.5 *cm*
From the collection of the Royal Photographic Society

Both the anonymous amateur here, and the Liverpool Pre-Raphaelite, William Davis depict an overgrown, labyrinthine retreat. Given the appeal of these buildings to the literary imagination, the photographer's solution to the problem of how to give the marker figure something meaningful to do, though conventional, seems appropriate.

To be read aright ruins must be seen properly, not lost in the distance, or with picturesque features exaggerated. How 'grand' the 'unexaggerated statement' could be, as distinct from the imaginative extemporization, was made clear by Ruskin in one phase of his thinking.

When considering 'Turnerian Topography' for the fourth (1856) volume of *Modern Painters*, Ruskin both sketched and daguerreotyped one of his favourite architectural effects: the ancient walls of Fribourg in Switzerland (figs. 82, 83). These range up and down steep slopes, interspersed with tall look-out towers. Turner swept scenes like this up into the trammels of his imagination: the result was a breathtaking amalgam of his own mind and what the eye saw. But only Turner could do this. For artists without Turner's

fig. 82 OVERLEAF

John Ruskin
The Towers of Fribourg (1856)

Engraving from sketch
$5\frac{1}{8} \times 3\frac{1}{2}$ in   *13 × 9 cm*

fig. 83 OVERLEAF

Engraving from daguerreotype
$1\frac{6}{16} \times 1\frac{1}{16}$ in   *3.5 × 2.7 cm*
Reproduced in Modern Painters IV   *The British Library*

Ruskin claimed that a painting based on his photograph of the Fribourg walls would not only be 'more right' but 'infinitely . . . grander' than the one based on his sketch (Ruskin, *Works*, VI, pp. 46–7).

powers there remained a question: should one exaggerate here and suppress there, or simply aim for a photographic likeness? Ruskin did not rule out either option. His own 'exaggerated' sketch had the advantage, he believed, of drawing attention to a particular feature of the Fribourg walls: that they had 'flexible spines, and creep up and down the precipices more in the manner of cats than walls' (an inspired comparison which showed of course that Ruskin's true talent was writing). And one feels that revealing the catlike nature of walls – in other words, seeing things in a fresh way – was substantially what Ruskin believed art was about. Nevertheless in contradiction to his later dismissal of Brett's 'mirror's work' and 'mere photography' he states his preference for a 'grand' depiction based on the daguerreotype: 'on a clear and calm forenoon, I daguerreotyped the towers ... and this unexaggerated statement, with its details properly painted, would not only be the more right, but infinitely the grander of the two.'[33]

The message to his disciples was clear: unless they had the temerity to compare themselves with Turner, the 'grandest' thing they could do was cultivate daguerreotype vision. When Inchbold and Brett moved on, there was a new generation of Ruskin acolytes associated with his projects such as the Working Men's College and the utopian Guild of St George: men like John Bunney, Thomas Matthew Rooke and Frank Randall. By this time Ruskin was so anguished by the demolition of ancient buildings throughout Europe that he no longer required young artists to transform themselves into Turners during a course of his 'hammering', but merely to furnish an accurate record. The photographic injunction, which as the Fribourg example shows, had been explicit in Ruskin's earlier recommendations to artists was strengthened, although no longer linked to serious theorizing about art. Ruskin made little distinction in his conservation work between the use of photographs and paintings. Having organized the section by section drawing and photographing of St Mark's Basilica in Venice, he set Bunney to paint the West Front (fig. 86). The job took six years, at the end of which the artist died. One day when Bunney had been hard at work Whistler had been spiteful enough to creep up and attach a card reading 'I am totally blind' to his back. The truth behind this jibe was that it did not need a human being with eyes to carry out Bunney's task. A machine could have done it.

Yet it was perhaps a half-truth. The camera itself is not a 'blind' eye. The photographic language, when employed by painters (whether or not appropriate) is even less impersonal. Bunney's work, the first masterpiece of 'photo-realism', advertized qualities of dedication and manipulative skill that other kinds of painting delight in concealing.

fig. 84

John Ruskin
The St Jean d'Acre Columns, with the south side of St Mark's (1879)

Pencil and watercolour heightened with white
$6 \times 3\frac{1}{2}$ *in*   *15.3 $\times$ 9 cm*
British Museum

fig. 85

Daguerreotype (c.1850)
$6 \times 4\frac{3}{8}$ *in*   *15.3 $\times$ 11.2 cm*
The Ruskin Galleries, Bembridge School, Isle of Wight

fig. 86

John Bunney
The West Front of St Mark's (1876–82)

Oil on canvas
57 $\times$ 89 in   144.8 $\times$ 226 cm
The Guild of St George, Sheffield

On occasion, Ruskin used the daguerreotype 'without scruple' (*Works*, XI, p. 312). This 1879 drawing reproduces the reversed image of the daguerreotype. It was perhaps an indication of a disturbed state of mind that one so valiant for truth imperturbably drew his favourite building the wrong way round. The year before he had been temporarily insane and the drawing was connected with an American exhibition of Ruskin's work arranged as a distraction by his friend Charles Eliot Norton. Bunney's early masterpiece of photo-realism, which took six years to complete, led to insults from Whistler and the artist's early death.

4 Journey to the East

fig. 87
William Holman Hunt
The Afterglow in Egypt (1854, 1860–3)

Oil on canvas
73 × 34 in   185.4 × 86.3 cm
Southampton Art Gallery

Invasion and Capture

For every pictorial mode there is an Ideal Subject: for the Impressionist, the banks of the Seine *en fête*; for a fifteenth-century Florentine, the pierced torso of St Sebastian; for the photographic or Pre-Raphaelite landscapist of the 1850s; a particular kind of terrain; static, devoid of rippling water, or trees which bend and quiver in the wind. This is a landscape of hard configurations, where a fierce sun casts a fretwork of shadows. There are no wreathed summits, but valleys curving majestically to fill the field of vision. Marks of the new world of steam and telegraph are absent; instead, there are crumbling habitations, ancient tracks, the patterns of primitive hillside cultivation. Human beings are scarce – for anything which moves is alien to this sensibility – but, when glimpsed, dark eyes and flowing robes contribute an unmistakable aura. The country depicted must above all be rich in associations so that every half-deserted village, abandoned tomb, or dried-up well tells a story; each story a particle of the Divine Word.

The photographers and painters of the 1850s who made Palestine their own were not admittedly the first in modern times to journey to this remote province of a vast, decaying empire. The very name the 'Holy Land' had a resonance which, as soon as travel became easier, had encouraged Europeans to dream of pilgrimage. By the mid-nineteenth century there was an established tourist route. It began in Constantinople and ended in Cairo, taking in Palestine (often referred to at this time as Syria) on the way. This was the route followed by Alexander Kinglake, whose stylish account of his journey, *Eothen* (1844), was only the most original of a growing body of literature on the area. Breathing a spirit of urbane curiosity and mild xenophobia belonging to the era of the Grand Tour, *Eothen* reminds us that the Tour was widening its scope: moving out beyond the confines of a Europe overrun with railways and middle-class tourists. Lucy Duff Gordon, who spent her final consumptive years in Cairo penning her sympathetic *Letters from Egypt* (1865, 1875), observed that the English milord, now 'extinct on the Continent', could still in this part of the world find treatment according with his dignified perception of himself: he was still 'greatly reverenced and usually liked'.

While one of the wittier of the species was enjoying the runaway success that would ensure him a lifetime of dinner invitations as 'Eothen Kinglake', a complete visual record of the Holy Land was emerging in the volumes of coloured lithographs made from the drawings of David Roberts. A Scottish Royal Academician, Roberts had carried out his drawings exhaustively, on the spot. He had made efforts to bend the ungrateful landscape of the Near East to the conventions of the Picturesque: foregrounds of colourful native figures, or fragments of ancient masonry, framed by trees, ruins, or escarpments; middle distances containing the main subject – a monastery, a mosque, the city of Jerusalem, backgrounds of misty hills. Roberts's activities signalled the fact-gathering mania that also lay behind the careers of his

contemporaries: William Bartlett, who is reckoned at his death to have produced over a thousand drawings of the Near East; David Wilkie, who died on his return from the area; the Bristol painter, William Müller; and that purveyor of an intricately-observed yet sanitized exoticism, John Frederick Lewis, who settled in Cairo for a decade. The interest in the region was also reflected in ambitious publishing ventures. *Finden's Illustrations to the Bible* (1836) was a comprehensive popular picture book; John Carne's *Syria, the Holy Land Asia Minor etc.* (1836–8) a systematic topographical survey. Popular interest soon prompted John Murray to bring the Near East into the orbit of his travellers' guides.

Thoroughgoing as the expeditions of the 1830s and 1840s were, an air of more intense endeavour surrounded the later Pre-Raphaelite and photographic incursions. The Pre-Raphaelite connection involved two men (unless like Ruskin, we include Lewis – who at this stage had not heard of the Movement – as a Pre-Raphaelite): Holman Hunt and Thomas Seddon. Seddon, the pious but excessively jocose son of a London cabinet-maker, was a friend of Madox Brown and the Rossetti brothers, and the would-be pupil of Hunt.

The relevant facts concerning Hunt and Seddon can be briefly told. Hunt left England for Egypt and Palestine in 1854 after exhibiting, amid

fig. 88

Julia Margaret Cameron
Holman Hunt in Eastern Dress (1864)
Collodion
$10\frac{3}{16} \times 8\frac{3}{16} in$ $25.9 \times 20.8 cm$
National Portrait Gallery, London

fig. 89

William Holman Hunt
Recollections of the Arabian Nights (1857)
Pencil
$6 \times 6\frac{1}{2} in$ $15.2 \times 16.5 cm$
Courtauld Institute of Art

Coventry Patmore most admired Cameron when she eschewed costumes and effects ['Mrs. Cameron's Photographs', *Macmillan's Magazine*, 13 (November 1865–April 1866), pp. 230–1]. Here 'colour' was probably included at the behest of the sitter. Hunt's delight in his 'Eastern Dress' was elaborated into outright fantasy in a drawing for the Moxon Tennyson.

fig. 90

William Holman Hunt
The Shadow of Death (1870–3)

Tempera and oil on canvas
$84\frac{5}{16} \times 66\frac{3}{16}$ in *214.2 × 168.2 cm*
City of Manchester Art Galleries

fig. 91

Frank Mason Good
Interior of a Workshop (late 1860s)

Collodion
$3\frac{15}{16} \times 3\frac{3}{16}$ in *10 × 8 cm*
The Palestine Exploration Fund

Good's workshop was adequately lit and contained the clutter of objects which appealed to the 'Pre-Raphaelite' photographer in him. A carpenter's shop had obvious hallowed associations. Good like Hunt hoped to sustain the Christian faith by recording the facts surrounding its origin.

controversy, *The Light of the World* (1851–3) and *The Awakening Conscience* (1853–4): the result of his novel combination of exalted themes and proliferating detail. The paintings brought him into the public eye and he sensed perhaps that the rewards just beginning to be preferred to his friend, Millais, might soon come his way and divert him into taking his profession less seriously. He stayed abroad for about a year and on his return, exhibited *The Scapegoat*, painted at the Dead Sea and in Jerusalem, and eventually his *tour de force* of biblical reconstruction, *The Finding of the Saviour in the Temple* (1854–60). While there he also painted a number of watercolours. His fascination with Palestine was to prove inexhaustible. He made further extended visits in the late 1860s and 1870s the chief products of which were *The Shadow of Death* (1870–3; fig. 90) and *The Triumph of the Innocents* (1875–85). These works are weirdly tasteless in conception and graceless in form. They test the faith of even Hunt's most devoted admirers, but the painful elaboration of pious subject matter emphasizes his remarkable ability to stick to his original Pre-Raphaelite principles.

On his first trip to the Near East he was preceded by Seddon. Waiting for Hunt in Cairo, Seddon had gone native, sartorially and in his enthusiasm for snakes. This irritated Hunt, as did his general levity, which had been encouraged by the brief companionship of Edward Lear. This bad start killed

fig. 92

Thomas Seddon
*The Great Sphinx at the Pyramids
of Gizeh* (1854)

Watercolour and bodycolour
$9\frac{3}{4} \times 13\frac{7}{8}$ *in   24.7 × 35.3*
Ashmolean Museum, Oxford

fig. 93

Francis Frith
*The Sphynx, and the Great Pyramid,
Gizeh* (1857)

Collodion
$6\frac{7}{16} \times 9$ *in   16.4 × 22.9 cm*
*From the collection of the Royal
Photographic Society*

Compared with Hunt, who eccentric-
ally painted the Sphinx from behind
Seddon and Frith contented themselves with a straight account.

fig. 94

Thomas Seddon
The Valley of Jehoshaphat:
Painted on the Spot, during the
Summer and Autumn Months
(1854–5)

Oil on canvas
$26\frac{1}{2} \times 32\frac{3}{4}$ *in* 67.3×83.2 *cm*
The Tate Gallery, London

fig. 95

James Graham
Kedron Valley (mid-1850s)

Paper negative
$7\frac{3}{4} \times 10\frac{3}{16}$ *in* 19.6×25.8 *cm*
The Palestine Exploration Fund

'Mr Graham photographs . . .'
wrote Seddon to his
fiancée. 'I hope to bring
some of [his views] to
England for him, so that I
shall be able to show them
to you and supply my own
want of sketches. They are
extremely valuable,
because perfectly true as
far as they go; however,
they will never supplant
the pencil, for there is
much in photographs that
is false . . .' [John Pollard
Seddon, *Memoirs and Letters of*
the Late Thomas Seddon
(London 1858), p. 111]

off the possibility of true friendship developing between Hunt and Seddon. Nevertheless, they applied themselves to the matter in hand. After tackling various Egyptian subjects, they made for Palestine. In Jerusalem they parted company to considerable mutual relief, though they continued to meet up for fraught, but not unenjoyable, expeditions into the hinterland. Hunt lodged in the city; Seddon encamped on a hillside nearby and embarked on *The Valley of Jehoshaphat* (1854–5; fig.94), the *ne plus ultra* of Pre-Raphaelite landscape (if this accolade is not merited by Brett's *Val d'Aosta*). Seddon left Palestine much earlier than Hunt. His earnestness was not in the same league and besides, he had left a girl behind whom he was anxious to marry. But he was as bitten with the urge to return to the Near East as Hunt; fatally, in his case as it turned out. Never a man of strong health, he succumbed to dysentery and died in Cairo in November 1856.

Photographically, it was at first the French who dominated Palestine – as was the case with her archeologically more awesome (and thus more obviously photogenic) neighbour, Egypt. There is a lingering Bonapartist air of educational fervour and colonial aggrandizement about *Les Excursions Daguerriennes* (1842–4), a set of engravings from daguerreotypes that included views of Jerusalem, Nazareth and Acre; similarly with the expedition of Maxime du Camp that resulted in the spectacular *Égypte, Nubie, Palestine et Syrie* (1852). Most people are likely to know of this expedition less through direct contact with du Camp's rare gold-toned calotypes, than through his companion, Flaubert's, scandalous written record of their adventures, chiefly sexual, *en route*. Nevertheless, du Camp was sent to the near East by the French Ministry of Education.

Flaubert in Egypt makes racier reading than the Rev. Dr Alexander Keith's *Evidence of the Truth of the Christian Religion* (1837), though the latter much reprinted work was no less characteristic of the nationality of its author. Keith was an Evangelical Scot, harnessing photography to his Mission. The very title of his vast work, which later contained engravings from now lost daguerreotypes, encapsulates the impetus behind British photography in Palestine in the first decades. The French sought enlightenment about remote civilizations: the British, Evidence – Protestant confirmation of the veracity of the Word. Calotypists in the early days varied between those, like Dr C. G. Wheelhouse, for whom Palestine was a stage in a Mediterranean pilgrimage, and others, like Hunt and Seddon's friend, James Graham. Graham, another pious Scot, was settled in Jerusalem and cultivated an interest in the biblical terrain as dogged as that of his Pre-Raphaelite fellows.

It was not until the wet collodion era, however, that this landscape, with its characteristic textures, was done photographic justice. By the late 1850s, an invasion was underway: Francis Frith, whose aim was to do Roberts over again for photography; Felice Beato who, with his brother-in-law James Robertson, exhibited fine studies in London in 1860; the Glasgow photographer John Cramb, whose views were published in *Jerusalem in 1860* by the Rev. Robert Buchanan; Francis Bedford, who toured the near East in the Prince of Wales's party in 1862; and Frank Mason Good, whose penchant for the

fig. 96
William Holman Hunt
The Plain of Rephaim from Mount Zion (1855–61)

Watercolour
14 × 20 in   35.6 × 50.8 cm
Whitworth Art Gallery, University of Manchester

fig. 97
Francis Bedford
The Village of Siloam, in the valley of Jehoshaphat, with the Hill of Evil Counsel, and the valley of Hinnom (1862)

Collodion
9 × 11 7/16 in   23 × 29 cm
The Palestine Exploration Fund

Bedford is fully equipped to record a landscape described by Hunt as having 'the proportions and lines of a human skeleton'.

unusual view took him to holes and corners off the normal itinerary. British photographic interest in the region inevitably culminated in the triumph of system: an *Ordnance Survey of Jerusalem* was carried out in 1865, involving extensive photo-documentation. More followed the setting up in the same year, of the Palestine Exploration Fund, an organization (still in existence) born of a characteristic blend of fact-finding, religious and hegemonist impulses.

Withdrawing the Silken Veil

A decade before Hunt and Seddon set foot on biblical soil, David Wilkie had called for an end to topographical inexactitude and Renaissance anachronisms in the treatment of historical or religious themes. Wilkie believed that in painting, as in theology, 'a Martin Luther' was called for 'to sweep away the abuses by which our divine pursuit is encumbered'. The Protestant ring to the remark well anticipates his Pre-Raphaelite successors. Seddon's intention in Jerusalem was to 'wield my brush in defence of the holy city from all misrepresentation'. Hunt thought that painters should go out to strange or historically interesting places 'two by two, like merchants of nature, and bring back precious merchandise in faithful pictures'. The 'triviality and superficiality' of the thousands of travel books produced every year was a reproof to his profession.

The response at home to Hunt and Seddon's work reflected these intentions. If contemporaries did not always like their work, they at least accorded it recognition as a valuable record of the facts. Especially was this the case with Seddon. Madox Brown, who found nothing 'of beauty, nothing to make the bosom tingle' in Seddon's Jerusalem picture, acknowledged that it embodied 'truthfulness seldom surpassed'. This was essentially Ruskin's response. Touched by Seddon's early death, he was eloquent in his praise of his 'truly historic landscape art'. Seddon united 'perfect artistical skill with topographical accuracy'. This involves 'self-restraint' – the subordination of the pictorial and dramatic effects sought by previous artists. 'In Mr. Seddon's works,' Ruskin concluded, 'the primal object is to place the spectator, as far as art can do, in the scene represented, and to give him the perfect sensation of its reality, wholly unmodified by the artist's execution.'[1]

This was also of course a precise statement of the photographers' aims. 'We may long have revelled in the *poetry* of the East,' wrote Frith's publishers, introducing his work for the first time, 'but this work enables us to look ... upon its realities.' Photography withdrew 'the silken veil' of Arabian Nights fantasy.[2] Just as efficaciously as Hunt and Seddon's work, it overthrew the pictorial conventions in representing the region. W. M. Thompson, who wrote texts for Bedford's work, confessed that 'almost the whole field' had been covered by Roberts; but only now, with photography, was it possible to perceive the 'hard, stern realities' of 'each mouldering ruin'. Done with

fig. 98
Francis Frith
Self-portrait, Turkish Summer Costume (1857)

Collodion
$6\frac{11}{16} \times 5\frac{1}{4}$ in   *17 × 13.4 cm*
From the collection of the Royal Photographic Society

Frith remarked on the advantage painters had over photographers in a country where 'Every man robes himself according to his own free, gorgeous fancy'. Without colour, photographers must bow to their 'brothers of the brush and palette, who may paint with little fear of exaggerating even to the verge of Pre-Raphaelite brilliancy' [Frith, *Egypt and Palestine*, I, n.p.].

'fervid imagination', we can sometimes seek, Thompson argued, a greater beauty and interest 'in the literal accuracy of the transcript set before us by the photograph'.[3] Such arguments carried an irresistible weight at this time. The *Athenaeum* critic found himself looking askance at Roberts in the light of photography. He could not get the right 'feelings of desolation, voidance and ruin' from Roberts's polished productions: 'We have seen photographs which were awfully grand in comparison.'[4]

Advantageously for both Pre-Raphaelites and photographers, the traditional British susceptibility to landscape was combining with Protestant devotion to the Bible to view the topography of Palestine as synonymous with the Word of God: to tamper with it was sacrilege. The *Art-Journal* thought the Holy Land 'the theme of all others best calculated for treatment' by photography. Here, 'any object ... would lose by being subjected to fancy'.[5] Likewise, subjects which would hardly have engaged attention at home, were transformed by their associations. Frank Mason Good, for instance, photographed a carpenter's shop (fig. 91) similar to that used by Hunt in *The Shadow of Death*. In Palestine, if not in Shoreditch, carpentry was a hallowed occupation. Ruskin lent his support to the choice of superficially unappealing subject matter, so long as it contributed to the spread of biblical knowledge. Hunt's Dead Sea might seem the dreariest imaginable setting for a painting, but actually it was ideal: 'exactly the scene of which it might seem most desirable to give a perfect idea to those who cannot see it themselves'.

The more wide-ranging the topographical investigations became, the more, as one writer said in 1865, they seemed to corroborate 'the minute accuracy of the Inspired Record'.[6] To those with a taste for Old Testament hellfire, the surest proof of biblical efficacy came from the dilapidation of modern Palestine. The Rev. Keith, compiling his '*Evidence*' with the daguerreotype, derived a grim satisfaction from the 'general desolation ... the mouldering ruins ... the cheerless solitude'. This was precisely what had been predicted if the Jews failed to recognize the Messiah. Photography, the product of modern atheistical science, merely gave Keith 'a still deeper conviction of the defined precision of the *sure word of prophecy*'.[7]

It is important not to put too simple an interpretation on the pious motives of those who journeyed to the Near East at this time. What the painters and photographers wrote should not necessarily be taken at its face value. Hunt's youthful journey was later incorporated in an elaborate personal mythology: in time, he viewed it through a veil of self-justifying nostalgia. In 1886, he remembered telling his friend, the painter, Augustus Egg, that he was going to Palestine 'to prove, so far as my painting can, that Christianity is a living faith'. But his memory was at fault. At the time, he had written to Millais professing to find it 'most amusing' that his friends thought he was intent on painting 'scriptural subjects'. He had not, he wrote, 'a single intention formed about my work of any kind'. Maybe this was no more absolutely true than his later pious avowals. Aware that his friends thought him a prig, Hunt, in writing to Millais, was perhaps anxious to project a more casual, even *risqué*, image of himself. Hence, his willingness also to confide an

amorous encounter on the journey – a 'little impropriety' in a 'French railway carriage'.

Though saintliness was no more widespread in the 1850s than at any other time, it was more common then than now for people to lead thoroughly muddled and barely virtuous lives in which religion was nevertheless a reality. To say that Hunt or Seddon, Frith or Graham, were drawn to portray the stony soil of Palestine purely from pious motives, would be to ignore the contradictions in their characters. Both Seddon and Graham had a tendency to laxity: Seddon, with his 'rattles' and 'violent fits' of laughter, mirthless practical jokes, and 'taste for pleasure and dissipation' acquired during student days in Paris; Graham, who, in the words of his enemies in Jerusalem, 'indulged too much in the society of worldly people',[8] and who, as an 'incorrigible procrastinator', disconcerted Hunt.[9]

But each subjected his instinct to the daily scrutiny of the watchful Christian. Seddon had persuaded himself in youth that his heart was 'desperately wicked'. In Jerusalem, he would put down his brush and pick up Keble's *Christian Year*. He was dedicated to the belief that his profession was the 'handmaid to religion and purity instead of mere animal enjoyment and sensuality'. He sought the company of Anglican clergymen (who were thick on the ground since the recent establishment of a bishopric).

Graham had a job which required no defence against accusations of animal enjoyment, rather of tastelessness. He was secretary of the London Society for Promoting Christianity among the Jews. Edward Lear certainly thought that the enterprise was as absurd as trying to 'convert all the cabbages and strawberries in Covent Garden into pigeon pies and Turkey carpets'. But the job gave Graham the chance to be about the Lord's business as much as his 'usual delays' would permit: preaching in outlying villages, routing out bad language, 'shocking and unnatural' practices, and the 'playing at marbles, ball, and other games on Sunday evenings' in the Diocesan school.[10] His Sabbatarianism was such that when camping in the wild, he would keep the other members of the party awake in the small hours of Sunday morning by taking 'upon himself the office of priest'. Sermons were his favourite reading and, although his opinions on photography are unrecorded, it is not difficult to imagine him agreeing with the Rev. Keith or Francis Frith that the truth of the new medium was a divine quality: one which might be expected to have the happiest influence on 'the morals of the people,' as Frith put it.[11] Certainly, photography seems for Graham to have mingled with religion as a daily pledge and obsession.

The religious motivation of these men is important because it confirms the evidence of their work: in laying a visually all-encompassing hold on the terrain and reducing or banishing the native inhabitants, they seemed, more than the more tasteful Roberts before them, to be claiming it as theirs, feeling deep down that it belonged to them. This feeling arose from a refined awareness of the country's spiritual associations and also, inevitably from a sense of racial superiority. The decay of the town and villages, which illustrated the unfitness of the inhabitants, strengthened the British

fig. 99
Francis Frith
Jerusalem. The Pool of Siloam (late 1850s)

Collodion
$8\frac{1}{16} \times 6$ *in*   *20.6 × 15.4 cm*
The Palestine Exploration Fund

It is tempting to regard this dazzling image as a celebration of the gift of sight itself: it was in the Pool of Siloam that the blind man in *John* 9 was bidden by Jesus to wash in order to see. It is unlikely that Frith, a religious man, would have been unaware of the New Testament episode.

Protestant's proprietariness. Later British politicians such as Milner and Curzon, who saw Britain as 'marked out' to rescue the region from barbarity and squalor, were merely inheriting the longstanding prejudices of British travellers, not least photographers and painters.

British policy in the Near East is comically foreshadowed by Holman Hunt who was forever giving Arabs a 'clout on the head', 'thrashing scoundrels', knocking 'half-savages' down two at a time, or seeing them off with the threat, 'We are English, and you had better be careful'. Inspiring terror and awe as he carved his imperturbable way through diverse populations with his alien machine, Frith, for his part, embodied the mentality of divide-and-rule: he had an equal contempt for all whom he met – the bigoted, ignorant, ruling Turks; the servile, vagabond Arabs; the 'hideous black children' and women of Nubian Egypt.[12] John Cramb, and the writer of Bedford's text,

fig. 100

James Graham
General View from Mount of Olives (1855)

Paper negative
$7\frac{7}{16} \times 9\frac{13}{16}$ in *19 × 25.3 cm*
The Palestine Exploration Fund

'Graham rented a tower on the Mount of Olives'; Hunt wrote: 'below were stables, kitchens and servants' rooms; above were sleeping and sitting chambers. At times the tenant went there to sleep in the fresh air; he gave me a free invitation . . .' [William Holman Hunt, *Pre-Raphaelitism and the Pre-Raphaelite Brotherhood* (London 1905), I, p. 431]. Graham's tower is identifiable as the nearer of the two in this photograph. During an 'invalid week', Seddon also exchanged his insect-infested hillside for the tower, rejoicing that Jerusalem lay 'like an open map' before him [Seddon, *Memoirs*, p. 119].

W. M. Thompson, were no less overcome with disgust: the Christian Arabs in Jerusalem were childish, the Jews idle and filthy. Cramb's remark that the only modernization in Palestine (some new roads) had come about through 'Russian gold', shows how little the fears and phobias of international relations have changed.[13]

If a man 'has no organ of veneration', wrote Frith, 'he had better stop at home and read "Eothen".' How could these rabidly observant travellers not feel possessive when every name recalled things learned at the parental knee? – 'an immortality,' as Frith phrased it, 'which has mingled vaguely with . . . thoughts since childhood'. The first journey from the port of Jaffa, across the narrow coastal plane and up through the hills to Jerusalem, was for them (no less than for the Diaspora Jew) an emblem of spiritual ascent and a series of rendezvous with things strangely familiar, culminating in the sight of the Holy City itself.

John Cramb, with his photographic equipment loaded onto mules (there were no wheeled carriages available in Palestine at this time), passed through villages both biblically resonant and 'quite unfit, according to our notions, for the habitation of the lowest animals'. Suddenly, he 'saw – JERUSALEM!' He was 'not poetical'; he could not, he wrote, 'go into ecstasies' – but what he felt during those few minutes was 'beyond description'. The sense of a profoundly personal revelation – at which point in travel memoirs the amused, superior tone breaks down – was commonplace. A few years before Cramb, Seddon had stood at the same spot: soon he would be within the city where Christ had endured so much suffering for *him*. 'I never was so affected in my life,' he wrote, '. . . and could hardly help from bursting into tears.'

The path to achieving an accurate representation of these hallowed spots by camera or brush was fraught with so many obstacles that there grew up an inevitable mythology of triumph-against-the-odds. The saga of Hunt's sojourn by the Dead Sea – where he endured horrors natural and supernatural, and 'frequent attacks from savage desperadoes' – has been told too often to bear repetition. Frith's difficulties were hardly less and were endured over much longer periods during three visits to the Near East. Things were especially bad in Egypt. The problems of preparing and developing the negatives, serious at any time, were multiplied. Once, it was so hot that the collodion actually boiled when Frith poured it onto the glass. Sometimes he was able to utilize a tomb or temple chamber as a dark room: but the floor would be covered in several inches of 'impalpable, ill-flavoured dust' and 'groups of fetid bats' hung from the ceiling. The subject Frith had come to photograph would elude him. He would be put ashore from the Nile in the vague vicinity of some treasure of Egyptology with a load of cumbrous apparatus and an unhelpful guide and would have to walk for miles over rough ground under the hot sun 'through dirty mud villages, suffocating us with noxious dust, and swarming with vermin, and curs and black children, naked and hideous' – before finally arriving at his goal.

Hunt had suffered hallucinations at the Dead Sea; Frith was driven by his privations into regarding his activities as 'so many mockeries and snares'.

Added to the physical endurance, and the burden of dealing with the under-races, this threat of derangement under a blistering sun adds the final link between a Hunt or a Frith and those whose escapades fed the myth of Empire: Livingstone, Gordon, Rhodes, and others. Their works are a testimony to crackpot courage and ingenuity as well as to the hold on the Anglo-Saxon imagination of an especially blessed and benighted region of the earth.

Mad Fools' Utmost Wishes

Hunt, Seddon and their photographic counterparts were also greatly excited by the physical qualities of the Palestinian landscape. Many pictures exploit a formula already familiar from our earlier investigations. Hunt in *The Plain of Rephaim from Mount Zion* (1855–61; fig. 96), *Nazareth* (1855–61; fig. 107) and other watercolours; Seddon in his Jerusalem *chef-d'oeuvre* and a watercolour, *The Mountains of Moab* (1854); Frith or Robertson and Beato in Jerusalem; Bedford at Siloam (fig. 97) – in purely compositional terms there is little to distinguish this work from Inchbold in Skye or Fenton in North Wales. Painters and photographers choose a high vantage point, whence they look across a valley to intricately-striated terrain rising opposite. The horizon is high and parallel with the top of the picture. The sun, low but strong, etches the shadows without which the landscape might appear characterless. There is no atmosphere; but here, more than at home, it could be argued that this accorded with the facts. 'I really believe that there was no more atmosphere at the time,' replied Seddon to criticism of his skeletally dry landscape. If there was a difference between this landscape and the Cuillin Ridge or Snowdonia, it was that it yet more ideally suited the demands and limitations of the new visual sensibility of the 1850s. The 'beauty independent of fruitfulness' referred to by Hunt was subject to a vision quite different from previous treatment. 'David Roberts *might* depict as he can . . . all he saw,' wrote Cramb with customary disdain, 'but how much was there he did not perceive.' He goes on:

Generally the air is so free from moisture that objects miles off are as sharp and *intense* as those in the immediate foreground of the picture. There is, generally, no atmosphere; for the artist's atmosphere is not air, but water. The mere photographic enthusiast, who desires clear definition throughout his entire picture, will have his utmost wish satisfied in such countries as Palestine. Planting his camera on the top of any house about the centre of Jerusalem and turning his lens towards Olivet, how delighted he will be to find the Church of the Ascension as clearly defined and as intense in shadow as the roof of the next house, though in reality some two miles distant.[14]

Cramb contrasts the 'mere photographic enthusiast' who liked clarity, a high vantage-point, and the cleaving of distant objects to near ones with the

fig. 101

Francis Frith
Philae: the Approach (late 1850s)

Collodion
$6\frac{7}{16} \times 9$ *16.4 × 22.9 cm*
From the collection of the Royal Photographic Society

The Ptolemaic and Roman ruins of Philae are sometimes scorned by Egyptologists, but they were a popular destination for Victorian travellers. Frith admitted that 'everybody' had sketched the island, 'many clever artists have painted it – Murray has engraved it for his "Guide".' [Frith, *Egypt and Palestine*, II, n.p.] But Frith's image made previous representations look almost washed out. The eye immediately focuses on the huge but minutely marked granite rocks and is then led firmly across to the ruins, dwarfed, crumbling, yet resilient in the fierce light.

atmosphere-entranced 'artist'. He seems little aware that there was in his time another kind of artist who relinquished atmosphere, sought definition, painted from a height, and (as hostile critics had often pointed out) allowed distant clouds to cleave to nearby heads: a kind of artist who just as much as the photographer had his 'utmost wish satisfied in . . . Palestine'.

Frith's study of the crumbling walls of the Pool of Siloam (fig. 99) show that he was as alive as any to the qualities which made Palestine so rewarding a subject for the wet collodion operator. Nevertheless, he was more truly at home in Egypt. The geometry of the ancient temples, emphasized by sharp morning light, never tired him. The flat terrain (which Hunt found no more appealing as a subject for art than Hackney Marsh) allowed the monuments to stand forth in colossal self-sufficiency, though maimed by the passing of time. There is little parallel here with Hunt and Seddon's work in Egypt, which, with the exception of bold studies of the Sphinx – Hunt's an idiosyncratic backview – were relatively conventional (figs. 92, 93).

All the same, comparison of Frith's treatment of the island ruin of Philae (fig. 101) with that of Roberts before him reveals the photographer's Pre-Raphaelite sensibility. For *The Island of Philae, Nubia* (1843), Roberts had positioned himself at a distance and looked down across the river at the entire temple complex: a vast, mysterious ruin in a softly sunlit, yet spectral landscape. No-one put into words the effect of Roberts's painting better than Frith when he was describing Philae for his readers: 'a vision of a giant fairy-land'. But from Frith's photograph we get no such impression. Huge granite rocks with minute, sharply etched markings dominate the foreground. By the disposition of the rocks, the eye is led firmly across the river to the temple and distant hills, all sharply defined, almost unnaturally so. Such poise and exactitude – the noble human artefact, though distanced, standing solid in the crisp light – rob Philae of all 'fairy' qualities. Not for the first time, a photographer had used words that had no connection with the new pictorial world embodied by his images.

Alerted by the obvious compositional similarity with Hunt's *The Scapegoat*, one is tempted to see Frith's *Crocodile on a Sandbank* (1857; fig. 103) as a comment on Hunt's portentous symbolism. Hunt's picture is (to some at least) unintentionally droll: there is something deliberately so about Frith's image. 'Look at this portrait!' wrote the photographer: his features are 'hideously grand', his teeth 'charmingly gothic', his hands 'almost as beautiful and delicate as a lady's'. In both pictures, a creature is posed centrally (Ruskin objected to Hunt's naïvety in this) against a strip of water with a harsh landscape rising beyond. The crusty hide of the crocodile is no less palpable than the numbered hairs of the goat. The crocodile is at once more prosaic and more exotic than Hunt's creature. The mysteries of animal life in such alien terrain require no anthropomorphic projection to exert their fascination. Hunt's kind of painting must make the facts *mean* something; Frith's photography asserts the sufficiency of the 'facts in themselves'.

In the light of these parallels, it is interesting to discover how much time the two Pre-Raphaelites, Hunt and Seddon, spent in Jerusalem in the company of a photographer: the dilatory James Graham. Both painters used to visit Graham's pied-à-terre on the Mount of Olives, a lonely tower easily identifiable in numerous contemporary photographs of the sacred spot (e.g. fig. 100). There they would divert themselves by raking the parched panorama with the Scotsman's telescope, or gaze at the Holy City, opalescent in the moonlight, while their host read aloud from a book of sermons. Along with another Scot, a Dr Sim, Graham, as 'caterer and paymaster', was Hunt's invariable companion on forays into the wild. While the painter would search for places to set up his easel, Graham, with 'a photographer's keenness', would confer with him on subjects for the camera. 'Graham was to photograph, Sim was to shoot, and I to draw . . .' wrote Hunt of an early expedition to Wadi Kerith. The territory was to be 'bagged' with the diverse implements of a superior civilization.

Graham frequently photographed close to where Hunt or Seddon were painting. He employed variations on Seddon's view of Jerusalem, and

fig. 102

William Holman Hunt
The Scapegoat (1854–5)

Oil on canvas
33¾ × 54½ in   85.7 × 138.4 cm
Merseyside County Council, Lady Lever Art Gallery,
Port Sunlight

fig. 103

Francis Frith
Crocodile on a Sandbank (1857)

Collodion
6⅛ × 9³⁄₁₆ in   15.6 × 23.4
From the collection of the Royal Photographic Society

'Of old,' wrote Frith of the Egyptian
crocodile, 'he was worshipped – one
regrets this, of course, but we can hardly
wonder at it. Look at his portrait! How
imposing – how grimly magnificent his
aspect!' Frith was particularly intrigued by
the 'great serrated jaws', the 'charmingly
Gothic' irregularity of the teeth, the
'jointed and overlapped' hide, and the
hands – 'as beautiful and delicate as a
lady's' [Frith, *Egypt and Palestine*, II, n.p.].
Frith's tactile appreciation is apparent in
the photograph. This quality combines
with the composition to recall Holman
Hunt's *The Scapegoat* – on the portentous
symbolism of which it appears a cheeky
commentary.

fig. 104

Francis Frith
The North Shore of the Dead Sea (1857)

Collodion
6¹⁄₁₆ × 8⁹⁄₁₆ in   15.6 × 21.8 cm
From the collection of the Royal Photographic Society

'. . . strangeness, and loveliness, and
unaccountability': these were the qualities
Frith saw in the Dead Sea [Frith, *Egypt and*
Palestine, I, n.p.]. Having deposited himself
at the less accessible south end, to be as
near as possible to the biblical Sodom for
The Scapegoat, Hunt took a more frenzied
view: 'No one can stand and say it is not
accursed of God . . . this is the horrible
figure of Sin – a varnished deceit – earth's
joys at hand but Hell gaping behind, a
stealthy, terrible enemy for ever'.

photographed once from further up the valley (fig. 95), once from further back. He took the Well of Enrogel (fig. 108) from the opposite side to Seddon, so that we can see where the painter positioned himself for his watercolour of the subject (fig. 106). In a letter to his fiancée, Seddon was frank: he would use Graham's photographs 'to supply my own want of sketches'.[15] Hunt was less so. It was left to a critic to point out that the hills in *The Scapegoat* appeared 'photographically studied'.[16] And yet the only instance of a discernible link between a surviving photograph of Graham's and a painting concerns Hunt. With his watercolour *Nazareth*, Hunt used Graham's photograph of the same name (fig. 108) as an *aide-memoir*.

Documentary evidence confirms the link between Hunt's watercolour and Graham's photograph. Long after Seddon had left Jerusalem, Graham accompanied Hunt on his last journey north from the city to Nablus, Jenin, Nazareth, and the Sea of Galilee. Here the two friends parted, Graham going across to Haifa to catch the steamer, Hunt leaving Palestine by the northern route to Lebanon. In his memoirs, Hunt states that they left Jerusalem on 17 October 1855. Having reached Nazareth, they stayed 'long enough (for Hunt) to undertake a large coloured drawing', leaving the town on 26 October. Graham's photograph of Nazareth is identical to Hunt's watercolour down to the cactuses and fall of the shadows, though Hunt includes two figures and a (symbolic) snake, and excludes a part of the view. But the photograph is dated 27 October, the day after the two men had supposedly left Nazareth. This mystery is cleared up by Hunt's diary. For whatever reason, Hunt gave the wrong date in his memoirs for the departure from Nazareth. On 27 October they were still in the town: it was in fact the very day on which, having worked for four exhausting days on the watercolour, he left off 'at night very sorry that I cannot carry my sketch of Nazareth to a higher state of completion'.[17]

The conclusion is inescapable: disappointed at not being able to finish his sketch, Hunt asked Graham to photograph the scene he had been painting. With his simple calotype machinery (still favoured at this time by many amateurs) it would have been easy for Graham to develop the negative and furnish Hunt with a print before they parted. We know from other sources that Graham was happy to give his photographs away.[18] Hunt would certainly have needed this assistance, given his literal style and the fact that he was not to take up the work again for some five years – it was finally exhibited in 1861. There was another published photograph of the same scene which he could have used: it appeared in Frith's *Egypt and Palestine* (1858–60), but it seems unlikely as the shadows all fall in the opposite direction.

Hunt was silent about a labour-saving operation which ill-accorded with his boasted diligence. But this is not what is important about the two *Nazareths*. It is rather that the existence of matching watercolour and photograph throws into yet sharper relief the photographic aesthetic of Pre-Raphaelites of the stamp of Hunt, Seddon, Brett, or Inchbold. Certainly these men had reservations about photography; but these were superficial cavils about its capacity *at that time* to act as a mirror to reality, not doubts about the

fig. 105

Thomas Seddon
The Well of Enrogel (1854)

Watercolour
$9\frac{3}{4} \times 13\frac{3}{4}$ in   24.7 × 34.3 cm
The Harris Museum and Art Gallery, Preston

fig. 106

James Graham
Meeting point of Valleys of Hinnom and Kedron with En Rogel in foreground (mid-1850s)

Paper negative
$7\frac{7}{16} \times 10\frac{1}{8}$ in   19 × 25.8 cm
The Palestine Exploration Fund

Mentioned in the books of *Joshua, Samuel* and *Kings*, the Well of En Rogel is typical of the kind of site chosen by painters and photographers to confirm 'the minute accuracy of the Inspired Record' [H. B. Tristram, *The Land of Israel* (London 1865), p. viii]. Seddon and Graham view the Well from opposite sides. The painter took the Pre-Raphaelite uninterest in the sky to its logical limit. Graham's horizon recalls the observation of another Scottish photographic pilgrim of the 1850s, John Cramb: 'the air is so free from moisture that objects miles off are as sharp and *intense* as those in the immediate foreground.' [*BJP*, 8, 2 December 1861, p. 425.]

And HE came to Nazareth, where HE had been brought up.
Luke IV. 16.

validity of attempting to mirror it. Seddon believed that photographs would 'never supplant the pencil'. He did not hold this out of any clear recognition of the greater imaginative scope of painting, but because 'there is much in photographs that is false' (chiefly that 'the greens and the yellows become nearly as black as the shadows').[19] Other theorists, like W. M. Rossetti and the critic P. G. Hamerton, were soon to perceive that photography's growing triumph over reality would lead painters back into the realm of the imaginary and the painterly. Seddon had no notion that the camera would render his approach obsolete.

Hunt was later to claim that the Pre-Raphaelites had never been 'realists'. It was true of him, at least in the sense that for his pictures his models adopted poses and expressions at the behest of his (singular) imagination; and that each detail formed part of an elaborate allusive pattern such as could never have existed in the reality. But there was no conscious desire to transform the appearance of objects, to extract the essence of light, form or colour and re-order them in painterly terms. When objects are represented in two dimensions, whether in painting or photography, they *are* transformed, but Hunt's ideal remained, so far as was possible, to mirror them one by one. Only the non-existence, as yet, of colour photography stopped him seeing how photographic his system was. Essentially the Pre-Raphaelites at this phase of the Movement's development were the 'mad fools' castigated in Baudelaire's celebrated outburst of 1859 against photography. Quitting (in the poet's phrase) 'the domain of the impalpable and the imaginary', the painters propagated implicitly the idea that 'photography and Art are the same thing'.[20]

Such accusations were strenuously denied. Hamerton, unusually aware for an Englishman of the time of current trends in French painting, aimed to cajole English artists out of a parochial literalism, not by enforcing the parallel with photography, but by denying it. '. . . *all* good painting,' he wrote, 'however literal, however Pre-Raphaelite or topographic is full of human feeling and emotion' — expressive powers absent in photography were inherent in the medium of painting. Hamerton rejected the criticism which the Modernists were constantly to level against nineteenth-century Pre-Raphaelite and Academic art: that subject transcended treatment, that models, fancifully arranged, were then simply 'copied'. 'Why,' he exclaimed, 'even the severest and most rigid pre-Raphaelites use the model as little more than a stimulus, an authority or a suggestion. Copy the model indeed!' To drive home the point Hamerton selected from the works of the great literalist pilgrimage — Hunt and Seddon's — the most elaborate exercise in factual reconstruction, Hunt's *The Finding of the Saviour in the Temple*: specifically the 'marvellous expression of beatitude that illuminates the sweet face of Mary'. He believed that no model would have been capable of assuming, let alone maintaining, this expression. It was the product of nothing less than 'the painter's soul'.[21]

Why does the admirer of Courbet and Manet here defend a type of painting with which he was not in truth profoundly in sympathy? The

fig. 107

William Holman Hunt
Nazareth (1855–61)

Watercolour
$13\frac{7}{16} \times 19\frac{5}{8}$ *in*   *35.2 × 42.8 cm*
Whitworth Art Gallery, University of Manchester

fig. 108

James Graham
Nazareth General view from north.
(Oct. 27 1855)

Paper negative
$8\frac{5}{16} \times 10\frac{3}{16}$ *in*   *21.2 × 25.8 cm*
The Palestine Exploration Fund

Graham's photograph is dated precisely the day Hunt abandoned his intention of completing his watercolour on the spot before leaving Palestine. Probably Graham took the photograph at his request: otherwise, why be content with an identical view? With the photograph in his possession there was no rush for Hunt to finish the watercolour: and indeed it was several years before he did so.

fig. 109
Roger Fenton
Nubian Model Reclining (late 1850s)

Collodion
11 × 15½ in   27.9 × 39.3 cm
Christie's South Kensington

fig. 110
John Frederick Lewis
The Siesta (1876)

Oil on canvas
37⅞ × 43¾ in   96.2 × 111.1 cm
The Tate Gallery

Lewis was not one of the Pre-Raphaelite
circle but Ruskin's championship and
his meticulous detail and bright colour,
connected him with the Pre-Raphaelites in
the public mind. His work, in which
exterior light invariably filtered onto
patterned tiles, carpets and dresses, created
a taste which Fenton here attempts to
cater to photographically. While admiring
the dreamy voluptuousness of Fenton's
'oriental' photographs, critics regretted (as
they did with Lewis) the inappropriate
European physiognomies.

fig. 111
David Wilkie Wynfield
Simeon Solomon (c.1870)

Collodion
7⅞ × 5⅞ in   20 × 14.9 cm
Royal Academy of Arts

Wynfield inveigled his artistic friends into
wearing costumes expressive of their
personalities. Solomon was the only Jewish
Pre-Raphaelite: in this he probably seemed
exotic to Wynfield and the wayward strain
in Solomon's personality would have
made him seem more so.

answer is that he had his sight set on another enemy, photography – or rather on the artistic aspirations that were at this time beginning to burgeon in photography. 'Look at even the most "photographic" painting,' Hamerton is saying, 'and see what a gulf separates even this from the paltry mechanic insensibility of an actual photograph.' Hamerton acknowledged that photography was useful to the painter: indeed its use 'indicates less a spirit of indolence than of awakened observation'. But any idea that a photograph, 'telling one truth for ten falsehoods', could itself constitute art, was anathema to him.

The 'Art Photography' that was beginning to appear on the exhibition walls in the late 1850s suggested to critics like Hamerton that photographers were getting ideas above their station. Coincidentally, one manifestation of this was the cultivation of 'exotic' subject matter for which the figure compositions of Hunt himself and, in particular, J. F. Lewis, had created a taste. It was one thing for oriental enthusiasts like Frith (fig. 98), Hunt (fig. 88), or the Jewish Pre-Raphaelite, Simeon Solomon (fig. 111), to have themselves photographed as a satrap. ('Eastern costume,' Frith observed, 'is one of the beautiful blunders of a luxurious, but half-civilized state of society.') It was another when consciously imaginative reconstructions of oriental scenes began to emanate from the photographic studios.

In 1858 the photographer, William Grundy, exhibited several 'Turkish scenes'. Fenton soon followed with photographs of Nubian Water Carriers, Pashas and Bayadères, and Dancing Girls. Critics complained of the Anglo-Saxon physiognomies beneath the turbans. But then the same criticism was made of Lewis after his return home. The studio-bound nature of the whole enterprise merely confirmed that the photographer was trying to steal the painter's clothes: literalism (in photography all but inevitable, in painting a matter of choice) in the service of exoticism. So potent in photography was this blend that it was to last for decades: through the work of Julia Margaret Cameron with her Zuleikas, Zenobias and Pharaoh's Daughters, to that of her follower, Mrs Eveleen Myers's *Rebecca* (c.1891; fig. 112). From the first there were photographic critics willing to urge photographers along this path. Hamerton's crucial point, that no model could summon a poetic demeanour before the camera, was contradicted by the reviews of Fenton's oriental scenes. According to the *Art-Journal*, his *Dancing Girl* (1858) 'has a strange quiet – an oriental dreamy air'.[22] The *Bayadère* (1858), echoed the enthusiastic critic of the *Athenaeum*, 'is a beautiful example of voluptuous tranquil beauty ... The mouth and eyes are of the tenderest and most siren-like grace'.[23]

Dreaminess, voluptuousness, siren-like grace, beauty itself: what do these epithets remind us of but the Pre-Raphaelitism that was now moving, exhausted with the effort, away from Ruskin and falling under the sway of the Rossetti Fantasmagoria. Just as, all but unconsciously, photography had earlier mirrored the earnest, leaf-counting Pre-Raphaelitism, so it now stood poised to emulate, rather more consciously this time, the escapist aestheticism of the Rossettian phase of the movement.

fig. 112

Eveleen Myers
Rebecca (c.1891)

Photogravure
$6\frac{7}{8} \times 4\frac{3}{8}$ *in*   *17.5 × 11.2 cm*
National Portrait Gallery, London

With cleaner lines than earlier 'oriental'
portraits by Fenton and Cameron, this
image shows the continuing taste for
robing Anglo-Saxon maidens as heroines
of exotic tales, biblical and otherwise. This
iconography eventually fed into the early
cinema. The moist-eyed *ingénues* and veiled
vamps of Hollywood were the ultimate
products of a Victorian vision.

The Portrait

fig. 113

William Holman Hunt

Dante Gabriel Rossetti (1853)

Oil on panel
$11\frac{1}{2} \times 8\frac{1}{2}$ in   29.2 × 21.6 cm
By courtesy of Birmingham Museums and Art Gallery

Changing Aspirations

In becoming more 'artistic', photography was in part merely following life itself. Attending a 'great Pre-Raphaelite crush' at the Madox Browns' in Fitzroy Square, the friend of photography and Pre-Raphaelitism, Mrs Howitt, was awed by the picturesque beauty of 'the uncrinolined women with their wild hair'. Life had taken on an Alice-in-Wonderland quality: it was 'very curious'; 'the gorgeous and fantastic forms moved slowly about'; it was 'like some hot, struggling dream'.

Similarly at Little Holland House, Sarah Prinsep (née Pattle) had, for twenty years, entertained the famous, housed the painter, G. F. Watts, and created an ambience conducive to discussions on the Beautiful: mealtimes were irregular, and the two most striking of the many Pattle sisters, Virginia (Lady Somers) and Sophia (Lady Dalrymple), floated in and out of view. Long before the Pre-Raphaelite 'look', these women had inaugurated, in opposition to contemporary fashion, a free-flowing style of dress based on simple lines, ample folds and rich colour. 'O what big eyes,' a child exclaimed on seeing Sophia for the first time, 'O what wide hair!' In later years Georgiana Burne-Jones could not think of Sophia without recalling 'the sound of soft, silken rustlings and the tinkle of silver bangles as she came and went'.

Little Holland House was important in the genesis of new aspirations in Victorian photography. Another Pattle sister was Julia Margaret Cameron. When in 1863 she took up photography, the camera had already become part of the 'Beautiful Life' at Little Holland House and, perhaps in a slightly narcissistic way, had even been necessary to it.

Cameron's brother-in-law, Lord Somers, took photographs. The professional photographer, O. G. Rejlander, was invited there for the same purpose (fig. 116). Lewis Carroll gained admittance, with some difficulty. Watts would follow Sophia about the house with his notebook, and when he noticed 'any particularly beautiful arrangement in posture or line would call out with a gesture of his hand, "Oh, pray, stay where you are for a moment".' But sometimes it was Lord Somers or Rejlander who would request the sisters (or their equally lovely children) to hold their pose: and Watts (as with *Britomart and her Nurse* – exhibited in 1878) would use the resulting photograph as the basis for a painting (figs. 114, 115).

Cameron's acknowledged mentor, David Wilkie Wynfield, believed that artistic portraiture could only be achieved by eschewing modern dress altogether: 'ransacking (as one hostile critic put it) the chests of the costumier for the moth-eaten drapery of a bygone, but more picturesque age'.[1] He dressed Millais as Dante (fig. 1). For one of her photographs taken on the lawn of Little Holland House, Cameron did the same with Lady Elcho (fig. 117). But the peculiar artistic feeling which now entered photography had its origin less in these effects than in a way of life. Hamerton denied photography artistic status, claiming that it 'makes no farther communication to the spectator than this simple one, "I, such an one, chose this

fig. 114

George Frederic Watts
Britomart and her Nurse (1878)

Oil on canvas
$66\frac{1}{2} \times 48$ *in*   *169 × 121.9 cm*
By courtesy of Birmingham Museums and Art Gallery

fig. 115

Anon.
The Sisters. Study for a Picture (c.1860)

Collodion
$4\frac{1}{2} \times 5\frac{13}{16}$ *in*   *11.43 × 14.8 cm*
Sir Hew Hamilton-Dalrymple, Bt.

Watt's broad handling, Titianesque colour and classical forms separate
him from Pre-Raphaelitism. Yet he was enmeshed in the Movement
socially – and intellectually, in that his work was also, in the words of
his biographer, 'a protest against materialism'. Sometimes, too, his
paintings include recognizably Pre-Raphaelite features, like the plant
here which recalls the potted lily in Rosetti's *The Girlhood of Mary Virgin.*
The photograph of Sophia and Virginia Pattle, provided Watts with
little more than a suggestion for his painting. It is interesting in its
own right as an attempt to escape the stiffness of studio portraiture.

fig. 116

Oscar Rejlander
*Group Portrait of Sophia Pattle, Lady Dalrymple
and G. F. Watts* (c.1860)

Collodion
$5\frac{15}{16} \times 4\frac{1}{16}$ *in*   *15 × 10.4 cm*
Sotheby's, London

'Artistic' portraiture grew out of a desire to capture the
Beautiful Life. The subjects here were both denizens of Little
Holland House, a centre of upper class bohemianism. A
diffused Pre-Raphaelite spirit was at work in this ambience.
Lady Dalrymple wears a 'medieval' gown. The composition,
as with many photographic portraits of the period, restricts
space with an ivy-covered wall in the manner of Millais's
A Huguenot.

fig. 117

Julia Margaret Cameron
A Dantesque Vision (1865)

Collodion
$10\frac{1}{8} \times 8\frac{7}{16}$ *in*   *25.8 × 21.5 cm*
Sotheby's, London

This photograph reveals many of the strands in Cameron's artistic
personality. In dressing Lady Elcho as a Dantean spectre, Cameron was
following Rossettian precedents, which she had absorbed partly through
Val Prinsep. Prinsep, a minor Pre-Raphaelite, was the son of Cameron's
sister Sarah, mistress of Little Holland House, where this photograph
was taken. Long before Cameron took up photography the medium had
been a part of life at Little Holland House through the enthusiasm of
Lord Somers, brother-in-law of Sarah and Julia Margaret. Cameron's
only acknowledged photographic mentor, David Wilkie Wynfield, had
earlier photographed Millais as Dante (*see* fig. 1).

subject"'.[2] But when the subject was the rich ambience of privileged bohemia, and the photographer was one of the enchanted circle, there occurred a dialogue, not witnessed before, between a rarefied existence and the magic of the instrument. The Little Holland House portraits, Lady Hawarden's studies of her daughters (figs. 137, 141), and the portraits of Jane Morris (figs. 129, 131, 133) share this arresting quality: the 'hot, struggling dream', stilled and perpetuated.

Although a large part of the impetus came from the genteel amateurs like Cameron, Hawarden, and Lewis Carroll, pressure to beautify photography came from other sections of the photographic community. The spread of photography had, it was said, 'lowered standards' all round. Commercialization had led to 'stupid, coarse brutality of taste and sentiment'. In 1858, shop windows in the Strand were exhibiting photographs of 'women more or less naked and generally leering at the spectator'; or – above the droll caption 'My Last Edition' – 'a woman in bed, with a man in his night-cap and night-shirt seated in a chair nursing a baby'. The *Photographic Journal* urged 'gentlemen who do not wish to see the degradation of Photography' to avoid exhibiting alongside these indelicacies.[3]

The issue of the artistic status of photography came to a head when the Commissioners for the 1862 International Exhibition placed photography not with painting and engraving but in the scientific section, 'in close proximity,' as the *Photographic Journal* complained, 'to the steam engine, patent mangle &c.'[4] Though some of the old guard painter-turned-photographers like Sir William Newton agreed with the Commissioners, most photographers were resentful.

Photographic journalism responded to slights in two ways. The first was to give continuous airing to the intrinsic claims of photography as an art. To the photographer Claudet, the interest of the Queen in photography proved that it was an art.[5] The *London Review* argued from less recondite evidence: the manipulations involved in photography; the necessity of adhering to artistic principles because of the vagaries of the chemical action of light, more difficult to master than 'all the arcana of "high art"'; and the parallel between photography's monochrome and that of sculpture and engraving. Rembrandt's chiaroscuro was also invoked.[6] It is hard to say whether these parallels were felt by photographers to confer dignity on their activities. Some photographers probably felt superior to art anyway, or at least to artists. 'Please to remember ... this is not a *common artist's* studio!' George du Maurier was advised when he entered a photographic studio in 1860, inadvertently smoking.[7]

The second response was to disseminate supposedly universal artistic principles among photographers. Many believed that this alone would dispel for ever the possibility of keeping company with steam engines and mangles. This crusade took time to gather momentum. In 1865 the photographic journals were said to be as full as ever of 'mere baths and processes, of frivolous novelties and experiments'.[8] But by 1868, the *Illustrated Photographer* had been founded expressly to raise aesthetic standards, while the other journals had all, it was said, 'suddenly become alive to the necessity of imparting to photographers a knowledge of art principles'.[9] 'The ideal which every photographer . . . should keep before him,' said the *Photographic News*, 'does not . . . differ from that of Phidias or Da Vinci.'[10] There were to be no limits to aspiration.

Taste was more conspicuously abysmal in portraiture than in any other branch of photography. The carte-de-visite mania of the early 1860s was mainly to blame. Perhaps critics would have minded less if the status of portraiture in art as a whole had not recently been elevated. Portrait painting had always been an English forte, but authorities had ranked it below religious and historical painting, which explains why Benjamin Robert Haydon could throw away the talent manifest in his portrait of Wordsworth on massively vapid exercises in 'High Art'.

The need for Carlylean 'heroes' had bred a new attitude reflected in the drive to establish a National Portrait Gallery during the mid-1850s. Moving the vote for the new gallery in Parliament, Palmerston argued that the features of the great were an 'incentive to mental exertion, to noble actions, to good conduct'. Others put it differently. In an essay on 'Rossetti and the Religion of Beauty' (1897) Frederick W. H. Myers (husband of the Cameronesque photographer, Eveleen), was to argue that the arts in the nineteenth century had returned to the spirit of Leonardo. They were finding in the human face and form above all else 'the utmost secret, the occult message' of 'all the phenomenon of Life and Being'. Palmerston's moral instrumentalism was absent. The depiction of the human form was just as surely exalted.

In this climate, the products of the photographic studios were wonderfully calculated to offend. Exaltation was impossible given the backgrounds against which the sitter must pose: 'sham stiles' as a writer in the *Quarterly* complained, '"practicable" rocks, precipices in flatted oils, and the "multum in parvo solid European accessory"'. (This could function as fireplace or piano, Gothic bookcase or Italian lake.) Like many Victorian writers from Carlyle down, this critic could hardly conceal his relish in what he excoriated. Cartes-de-visite propagated a surreal distortion of life in England:

. . . a country abounding in terraces, gardens, lakes, and wild sea-shores, in which the inhabitants might generally be seen sitting in the open air uncovered, looking away from the view, or playing hide-and-seek (at the manifest risk of their lives) behind curtains attached to pillars which, for some unexplained reason, were generally erected upon the brinks of tremendous precipices.[11]

To counteract this unnerving vision, some critics pressed photography to purloin a basic, traditional aesthetic from painting. H. P. Robinson was the most assiduous in advocating a classical simplicity in portraiture. He urged the banishment of vases of flowers, elaborate table-cloths, books, 'trifles': all but the most unobtrusive accessories. Reynolds had urged painters to study the best portraits of Raphael, Titian, and Van Dyck. Photographers, Robinson argued, should do the same. Other theorists recommended the scrutiny of 'antique models'.

This ideal might most accurately be termed 'photographic Raphaelesque'. Robinson bowed repeatedly in the direction of obsolescent theorists – Dufresnoy, Gerard de Lairesse, Thomas Burnet – for whom Raphael was the pinnacle of art. He advocated for photography the balanced curvilinear grace of the Umbrian. At times Robinson sounded as if he was writing a prescription for a photographic *Belle Jardinière* or *Madonna of the Field*. The essence of portraiture was simple form, balance of light and shade, suitable expression, and 'harmonious flow of lines'. The most perfect general form was 'an irregular pyramid with a curved base'. Robinson sensed that photography had 'traced a path for itself'; that it had 'nothing to do with Dutchman or Italian'. But he was at a loss to uncover principles deriving from the unique freedoms and constraints of photography itself.[12]

A decade or so after the formation of the Pre-Raphaelite Brotherhood, recognition dawned. This movement, which placed 'fidelity' above tradition- al 'selection' and 'generalization', might (if any lessons were to be taken from painting at all) have more to teach photography than Raphael. Photography's hostility to Pre-Raphaelitism, born of conservatism and rivalry, began to soften.

This was partly because the Pre-Raphaelites were now more fashionable. Rossetti had been premature when in 1853 he had observed that the Brotherhood's position had 'greatly altered' from 'reckless abuse' to 'general and high recognition'. But various events over the next few years signalled that the Movement was widening its scope and reputation: the continuing championship of an ever more authoritative Ruskin; the inauguration of a second phase when the young William Morris and Edward Jones fell under the spell of Rossetti, and the Oxford Union rang with the 'jovial' cries of inexperienced muralists; the Moxon Tennyson; the 1857 'American Exhibition of British Art' and the exhibitions of the Hogarth Club; the growth of provincial Pre-Raphaelitism, particularly in populous cities like Liverpool; and by no means least important, the outstanding popular success of avowedly Pre-Raphaelite works like Millais's *A Huguenot* and Henry Wallis's *Chatterton* (1855–6; fig. 156), widely disseminated in the form of engravings. Some, such as Russell Sturges, writing in the *Nation* in 1865, argued that the Movement had phased itself out of existence by its very success. It was no longer possible to distinguish 'the great chief' (as Dante Gabriel had become known to some) from a host of artists committed to 'Realistic, painstaking, purposeful work'. The fact that Rossetti was neither especially realistic, painstaking, nor indeed purposeful, shows the difficulty of pinning down what was nevertheless universally recognized at this early date: the impact of Pre-Raphaelitism on British painting since the mid-century.

In 1858, a photographic critic praised the crisp definition of the latest products of photography at the expense of the 'mere blotting haste of the idle generalizing school'.[13] This was the very language used by the young Brethren ten years earlier. Since they were hounded as much as the Pre- Raphaelites for their 'sordid' interest in every wart and pimple, the photographers were bound in the end to produce the same counter

fig. 118

John Everett Millais

A Huguenot, on St Bartholomew's Day.
Refusing to Shield Himself from Danger by
Wearing the Roman Catholic Badge (1851–2)

Oil on canvas, arched top
36½ × 24¼ in   92.7 × 62.2 cm
Royal Academy of Arts

fig. 119

Lewis Carroll

Arthur Hughes and his Daughter Agnes (1863)

Collodion, arched top
5 5/16 × 4 5/16 in   13.5 × 10.9 cm
Howard Grey

Photographically, 1863 saw Lewis Carroll's
'Pre-Raphaelite autumn'. He moved his
camera among the circle in London: he
met Holman Hunt, photographed the
Munros, and spent many hours
photographing in Rosetti's garden. He also
took photographs of Munro's sculpture
and Rossetti's drawings. Carroll's journal
for 12 October records: 'Mr. A. Hughes
came over to be photographed with his
children ... Got a splendid picture of him
with Agnes' [*The Diaries of Lewis Carroll*, ed.
Roger Lancelyn Green (London 1953), I,
p. 206]. Carroll was staying with his friend,
George MacDonald, in Hampstead, and
the Hughes picture is one of a number
taken in the garden using the *Huguenot*
formula.

arguments. Solidarity manifested itself with new theorists of photography, such as Alfred H. Wall of the *Photographic Journal*, propagating what was in effect a Pre-Raphaelite aesthetic for photography. With no option but to accept nature as it was, the camera seemed to Wall a preternaturally Ruskinian instrument. Had not the great critic argued that only 'powerless indolence or blind audacity' led an artist to alter nature? Great art was all-accepting. It directed (as Ruskin put it) 'the eyes and thoughts to what is perfect' – just like a camera, Wall thought. He believed that other critics, Thomas Sutton, the polemical editor of *Photographic Notes*, for example, indulged in a too 'extravagant advocacy of the ideal'. The work and theories of H. P. Robinson implied a similar hankering after improving nature.[14]

Writers of Wall's way of thinking now approached the studio concoctions of the 'art photographers' in the same spirit as Ruskin examining the latest Academy exhibits. The blossom in Robinson's *Bringing Home the May* (1862; fig. 170) was judged 'a ridiculous looking stuff, more like sponge than hawthorn blossom'.[15] Photographers were exhorted to take note of Pre-Raphaelitism, for, as the *Photographic News* declared, 'no one can deny the position which these works have attained'.[16]

The Fog Descends

A Huguenot, on St Bartholomew's Day, Refusing to Shield Himself from Danger by Wearing the Roman Catholic Badge: this elaborately titled and immensely popular painting by Millais spawned more photographic progeny than any other single Pre-Raphaelite work. Its formula, handsome figures before a plant-traversed wall, was followed by Fenton, Lewis Carroll, the aristocratic Scottish amateur Ronald Leslie Melville, Rejlander, and others. There was a technical reason for this: such a background was necessary for those photographers who disliked a blur in any part of the image. Millais's treatment also seems to have appealed to photographers as a particularly attractive way of restricting space.

Ivy, in particular, was rich in meaning. It stood for the passing of time and friendship in adversity. When clinging to wall, it further connoted female sexuality, as perceived. Trollope observed in *Barchester Towers* (1857) that only when 'the ivy has found its tower, when the delicate creeper has found its strong wall' did surrounding plants grow and prosper. Millais lavished as much time on the background of *A Huguenot* as on the figures. His companion, Charles Collins, 'gave up painting in despair' when he found no foreground subject could engage his attention as much as the old shed and leaves he had been working on. 'If you have human beings before a wall,' Tennyson told Millais, 'the wall ... must not be made intrusive by the bricks being *too* minutely drawn.' The poet worried that the Pre-Raphaelites were in danger of putting walls before people.

But he was probably alone in finding the wall and vegetation in *A Huguenot* intrusive. In fact they foster a peculiar feeling of intimacy. The picture is vitiated, if anything, by that obviousness of sentiment that was to be Millais's downfall as an artist. Happily free of the pressure to tell a story, the photographers successfully employ the wall as a foil. With plants idly trailing or thickly tangled, it stands in itself for a dialogue between nature and humanity. In Fenton's studies of children at Tintern (fig. 120), or Melville's portrait of Mrs Godfrey Clarke (fig. 2), the wall provides a magical seclusion: a most sensitive environment in which inward qualities are heightened. In Carroll's portrait of Arthur and Agnes Hughes (fig. 119), the background contributes particularly to the subtle feeling of mutual dependence of father and daughter.

Photographic portraiture took on a more complex Pre-Raphaelite colouring. The complexities arose from the way in which Pre-Raphaelitism itself was changing. The strict fidelity rule was in eclipse. The new preoccupation was balance. Theoretically, the Brethren had agreed on balance at the start. Hunt recorded that he and Rossetti concurred in the winter of 1848–9 that a painting should not just be the 'icy double of the facts', but the 'reflex of a living image' in the mind. An art of mere imitation or 'realism' misrepresented the world, depicting it as 'without design or finish, unbalanced, unfitting'.

fig. 120

Roger Fenton
Interior of Tintern Abbey (late 1850s)

Collodion
$7\frac{1}{2} \times 9$ in   *19 × 22.8 cm*
Christie's South Kensington

It is uncertain whether Fenton and other photographers who used the compositional device of Millais's *A Huguenot*, were consciously influenced by this popular Pre-Raphaelite work. The formula proliferated in every corner of art from the Academy to the illustrated periodicals. The elements – crumbling masonry, creeping vegetation, and humanity – could be endlessly varied to create a distinctive pathos. In photography, those 'Pre-Raphaelite' practitioners like Fenton who disliked a blur in any part of the image were particularly attracted to the formula.

This unanimity was only skin deep. Hunt's art (though it sometimes gains impact from his idiosyncratic conceptions) never evolved beyond the production of 'icy doubles'. But Rossetti edged the Movement towards that equilibrium of outward truth and inner vision theoretically agreed upon at the beginning. He took up a new medium, watercolour, and a new subject, medieval fantasy. These helped him escape from the strict imitation for which he was in any case temperamentally unsuited. By 1860, he was able to announce to Bell Scott that he had given up Pre-Raphaelite 'niggling'. Millais had also broadened his manner by then – which might have been no bad thing if he had had something to say – and the *Athenaeum* announced that Pre-Raphaelitism had changed. Having 'taught us all to be exact and thorough'; the Movement was 'fast modifying and softening'.

The works of Rossetti, Burne-Jones, and their followers would always contain passages of careful natural detail reflecting the original ideas of 1848 and the unavoidable influence of Ruskin. In *The Blue Bower* (1865), for example, Rossetti included exquisitely observed oriental tiles and passion flowers. But F. G. Stephens remarked that there was beyond that 'nothing to suggest subject, time or place'. (We may disagree and decide that the picture very adequately suggests bohemian Chelsea in the mid-1860s.) According to this conception of Pre-Raphaelitism, the release at a certain point from 'subject, time or place' is crucial to the projection of the artist's 'living image'. 'Where we thus leave off,' as Stephens put it, 'the intellectual and purely artistic splendour of the picture begins to develop itself.' There are conflicting views about the merits of many works produced in this phase of Pre-Raphaelitism, but the shift away from 'icy doubles' to inner vision was not in itself a derogation of the principles of 1848.

The same evolution is apparent in the Pre-Raphaelite treatment of the human form: a shift of emphasis from external to internal. In the early days the Brethren recorded the details of each other's physiognomies with dedication. If they mostly seem remarkably good-looking, this was not through idealization but because they were so. Yet by the 1860s William Michael Rossetti was arguing strenuously that the outward form was not enough: a portrait should reveal 'the divinity that is within us'. Watts, too, was fired with the idea that it was possible to fuse accurate record with spiritual insight: hence his decision to embark in 1860 on his portraits of great contemporaries on which his reputation now principally rests.

To William Michael, however, it was not Watts but one of the original Pre-Raphaelite Brotherhood, the sculptor Thomas Woolner, who came nearest to this 'modern ideal'. In his portraits of Wordsworth and Tennyson (fig. 122), Woolner had combined fidelity to dimples and strands of hair with revelation of the inner man. Another admirer of Woolner was Julia Margaret Cameron. Not afraid to compare her photographs with 'Woolner's ideal heroic busts', she aimed to transfer to photography the current portraiture ideal. Apart from Woolner and Watts (a close friend), the key figures here were Dante Gabriel Rossetti, whom she showered with her photographs, Arthur Hughes, whose *April Love* (1855) was a particular inspiration, and her nephew Val

Prinsep, a second generation Pre-Raphaelite: '... my whole soul,' Cameron wrote, 'has endeavoured to do its duty ... in recording faithfully the greatness of the inner as well as the features of the outer man.'[17] The analogy with the aims of Watts, the Pre-Raphaelites, and the ideas of William Michael Rossetti, only breaks down when the inevitable mirror-like component in Cameron's images is brought to mind. With her medium, the 'real' side of the equation was no matter of choice. It was unavoidable.

There is a further complication. Cameron's sympathizers, the 'soft' school of photography, had a favourite term of abuse for their 'hard' opponents. It was, of course, 'Pre-Raphaelite'. They took little note of how Pre-Raphaelitism had changed, had become less precise, dreamier, indeed softer. To them it remained what it had been to Dickens in the early 1850s: all misshapen forms and wrinkled unsightliness. 'We know that nothing is more offensive to the artistic eye,' wrote the *Photographic News*, 'than a hard-lined, seared, wrinkled visage, rendered with a more than Pre-Raphaelite faithfulness ...'[18] While some photographic writers used 'Pre-Raphaelite' in this anachronistic sense, others were aware that it was better applied to Cameron's Rossetti-inspired subjects. However the term was used, the controversy over hard and soft in photography strikingly recalled the divergence within Pre-Raphaelitism between the Hunt and Rossetti wings – between 'icy doubles' and the mind's 'living image'.

It is worth noting that this controversy is perennial in photography. It began with the furore in the Photographic Society when in 1853 Sir William Newton recommended blurring the image for artistic effect. With Cameron's work providing the stimulus for another round in the 1860s, the debate continued with Emerson *contra* H. P. Robinson. Robinson was a photographic manipulator who employed the sharp focus of the purist; Emerson, a 'naturalist' who used tasteful soft focus knowing that the eye does not see as sharply as the lens. The highly deliberate artistry which infused photography towards the end of the century with the Linked Ring Brotherhood in Britain and the American Photo-Secession favoured a general mistiness in the image, but there developed gradually a reaction against this. The argument flared up again with the dispute in the 1930s between the 'fuzzy-wuzzies' (led by William Mortensen) and the f.64 Group, including Ansel Adams and Edward Weston.

Photography is a variable language, but it appears that there will always be those on the one hand who insist (with Weston) that the photographer's duty is to 're-create his subject in terms of its basic reality' (i.e. in sharp focus with the clear textures of which photography is capable) – 'the thing itself revealed for the first time;' and those who, on the other hand line up with Mortensen. For them, detail causes the facts to obtrude. Photography's business is to create 'large simple forms and open planes wherein the mind can move freely'. This simplicity and openness conveys 'the basic truth that the final concern of art is not with facts, but with ideas and emotions'.[19]

The writer in the *Quarterly*, referred to earlier (the scourge of studio backdrops), foreshadowed the f.64 view. He believed in a 'cleanly taken, and

fig. 121

Julia Margaret Cameron
The Dirty Monk (1869)

Collodion
$4\frac{15}{16} \times 3\frac{15}{16}$ in   12.6 × 10.1 cm   (rounded top)
From the collection of the Royal Photographic Society

fig. 122

Thomas Woolner
Alfred Tennyson (1855–6)

Plaster medallion
10 in   25.4 cm   diameter
National Trust, Wallington, Northumberland

Cameron aimed at the balance of outer and inner truth that Woolner was particularly admired for in the 1860s. The title, *The Dirty Monk*, given by Tennyson himself, reminds us that photography often gives an unexpected slant on, rather than dignified homage to the sitter. This print also shows Cameron's misguided purism: her refusal to touch out the spots which were not intrinsic to the medium, but the result of her slipshod handling.

fig. 123

George Frederic Watts
Choosing (1864)

Oil on panel
$18\frac{1}{2} \times 14$ in   47 × 35.6 cm
National Portrait Gallery, London

fig. 124

Julia Margaret Cameron
Alithea (1872)

Collodion
$12\frac{1}{2} \times 9\frac{5}{16}$ in   31.7 × 23.7 cm   (oval)
From the collection of the Royal Photographic Society

Watts was Cameron's intimate friend and artistic adviser. His portrait of his young wife, Ellen Terry, probably influenced this photograph of Alice Liddell though, largely as a result of Rossetti, the taste for 'female heads with floral adjuncts' was pervasive.

properly focused' image. He held that the blur was a nonsense, particularly when special measures were taken to achieve it – requiring the sitter to move or taking the photograph deliberately out of focus. These measures invested the sitter 'with a blurred, hazy margin, which is presumably "artistic"'. It was nothing of the sort. It just made him look like a man 'standing a few feet off in a thick fog'.[20]

To Cameron, against whom such criticisms were mainly directed, the 'fog' was the very means by which the vital balance between real and ideal was established. 'What is focus –' she demanded, 'and who has a right to say what focus is the legitimate focus?' To 'ennoble photography', to raise it to the level of 'High Art', it was necessary to escape 'mere conventional topographic photography – map-making and skeleton rendering of feature and form'.[21] Rossetti had abandoned the 'map-making' and pristine colours of the early Brotherhood for the breadth and solemn harmonies of the Venetian masters. Similarly, as Hamerton pointed out at the time, Cameron 'deflated the obtrusiveness of photographic detail' by cultivating 'a massive breadth not unlike the gloom and obscurity of some old pictures'.[22]

Photographic detail and the sheer presence of objects have their intrinsic poetry, as a shell painted by Ruskin or photographed by Weston reveals. But Cameron was far enough away from this sensibility to be oblivious of this. Her 'devotion to Poetry and beauty' meant the blending of the facts with obscurities in which the mind can indeed, in Mortensen's phrase, 'move freely'. Her work was the 'embodiment of a prayer': a conception it must be said she did justice to when she kept the forms simple and did not too much insist on the narrative. In an image like *Call, I follow, I follow – let me die* (c.1867; fig. 126), Cameron approached that hinterland where Pre-Raphaelitism shades into Symbolism: the 'Dream-land' evoked by the critic and essayist Walter Pater (describing Rossetti's poetry in *Appreciations* 1889): 'its "phantoms of the body," deftly coming and going on love's service ... people of a remote and unaccustomed beauty, somnambulistic, frail, androgynous, the light shining through them'.

The parallel might seem questionable. But for Pater, the 'perfection' of lyric poetry (to him the highest kind of poetry) depended 'on a certain suppression or vagueness of mere subject, so that the meaning reaches us through ways not distinctly traceable by the understanding'. Anyone who has been touched by the poetry of Cameron's best imaginative work – anyone, that is for whom her vague forms free the imagination rather than fog the brain – will find this a fair summary of its effect.

After two decades it was possible to look back and speculate on the influence photography had exerted on Pre-Raphaelitism. A Pre-Raphaelite associate like Lowes Dickinson knew that many in the circle had copied photographs at one time or another. Perhaps he was also aware how much a work in progress like Rossetti's *Beata Beatrix* (c.1864–70; fig. 125) owed to the artist's enthusiasm for Cameron's portraiture: dead Lizzie Siddal's head haloed in the manner of a top-lit photograph. But Dickinson believed that photography's influence on the Movement had been mainly unconscious,

fig. 125

Dante Gabriel Rossetti
Beata Beatrix (c.1864–70)

Oil on canvas
34 × 26 in   86.4 × 66 cm
The Tate Gallery, London

fig. 126

Julia Margaret Cameron
Call, I follow, I follow – let me die (c.1867)

Brown carbon, autotype
$15\frac{3}{16} \times 11\frac{3}{4}$ *in   38.7 × 29.9 cm*
From the collection of the Royal Photographic Society

The blurred background and glow around the head in this idealized portrait of the artist's dead wife, Elizabeth Siddal, have been attributed to the influence of Cameron's photography. The image was published by the Autotype Company at the time Rossetti was working on *Beata Beatrix*. It may have impressed him since it has a plasticity rare in her imaginative work and illustrates appropriately morbid lines from Tennyson's 'Lancelot and Elaine'. The unusually cleaned up appearance of the image is the result of retouching by the Autotype printers.

though nonetheless important for that: 'it is at least a question,' he wrote, 'whether what is called pre-Raphaelitism is not due to (photography) acting upon a few minds unconsciously impressed by the clear manifestations of important truths hitherto smothered under broad conventionalisms'. Dickinson cited Woolner's 'admirable portrait busts', again stressing the unconscious element in photography's influence: 'Mr. Woolner is probably wholly unconscious how many of the really valuable results of photography he has appropriated and embodied in his work.' Needless to say, Dickinson saw these 'valuable results' as relating merely to photography's outward truths. The medium was still primarily associated with external appearances despite Cameron's efforts to invest it with the aura of spiritual insight.[23]

Pre-Raphaelitism and photography were in complex symbiosis. Given the complications, particularly those which result from the evolutionary character of Pre-Raphaelitism, it may be a relief to concentrate solely for a moment on an area of photography where a particularly blatant Pre-Raphaelite iconography was at work: female portraiture.

6

The
Pre-Raphaelite
Goddess

fig. 127
Dante Gabriel Rossetti
Fazio's Mistress (1863)

Oil on panel
17 × 14 $\frac{7}{16}$ in   43.2 × 36.8 cm
The Tate Gallery, London

Original or Copy?

On a fine July day in 1865, Dante Gabriel Rossetti presided over a photographic session at his Chelsea home. The sitter was Jane Morris, wife of his one-time admirer, William. As far as we can gather, the man behind the camera was John R. Parsons. Parsons was a professional photographer and friend of the mendacious entrepreneur of Pre-Raphaelitism, Charles Augustus Howell (called by Madox Brown 'the Baron Munchausen of the Circle'). In time, first Parsons, and then Howell, fell out with Rossetti. In 1873, when Rossetti severed connections with Parsons, he wrote to Howell: would he get back the 'negatives of my things (about 30 including those portraits taken from life in my garden) which are in Parsons' hands'?[1] Jane's daughter, May, later confirmed that Parsons was the Cheyne Walk photographer.

Rossetti's anxiety to acquire the negatives was understandable. Possibly, the original prints had gone astray – at any rate they have never since been found. The images had provided inspiration for his work. He had probably pored over them as a substitute for Jane's presence. These were the very years of his 'regenerate rapture': a love which rescued him from both the morbidity and the cheerless sexual indulgence following his wife's death, reviving also his passion for writing verse. Besides this, the photographs were remarkable in themselves.

Due to whatever blend of artistry on the part of Parsons and Rossetti, they capture Jane Morris more successfully than any other visual image or description which has come down to us. In the well-known later set of photographs by Frederick Hollyer, she is embedded in her own and the Burne-Jones family. In Rossetti's numerous portrayals, she becomes an obvious fantasy-figure. The written record about her is contradictory, but here in the photographs, there is a sharp revelation. This results from a contrast between a preoccupied sitter and the blithe accidents of environ-ment which monochrome photography is well-fitted to articulate. The lack of constriction – the pervasive airiness, the freedom of unloosed hair and flowing gown – is something of which the subject's highlighted features fail to partake. The garden is dappled, the makeshift marquee or studio is light-filled: they might have encouraged her personality to take wing. Instead, they suggest a curious entrapment.

In his drawings and paintings Rossetti either banished or mythologized the disturbing quality in these images. *Reverie* (1868; fig. 128) and *The Roseleaf* (1870; fig. 132) are both exercises in prettification of photographs. One elongates a neck already remarkable for its length, removes an anxious angularity from the wrists, and expels the disorder in the eye; the other lifts the hair to make room for a perfect make-up-artist's eyebrow. Sullen lips are re-shaped. A final fashion-plate touch is supplied by a graceful yet obviously appended arm and by the sprig which gives the picture its name.

Depicting Pandora (in several versions) Rossetti adapted the photograph in which Jane had appeared most vulnerable (fig. 131). Timorous pose and

clasped hands had suggested one trying to contain a nameless fear. The hands were slightly rearranged to clench the box from which evil has been unleashed upon the world. '. . . clench the casket now!' Rossetti apostrophized Pandora in his accompanying sonnet, again emphasizing the hands. The fetishism is characteristic. With the photograph as a starting point, the hands have become the focus of passion from which, as he intuited, only despair could result: headed where 'Thou mayst not dare to think', knowing only 'impassioned hours prohibited'.

Rossetti transforms his lover into a figure of adoration or dread. But there is no easy polarity between a fictional, recreated Jane Morris and a 'real' Jane Morris, photographed at Cheyne Walk. Rossetti could not metamorphose her in the photographs, yet maybe she could not escape being 'interpreted' by him. Was she in fact the rather 'ordinary woman' (in Graham Robertson's phrase) who talked of suet puddings and quince jam? Or was she intelligent and cultivated, as others believed; only reduced to statuesque silence by intolerable conflicts? The photographs do not help us decide. Her sombre mien is suggestive, but with long exposures one *did* look sombre. Was there perhaps also an element of obedience to a fashionable demeanour — life reflecting something from Pre-Raphaelitism, as it were? Henry James wondered about this. 'It's hard to say whether she's a grand synthesis of all

fig. 128

Dante Gabriel Rossetti
Reverie (1868)

Coloured chalks, 33 × 28 in   83.8 × 71.1 cm
Courtesy of Christie's

fig. 129

John R. Parsons
Jane Morris (1865)

Collodion. Negative size
$7\frac{13}{16} \times 5\frac{13}{16}$ *in   19.9 × 14.8 cm*
Victoria and Albert Museum, London

The element of witchcraft in photography no doubt appealed to Rossetti: the performance of arcane procedures, the miraculous appearance of the icon of a loved one. He was not interested, however, in reproducing photographic effects. With Jane Morris, he softened and etherealized.

the Preraphaelite pictures ever made – or they a "keen analysis" of her – whether she's an original or a copy.' This is the elusive quality of the photographs. We cannot tell ultimately how much she is 'herself', and how much playing up to Rossetti's idea of her.

The role of Adored One was no doubt irksome in some ways. After the death of the two men who loved her, Rossetti and her husband, Jane seems to have come into her own. William Rothenstein noticed that she was 'an admirable talker, wholly without self-consciousness'. Like the 'disdainful reserve' noted in Lizzie Siddal, Jane's earlier silence had had its origin in social and intellectual insecurity. But one speculates that it was also expressive of rage at masculine indifference to her needs: an unconcern all the more devitalizing maybe, coming cloaked in adulation.

'To kiss her feet,' said Swinburne, 'is the utmost men should think of doing.' He had just been told of William Morris's plan to marry Jane. No doubt the excitable poet was an extreme case. The beauty of another Pre-Raphaelite Goddess, Marie Spartali – the 'Mrs. Morris for beginners' – (fig. 164) made him want to 'sit down and cry'. But his infantilism is indicative. Society subjected women: it also debilitated young males by rearing them in ignorance of the female sex and of the female within themselves. The silence of Siddal, Morris, and other women of their kind was the seeming vacuum into which flooded images of femaleness created by masculine craving. The women were – it is a truism – objects of peculiarly intense anima projection.

The artists went out in worshipping posses. At a party given by Alexander Ionides in 1862, Rossetti, Legros, du Maurier and Whistler 'were all à genoux' before the Spartali sisters: 'and of course,' Thomas Armstrong recalled, 'everyone of us burned with a desire to paint them.' And Heaven itself – how else could that be envisaged but as a 'rose garden full of stunners'? Falling over each other to prostrate themselves, these men could barely focus on their idols. Intelligence and talent lay hidden. Wounded silence was misconstrued in various ways: as guileless innocence, as occult wisdom, as the masochistically gratifying scorn of an 'indifferent, equable, magnetic' deity. Christina Rossetti perceived the tenuousness of the connection between these shenanigans and the actual women. 'One face,' she wrote of her brother's early obsession with the image of Lizzie Siddal, 'looks out from all his canvases ... Not as she is, but as she fills his dream.'

'The camera cannot lie': the adage is only ever mentioned now to be instantly dismissed. We all know that the camera is at most a partial truth-teller, that it can whisper deceptions and fill dreams. How inevitable, therefore, that it should be caught up in this, its first of many attempts to purvey an erotic stereotype. The pallid face and enigmatic gaze, the hair and garments all unloosed, the medieval jewel: the Pre-Raphaelite Goddess is found in photographers as diverse as Rejlander and Melville, as distanced in time as D. O. Hill and J. Craig Annan. In the photography of Lewis Carroll, the phantom is transmuted and appears in the guise of a child. With the women photographers, Hawarden and Cameron, she is lovingly and supportively caressed.

'You, I suppose, dream photographs,' said Tennyson to Carroll, having confessed that he himself dreamed long passages of poetry.[2] The aside was more astute than the Laureate imagined. This was a natural marriage between fancy and photography: between the inclination to rob the female of a dimension to nourish a dream, and a medium which could play tricks with reality while purporting to serve it — redefining the world in chiaroscuro, distorting space, highlighting trappings and adornments, eliminating life's glow and pulse.

The Divine Attributes

Tousled, tumbling the length of the back or half-across the wan and enigmatic face, hair was the chief attribute of the Goddess. Like sheaves of corn, or the leaves on a tree, a head of hair was an intrinsically rewarding subject for a photographer. A painter might wrestle in vain with that body formed elusively from the play of light on innumerable strands. Alone the photographer could do justice to the whole, while registering the parts.

> But shouting, loosed out, see now! all my hair,
> And trancedly stood watching the west wind run . . .

Thus exults Guinevere in William Morris's vision, recalling the springtime of her passion for Lancelot. Hair, uncut and unloosed, signified abandonment to feeling. Pre-Raphaelite interest in women's hair was pervasive. It extended from Rossetti's *Hist! said Kate the Queen* (*c.*1850), where maids comb the royal tresses as the love-sick page moons on the balcony; to Millais's *The Bridesmaid* (1851), golden hair massively unloosed in superstitious expectation of a lover; to that legion of *femmes fatales* who twist or comb their locks while men suffer — typified by the milkmaid temptress who waylays the prince in Christina Rossetti's 'The Prince's Progress' (1866):

> Who twisted her hair in a cunning braid
> And writhed it shining in serpent-coils,
> And held him a day and a night fast laid
> In her subtle toils.

It was Dickens who defined the connection between unloosed hair and freedom from Puritan restraint. In an 1865 article on 'Beautiful Girls', he declared that no woman could 'be ugly, or even plain, if she have a profusion of hair'. The determination of the previous generation to tie the hair up, to 'plaster it down and put it out of sight' was in keeping with its 'cold, stiff, and artificial' manners. Now, Dickens rejoiced, a girl 'combs it out and lets the sun into it'. The 'great wealth of beauty that lies in the hair' is permitted to 'flow out in natural luxuriance to delight the eyes of men'.[3]

fig. 134
David Octavius Hill
Prayer (1850s)

Paper negative
8¼ × 6 in   15.6 × 11.5 cm
National Portrait Gallery, London

fig. 135
Charles Allston Collins 1828–73
The Devout Childhood of St Elizabeth of Hungary (1852)

Pencil
10¾ × 6⅛   27.6 × 15.5 cm
The Tate Gallery, London

No doubt the purpose of some photographers was merely to tickle masculine delectation, but often the flowing hair of their sitters stimulated a narrative impulse. Photographers wanted to suggest the reason for the intense feeling conveyed by unloosed locks. D. O. Hill has his daughter on her knees in prayer (fig. 134). With Rejlander, long hair and contrived 'classical' pose suggest the grief of Andromache or Electra (fig. 136). In one Hawarden image, her daughters fall on the floor apparently overcome by emotion, though doubtless they were merely entertaining themselves.

This Hawarden photograph is indicative: as well as long hair, another way of conveying the idea that the subject was in the grip of strong emotion was

In the early days of Pre-Raphaelitism, the untying of hair was tentative, the unchecked feelings implied, devotional. St Elizabeth was a heroine of High Church Pre-Raphaelites. Collins's drawing can be linked to James Collinson's major oil painting, *The Renunciation of Queen Elizabeth of Hungary* (1851). Hill's photograph shows his daughter Charlotte. The dating of the photograph depends on the assessment of her age. Hill did occasionally take photographs after Adamson's death in 1848.

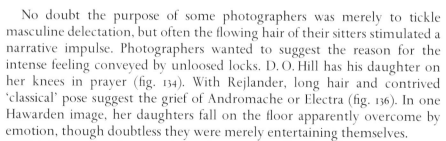

fig. 136

Oscar Rejlander
Grief (1864)

Collodion
$7\frac{1}{4} \times 5\frac{3}{16}$ *in*   *18.5 × 13.2 cm*
*Gernsheim Collection, Harry Ransom Humanities
Research Center, University of Texas at Austin*

This was one of those occasions, like Lizzie
Siddal's bathtub immersion for Millais's
Ophelia, when women risked catching cold
in the service of the idealization of their
sex: the statuesque, clinging drapery was
secured by using thin, damp fabric.

fig. 137

Clementina, Lady Hawarden
Study of Two Girls (c.1860)

Collodion
$9\frac{7}{16} \times 10\frac{5}{16}$ *in*   *24 × 26 cm*
Victoria and Albert Museum, London

The effulgence of Hawarden's vision seems
barely of its time. What is more mid-
Victorian (and Pre-Raphaelite) is the
claustrophobia, the abandonment to
feeling conveyed by the throwing off of
crinolines, unloosing of hair and (not
infrequently) collapse.

to suggest an inability to stand up. Hawarden's girls descend in a flurry of
drapery and hair. They also often collapse over dressing tables. Cameron
permitted her male sitters to face the camera bold and erect. They are dared
to reveal the entirety of their personalities. But the women droop. There is
little sense of a rounded personality. They fall victim to a single emotion –
love, regret or pity:

Everything . . . which droops . . . has a sorrowful and beautiful expression. Hence it is,
that the painters when they would fill the mind with images of grief, not only
dispose the heads and limbs of their figures as grief would dispose them, but take
care that the hair and the drapery shall also droop . . .

This is the Cameron female icon surprisingly anticipated by her husband,
Charles, in an early (1835) 'Essay on the Sublime and the Beautiful'.[4] But the
sorrowful curve also came from Pre-Raphaelitism. It was a leitmotiv in the
Moxon Tennyson, employed most notably by Millais to convey the despair of
Mariana (fig. 139). In emulation, Cameron's Mariana curves herself over a
carved chest (fig. 138). Cameron also modelled the long curve of trunk and
arm in her tender portrait of *May Prinsep* (1870, front cover) on Holman Hunt's
Isabella and the Pot of Basil (1866–8, back cover). This image is titled *Pre-Raphaelite
Study*.

fig. 138

Julia Margaret Cameron
Mariana (1874)

Collodion
$13\frac{7}{8} \times 11\frac{1}{8}$ in   35.4 × 28.1 cm
Victoria and Albert Museum, London

fig. 139

John Everett Millais
Mariana (1857)

*Point of brush, with wash and pen in black
watercolour*
$3\frac{3}{4} \times 3\frac{1}{16}$ in   9.6 × 7.9 cm
Ashmolean Museum, Oxford

Tennyson reacted coolly to Edward
Moxon's edition of his poems which
included drawings by the Pre-Raphaelites.
He had greater faith in Cameron's
photography and himself suggested that
she illustrate his Arthurian narrative, *Idylls
of the King*. She was daunted but thrilled.
'Now *you* know, Alfred,' she told him, 'that
I know that it is immortality to me to be
bound up with you' [Helmut Gernsheim,
Julia Margaret Cameron, 2nd ed. (London 1975),
p. 42]. Mariana, abandoned and footloose in
the moated grange, is a Victorian
archetype. Cameron inclines the body in
the Pre-Raphaelite droop but, more starkly
than any painter of the time, conveys with
the model's expression an angry turning in
on the self.

Then there was the mirror. The key figure here is Tennyson's Lady of
Shalott, a woman forced by a curse to depend on a mirror that 'crack'd from
side to side' when she looked out on to the world. A crucial emblem in the
poem, the mirror emphasized the Victorian preoccupation with the tensions
between art and life. Art, as we know from another Tennyson piece, 'The
Palace of Art' (1839), was always in danger of removing itself from life, turning
in on itself in precious, etiolated self-sufficiency. This subject was popular
with painters throughout the second half of the nineteenth century. Rossetti
had made a sketch for the Moxon Tennyson, but the final illustration was
drawn by Holman Hunt (fig. 140). His dedication to the subject culminated in

Sometimes Hawarden's daughters rifled the dressing-up cupboard and play-acted the doomed damsels of medieval myth. Costume and mirror here may be intended to evoke Tennyson's immensely popular poem, *The Lady of Shalott*. This parable of the terrors of waking to a real life was illustrated by Millais and Rossetti, and obsessed Holman Hunt (though he interpreted it idiosyncratically). At the heart of the poem lies the mirror which 'crack'd from side to side'. The mirror in Victorian culture signified the tensions between art and life and a more general fascination with resemblances.

his excessive but unforgettable oil painting based on the original published Moxon design. Oddly enough, however, Hunt never seems really to have understood what the poem was about. To him it was a Victorian parable on dereliction of duty. The Lady should have stuck to her weaving and not been diverted by Lancelot's waving plumes. To most people 'The Lady of Shalott' is a typically Tennysonian metaphor on the perils of waking to real life. The world as represented in the mirror is no snare but a healthy, natural arena for action, daunting only to those enfeebled by absence from it.

Among those thus debilitated might be artists – or habitual sinners. Hunt himself explored this notion by mirror imagery in *The Awakening Conscience*. Here the morally contaminated love nest is set off by a large looking glass reflecting the world of nature behind the spectator's back, as it were. The same contrast is found in Rossetti's *Lady Lilith* (1868). The lolling temptress's boudoir is fitted out with a mirror reflecting a garden. For his part, Rossetti's interest in mirrors also connects to the doppelgänger idea, pervasive in his poetry, and treated in his eerie drawing, *How They Met Themselves* (1860). It also relates to narcissism, that key attribute of the fatal woman – Lilith has a hand mirror as well into which she gazes, listlessly self-entranced.

Photographers were technically hampered in elaborating these themes. Yet Hawarden, placing her daughter by a looking glass, robes her in medieval fancy dress. Rossetti, posing his mistress, Fanny Cornforth, for the photographer, Downey, brings a mirror out into the garden, thus broaching (without the benefit of a well-focused reflection) the theme of nature

mirrored (fig. 142). Likewise at Little Holland House a mirror is imported into the conservatory and placed behind a crouching Virginia Somers (fig. 143). There were obvious practical advantages in the occasional use of a mirror for portraiture: it filled up the composition; it offered a double portrait – the face seen from different angles, a silhouette combined with front view. But the mirrors were not just a formal device. In the closely-knit world where aristocrats, bohemians, and photographers intermingled, mirrors, since Tennyson, since the Pre-Raphaelites – even more since Alice stepped through one – had a speaking voice. They hinted of other worlds.

Musical instruments must be viewed in the same light. When Cameron evoked first Tennyson's Enid (from *Idylls of the King*) and then *The Princess* (fig. 145) with a photograph of a girl plucking at the strings of an instrument, she was partly responding to the demands of the narrative. But there was something deliberate about selecting the moment in 'Geraint and Enid' when 'Enid sang'; and illustrating *The Princess* from one of its lyric interludes, 'The splendour falls on castle walls', with its musical echoes rolling 'from soul to soul'. But in a special sense music was then 'in the air'.

fig. 142

W & D Downey
Fanny Cornforth (1863)

Collodion
$6 \times 5\frac{1}{6}$ in 15.3×13.3 cm
Jeremy Maas

Rossetti's down-to-earth mistress is invested with a true Pre-Raphaelite aura.

fig. 143

Anon.
Study of a Woman (c.1860)

Collodion
$4\frac{3}{16} \times 6$ in 10.6×15.24 cm
Sir Hew Hamilton-Dalrymple, Bt

Virginia Somers, mirrored and 'medieval', poses at Little Holland House.

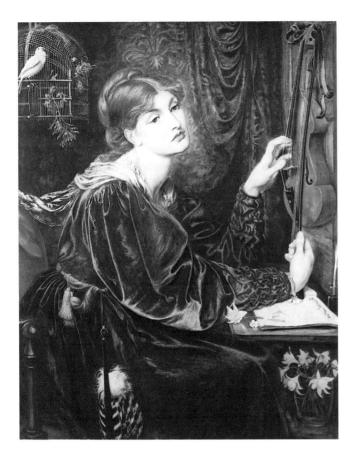

fig. 144
Dante Gabriel Rossetti
Veronica Veronese (1872)

Oil on canvas
43 × 35 in   109.2 × 88.9 cm
Delaware Art Museum, Samuel and Mary Bancroft Memorial

fig. 145
Julia Margaret Cameron
The Princess (1874)

Collodion
13⅝ × 11 1/16 in   35 × 28 cm
Victoria and Albert Museum, London

To illustrate Tennyson's long satire, *The Princess*, Cameron ignored, in the spirit of Rossetti, the many narrative possibilities hoping that an image of music-making would convey profundities otherwise incommunicable.

The 1870s saw the clearest articulation of the idea that of all the arts, music was most attuned to the deepest stirrings of the soul. This longstanding belief had found fresh currency in German philosophy, in Schiller and Hegel, and then in Schopenhauer, whence it reached polemical excess in the writings of Wagner. The idea first came to England through Carlyle ('Observe . . . how all passionate language does of itself become musical'); also through Baudelaire, whose enthusiasm for Wagner's ideas was known by those initiates who had read *L'Art Romantique* (1868). Among these was Walter Pater. In the preamble to his essay, 'The School of Giorgione', Pater co-ordinated a bundle of previous sources and elaborated with unprecedented subtlety the notion that all the other arts aspire 'to the condition of music' – aiming perpetually to obliterate the distinction between matter and form. Pater became a cult figure among undergraduates for his 'pagan' opinions in the late 1860s. He attained a more widespread notoriety with the publication of *The Renaissance* in 1873. The following year Tennyson asked Cameron to illustrate the *Idylls*.

Meanwhile, between 1872 and 1874, Rossetti, always admired by Cameron, completed no less than four works in which women sorrowfully fingered stringed instruments, *Veronica Veronese* (fig. 144), *The Bower Meadow*, *Ghirlandata*, and *Roman Widow*. '. . . let a distant stream/Of music lull me,' wrote his sister in

1849 in 'Looking Forward', 'languid as a dream/Soft as the whisper of a summer sea . . .' Cameron hoped that the unheard melody, the hand trailing over the strings would lull her audience into acceptance of her novel art. Her choice of musical theme arose out of her milieu. At no other time would musical images have so clearly signalled the mysteries of life, the aspiration towards otherwise incommunicable profundities.

The Flowers' Sweet Companions

The sitter's willingness to take part in a charade was an integral part of this iconography. That is why Lewis Carroll's photography seems to belong to it. A child could represent a particularly pure form of the Pre-Raphaelite Goddess: submissive to commands, offering no intellectual challenge, inhabiting a half-forgotten dreamworld. Alice Jane Donkin poised on a window-sill for *The Elopement* (1862); Xie Kitchin, *A Chinaman* (1873), resting on a pile of lacquered tea-chests: a few of Carroll's images highlight the fantasy quality of his photographic enterprise. 'Still she haunts me phantomwise,' wrote Carroll on the last page of the *Alice* books, 'Alice moving under skies/Never seen by waking eyes'. 'Alice' was a phantom, bearing only a partial relation to Alice Liddell. In photography he also transformed her in part – just as he did the other dons' and bishops' daughters who sat for him. He had an impressive rapport with children. He used this as well as the mesmeric power of the still unfamiliar invention – with its paraphernalia of black hoods and witches brew chemicals – to still natural effervescence and bring out the canny, pensive qualities that intrigued him in children.

Less ambitious as a photographer, but an example of how the medium could be harnessed to such innocent passions, was the painter and designer Henry Holiday. 'What,' asked the conservative artist, J. D. Harding, of Holiday in 1858, 'are you a Pre-Raphaelite?' To which the artist steeled himself to reply, 'I am' – and Pre-Raphaelite he remained in his use of every means of accurate representation to further what was nevertheless a fantasy. Holiday was a thoroughgoing medievalist. In the early 1870s he was commissioned to paint a vast (13ft × 35ft) picture of the signing of the Magna Carta. He ransacked the Templar's remains to get every detail of the armour right. This gave him a taste for armour which he could not resist taking to the limit. He had a complete set of chain mail made 'with all accoutrements'.

Meanwhile, Holiday had met two people who were to bring together photography and chain-mail drollery. One was Lewis Carroll with whom he established an immediate rapport, based mainly on a shared love of young girls. Carroll encouraged him to take up photography, advising him that the only prescription for the perfect photograph was 'Take a lens and put Xie before it'. The other person was the young Effie Newall from Gateshead. He played duets with her, drew her, persuaded Watts too that she was an 'irresistible' subject for a portrait – and got her to put the chain mail on. Sword in hand and eyes downcast, Effie was photographed in April 1871 (fig. 147). But though she was his special love, the chain mail was not reserved for her alone. He of course wore it himself and was photographed in it. On a later occasion, Marion Terry, sister of Ellen, wore it. This time Lewis Carroll photographed and Holiday 'drew her lying on the lawn in the same' (fig. 146).[5]

fig. 146

Henry Holiday
Marion Terry (1875)

Line drawing reproduced in Reminiscences of
my Life *(London, 1914)*
The British Library

fig. 147

Phoebe ('Effie') Newall (1871)

Collodion
$5\frac{7}{16} \times 3\frac{15}{16}$ in   13.8 × 10 cm
Jeremy Maas

Henry Holiday, like his friend Lewis Carroll, dealt with his powerful feelings for young girls by resorting to charade – and photography. His medieval tastes, the heritage of his early Pre-Raphaelitism, led to the purchase of a bespoke chainmail suit. Anyone he was fond of was obliged to put it on. If, like Effie Newall, they could all the better summon a St Joan-like demeanour before the camera. On the occasion when Holiday drew Marion Terry (sister of Ellen) lying on the lawn dressed in the armour, Carroll was also present and photographed her.

The trappings of these young sitters invariably point to pre-Freudian assumptions of childhood purity. Mark Anthony, landscape painter, friend of Madox Brown, and photographer, arrayed a young girl in wild flowers in an early example of the genre (fig. 148). This was a conventional way of conveying the unsullied beauty of the child's mind. But the photographer failed to supply a background, and thus the sense that she truly belonged

fig. 148

Mark Anthony
Wild Flowers (1856)

Collodion
$8\frac{3}{16} \times 6\frac{3}{16}$ *in   20.8 × 15.7 cm*
From the collection of the Royal Photographic Society

fig. 149

Arthur Hughes 1832–1915
Girl with Lilacs (1863)

Oil on wood
$17\frac{1}{2} \times 8\frac{7}{8}$ *in   44.5 × 22.6 cm*
Art Gallery of Ontario, Toronto

Girl with Lilacs was owned by Lewis Carroll. Hughes delivered it to him on the day he was photographed by Carroll with his daughter, Agnes (fig. 119). The painting is an example, in a naïve style, of the susceptibility to virginal purity which Hughes shared with other Pre-Raphaelites and with Carroll. The association between the innocent bloom of youth and flowers was conventional but much explored at this period. Anthony was a painter-photographer on the fringes of Pre-Raphaelitism. *Wild Flowers* is poised between the conventions of sentimental genre and the intentness of Pre-Raphaelitism.

with nature – the feeling we get for example with Arthur Hughes's painting, *The Woodman's Child*, is absent. Here the infant is so uncorrupted as to warrant protection, while she sleeps, from a robin and a squirrel.

As we saw earlier, J. D. Llewelyn photographed children in woods. A simpler way of bringing children into proximity with vegetation was to employ the Pre-Raphaelite wall. Lewis Carroll's use of the *Huguenot* formula underlines his view of childhood as a time 'Of innocence, of love and truth!' He is oddly anticipated by the imagery of another Pre-Raphaelite, the doomed Walter Deverell, in a poem written for *The Germ*, 'A Modern Idyll'. The girl in the poem (Deverell's cousin) is a child of nature: she 'loves the earth and skies'; she is 'the sweet companion of these flowers'. With her 'earnest eyes' she sits against a 'grey and mossy wall' while 'the tendrils shook around her'. It is when he poses his sitter in just this way, that Carroll best conveys the guileless sincerity in which he wished to believe.

But Hughes is the most important Pre-Raphaelite connection here. (Carroll's use of the *Huguenot* formula in his Hughes family portrait was perhaps a tribute to the artist's Pre-Raphaelitism.) A frequent painter of children, he also loved to depict young women in a state of vulnerability bordering on the childlike. His penchant for virginal purity was shared by other Pre-Raphaelites, it is true. We think of Rossetti's early pictures of the Virgin Mary, of Millais's *Ophelia* and *Autumn Leaves* (1855–6). But Hughes's treatment was unique. It took yet another admirer of virginal beauty, Ruskin, to see why. The girl in *April Love*, Ruskin wrote, was 'most subtle in the quivering expression of the lips, shaken like a leaf by the winds upon its dew'. The artist had captured the moment when threatened innocence was 'hesitating back to peace'. At its most refined, Hughes's art could capture, like no other, innocence in bittersweet suspense.

Hughes was a friend of Carroll's; he painted the only picture of any significance that Carroll owned, *Girl with Lilacs* (1863; fig. 149). This too puts a girl and flowers together to form a vision of innocence. Carroll drew from it for his illustration of Alice for the original *Alice in Wonderland* (*Alice's Adventures Under Ground*, 1862, which he gave to Alice Liddell). Carroll's liking for the picture confirms that he shared with Hughes a feeling for the *fragility* of beauty and innocence. The *Alice* books are full of metamorphoses and fadings away: the pack of cards that becomes dead leaves floating down from the trees; the rushes that 'melted away like snow'. To Carroll, it was a peculiar anguish to contemplate the brevity of childhood against the long, slow decay of adulthood:

> I'd give all the wealth that years have piled,
> The slow result of Life's decay,
> To be once more a little child
> For one bright summer-day.

Photography – which seizes the felicities of the here and now only to assail us later with the knowledge of what has been lost – was the natural medium for one so unreconciled.

Despite his occasional use of fanciful costumes, Carroll liked his children above all to be natural in front of the camera. He 'never could bear a dressed-up child', one of his sitters later recalled, preferring 'ruffled untidy hair' and even on occasion, nakedness. Staying with the Camerons on the Isle of Wight he went to some pains to be introduced to a 'little gipsy beauty' he had seen on the beach (she turned out to be a colonel's daughter).[6] This taste for naturalness – for the spontaneous, complex child, prescient of the world's sorrows – reduces the charade, undercuts idolatry, and defeats sentimentality. In his best images he explored rather than confined his sitters. His most famous photograph of Alice Liddell (fig. 150) brings out the 'gipsy' quality. His description of her as the 'Child of the pure unclouded brow' is belied: there is no youthful oneness with a beneficent nature here; much more a reminder of Matthew Arnold's *To a Gipsy Child by the Sea-Shore* (1849), that deliberate attempt to subvert the Wordsworthian orthodoxy:

> Who taught this pleading to unpractised eyes?
> Who hid such import in an infant's gloom?
> Who lent thee, child, this meditative guise?
> Who mass'd, round that slight brow, these clouds of doom?

The clouds massing round the brow of childhood dispersed, at least, in sleep. Who knew but that when she closed her eyes she did not escape to a land of brighter radiance? D. O. Hill photographed girls sleeping among the antimacassars of a middle-class interior (fig. 152); the Hampshire photographer, John Whistler, showed them nodding off in the backyard among wood-chippings (fig. 151). It would be helpful to know whether either photographer believed that their subjects were drinking at the source of an anterior wisdom. The particularly tender mood of these images and the special popularity at this time of the perennially touching sight of children asleep encourages speculation.

Sleep itself had a mystique to which none contributed more than the Pre-Raphaelites. 'Let the day come or go,' wrote William Bell Scott in *The Germ*, 'there is no let/Or hindrance to indolent wilfulness/Of fantasy and dream-land ...' But it was later, with the Burne-Jones generation, that sleep truly came to be seen as the begetter of all solace and wisdom. Burne-Jones and Albert Moore simply painted large numbers of people asleep in order to propagate the notion. Simeon Solomon made the personified figure of Sleep the hero of his tortured allegory, *A Vision of Love Revealed in Sleep* (1871). Sleep vouchsafed his crowning vision of 'the Very Love, the Divine Type of Absolute Beauty'. Sleep signified an end to conflict: 'looking upon him, our wave-tossed spirits found their haven, and rest fell upon us'.

The sleep of the innocent elicited special sympathy. Henry Holiday found that an 'image of perfect repose' came to him 'in the form of a sleeping girl'. (He proceeded to body her forth in sculpture.) As Solomon's emphasis on an end to conflict makes clear, underlying the mystique of sleep was the association with death. Many photographs of sleeping children echo the formulae of the numberless paintings and drawings which assuaged the

fig. 150

Lewis Carroll

Alice Liddell as a Beggar-girl (c.1859)

Collodion
$6\frac{3}{8} \times 4\frac{1}{4}$ in   *16.2 × 10.8 cm*
Howard Grey

Carroll met Alice Liddell, the daughter of the Dean of Christ Church, Oxford, when he was looking for young photographic models. It was for her benefit that he whiled away the summer of 1862 elaborating the fable which ensured his immortality. When she was grown up she still haunted him:

> Still she haunts me, phantomwise.
> Alice moving under skies
> Never seen by waking eyes.

It says something for Carroll's way with children that he was able to get them to remain still for his usual exposure time of forty-five seconds. The results often reveal a solemn infant perceptiveness. Here this is emphasized by the starkness of the figure in shallow 'Pre-Raphaelite' space. The suspicion lurks in Alice's eyes that she is the victim of an obscure adult jest.

fig. 151

John Whistler

Sleep (c.1855)

Paper negative
8 × 10 3/16 in   20.5 × 26 cm
Sotheby's, London

This image seems to record genuine rustic exhaustion. It does not conform to the idealized vision of rural life found in much photography of the time.

fig. 152

David Octavius Hill and Robert Adamson

Sophia Finlay and Harriet Farnie (c.1848)

Paper negative
8 1/4 × 6 in   15.6 × 11.5 cm
National Portrait Gallery, London

fig. 153

Arthur Hughes

The Woodman's Child (1860)

Oil on canvas
24 × 25 1/4 in   61 × 64.1 cm
The Tate Gallery, London

From Rossetti's early drawing of Edgar Allen Poe's 'The Sleeper' to the paradisaical slumberlands of the late Burne-Jones Sleep intrigued the Pre-Raphaelites. Setting a squirrel and a robin to guard the sleeping woodman's daughter, Hughes emphasized innocence and oneness with nature. Photographers, whatever their deeper motives, found it a useful solution to the problem of long exposure in portraiture. Like tree silhouettes and ruined abbeys, it was a natural subject for early photography.

fig. 154

Julia Margaret Cameron
Study of a Dead Child (c.1868)

Collodion
$8\frac{1}{3} \times 13\frac{1}{2}$ in   21.4 × 34.5 cm
National Portrait Gallery, London

Pre-Raphaelites like Hunt, Shields, Sandys and M. J. Lawless illustrated deathbed scenes for an avid periodical market. Photography scored a morbid success in H. P. Robinson's *Fading Away*. Is Cameron's child posing or really dead – or just asleep? Much verse of the period shows that the imagery of sleep and death was intermingled ('Sleeping at last, the struggle and horror past,/Cold and white . . .' – Christina Rossetti, 'Sleeping at Last', 1896).

contemporary horror of infant mortality: the sick, dying, and dead young people thronging the exhibition walls and the pages of the illustrated magazines like *Once a Week* and the *Cornhill*; the procession which had its literary counterparts in Little Nell, Paul Dombey, and Rossetti's 'Sister' who 'fell asleep on Christmas Eve'. With Cameron's *Study of a Dead Child* (c.1868; fig. 154), and more famously with Henry Peach Robinson's *Fading Away* (1858), photography contributed directly to the genre.

But it is doubtful whether it gained much by traversing a field so thoroughly tilled by others. As Barthes tellingly argued in *Camera Lucida*, photography – the photography which moves us most though it may lack documentary interest or artistic worth – is of its nature bound up with mortality. It has no need to treat the theme overtly. A photograph – as distinct from a work of art that attempts to make sense of experience – can bring about a frenzied confrontation with existential absurdity. Photography is the prompter of Pity for the human condition – for all those, simply, who have died and will die. Why respond especially to photographs of corpses when, looking at images of the living or the once-living, we take into our arms 'what is dead, what is going to die, as Nietzsche did when . . . he threw himself in tears on the neck of a beaten horse: gone mad for Pity's sake'?[7]

7 *Telling a Story*

fig. 155

Dante Gabriel Rosetti
The Wedding of St George and Princess Sabra (1857)

Watercolour
$14\frac{1}{4} \times 14\frac{1}{4}$ in   36.2 × 36.2 cm
The Tate Gallery, London

Ingenuity and Pre-Raphaelitism

In 1862, the *British Journal of Photography* boasted that photography had 'undoubtedly' encouraged the spread of the now fashionable Pre-Raphaelite movement, verifying also that 'unquestionably the prae-Raphaelite painters have reacted on some of our photographers'.[1] Nevertheless, this journal probably little appreciated the extent of the Pre-Raphaelites' and photographers' joint endeavour: the evidence available to the present-day researcher of a common obsession with minutest tracings of leaf veins and rock fissures, and of a Pre-Raphaelite photographic portraiture. Writing of Henry Peach Robinson, the magazine was concentrating on only one strand in the web: the impetus Pre-Raphaelitism had given to photography's narrative aspirations. Since about the mid-1850s photography had linked itself with the venerable English tradition of 'telling a story' with a picture. By the 1860s, the story it often told was a 'Pre-Raphaelite' one.

Anxious to comply with the narrative tradition but with no precedents in their own medium, the photographers naturally looked to painters. At first, they looked in all directions. Rejlander, having studied in Rome, incautiously followed Raphael. His ambitious allegory, *The Two Ways of Life* (1857) aimed to harmonize groups of figures in the manner of *The School of Athens*. Grundy was more modest. His *Dutch Fisherman* exhibited in 1858 was compared by everyone to Teniers. The blind fiddlers, ragamuffins and pretty maids of the recent English school of sentimental genre helped form the vision of Robinson. Rejlander, despite his one High-Renaissance effort also settled into this tradition, as other titles from the 1850s like *The Washing Day*, *Don't Cry, Mama* and *Drunken Barnaby Leaving the Tavern* make clear.

William Lake Price's early Robinson Crusoe series, meanwhile, was praised for its 'ingenuity and pre-Raphaelitism'.[2] Apart from the fact that Crusoe was recorded with a lot of clutter in sharp focus, there was nothing very Pre-Raphaelite about the series. But it is true that photography's narrative ambitions were kindled just at the point where the Pre-Raphaelites were becoming acceptable. Photographers began to try their hand at the Arthurian, the Tennysonian, and the Christian-symbolic: the new-old world of romance the Pre-Raphaelites had helped to usher in. Barnaby and the washerwoman made way for Lancelot, St Agnes and the Lady of Shalott.

This was partly from commercial pressure. The competitive stereographic industry was voracious. When done with shipwrecks, Turkish harems, Little Nell and saucy monks, stereo photographers looked to the walls of the Academy for ideas. Grimacing models and cardboard sets were pressed into service in tawdry imitations of popular paintings. By the mid-1850s these acclaimed works were often by Pre-Raphaelites. Robinson of Dublin staged a scrupulous mock-up of Henry Wallis's *Chatterton*, and was only prevented from marketing the stereo by legal action from the man who had bought the lucrative engraving rights to the picture. This Robinson should not be confused with H. P. Robinson — although he, too, took a lot of notice of

fig. 156 OVERLEAF

Henry Wallis
Chatterton (1855–6)

Oil on canvas
$23\frac{11}{16} \times 36$ in 60×91.2 cm
The Tate Gallery, London

fig. 157 OVERLEAF

James Robinson
The Death of Chatterton (1859)

Collodion, one of a tinted stereographic pair
$2\frac{13}{16} \times 2\frac{15}{16}$ in 7×7.4 cm
John Jones

'Examine it well inch by inch,' Ruskin advised on seeing Wallis's painting of the dead poet. No-one obeyed more scrupulously than James Robinson. In his eagerness to profit from the success of the painting, he assembled every prop, from the torn manuscripts and burned-out candle to the potted rose. The result is at once bizarre and tawdry, though doubtless photography had been encouraged to turn in this direction by the obsessive literalism of painting at this time. Painting and photography could go no further than this in their exchange of identities.

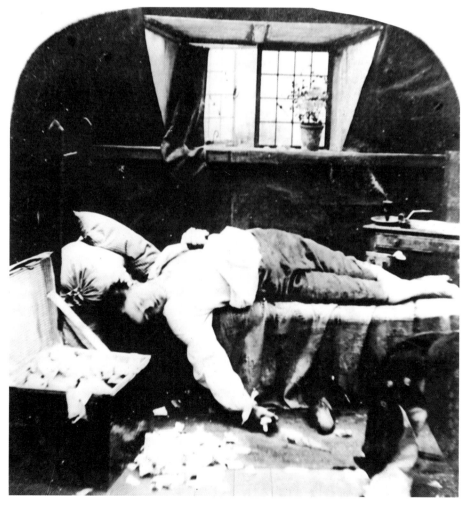

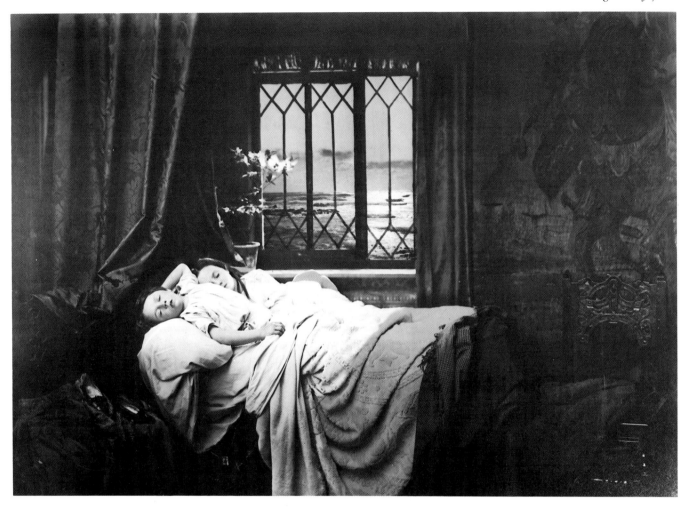

fig. 158
Henry Peach Robinson
Sleep (1867)

Collodion, combination print
14 15/16 × 22 in   37.9 × 55.9 cm
From the collection of the Royal Photographic Society

The *Photographic News* had literalist
objections to this illustration of Matthew
Arnold's *Tristram and Iseult*: the light cast by
the moon was not bright enough – and
where were the shadows of the window
bars? [*PN*, 11 (22 November 1867), p. 560].

Wallis's painting. Both his *Fading Away* and his later *Sleep* (1867; fig. 158) (based on an Arnold poem and reverting to the theme of sleeping children) repeat the formula adopted in *Chatterton* of a centrally placed window with inert humanity beneath.

Usually the commercial photographers took the trouble to vary the themes supplied by popular paintings. *Broken Vows* was the title of an 1856 painting by Philip Calderon (fig. 159) and of a stereo by James Elliott produced around the same time (fig. 160). The heroine endures her lover's faithlessness in different (but equally Pre-Raphaelite) settings: against an ivy-covered wall in Calderon's version, in a Gothic church with Elliott's. Occasionally commercial productions anticipated the work of more consciously artistic photographers. Alfred Silvester's stereo, *Guardian Angels* (c.1856) is a coarse treatment of a theme later taken up by Cameron, that of divinely protected sleeping infants – although she, too, was not above sticking papier mâché wings on her models.

A further Pre-Raphaelite infusion came from the amateur, aristocratic wing of photography. Narrative photography, as practised in country houses, emerged out of the tradition of the *tableau vivant*. This bizarre form of entertainment was popular throughout most of the nineteenth century and artists as eminent as Wilkie, Millais and Leighton designed for it. It was enjoyed by that refined element in the upper class that was not wholly given over to more barbaric recreations – the very people who were most drawn to the hierarchical world of Tennysonian romance. Very different from the commercial ambience of Silvester's and Elliott's studios, was the house party of the Earl and Countess of Fife at Mar Lodge in 1863. The *tableaux* were devised by the Hon. Lewis Wingfield and Victor Prout. Among the subjects was the demise of the age's central symbol of selfless virgin love, Elaine, 'the lily maid of Astolat'. As she lay on her bier for the edification of the assembled grandees, Victor Prout photographed her. This was a logical alliance between a photography that still required long exposures and an art form asking little more of its practitioners than a capacity to hold still and restrain mirth. D. O. Hill had earlier photographed a Walter Scott *tableau*. Melville was to follow with Tennyson, Scott and Shakespeare (figs. 161, 162). It has been said

fig. 159

Philip Hermogenes Calderon
Broken Vows (1856)

Oil on canvas
$36 \times 26\frac{3}{4}$ in 91.4×67.9 cm
The Tate Gallery, London

fig. 160

James Elliott
Broken Vows (c.1856)

Collodion, one of a tinted stereographic pair
$3\frac{1}{16} \times 2\frac{9}{16}$ 7.8×6.5 cm
William C. Darrah

Calderon was not a Pre-Raphaelite, being a member with D. W. Wynfield of the eccentric St John's Wood Clique. Nevertheless *Broken Vows* was Pre-Raphaelite in its use of shallow space and counting of ivy leaves. Stereo photographers

capitalized on such Academy successes.
Elliott took the story on a stage and
maintained with his cardboard Gothic a
vaguely Pre-Raphaelite atmosphere.

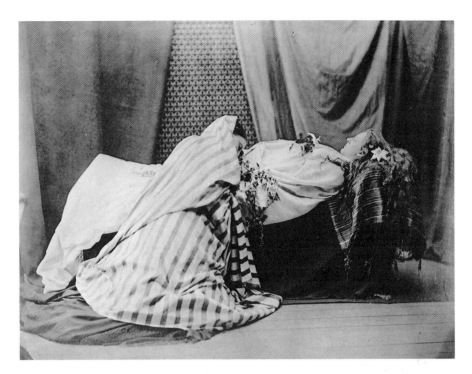

fig. 161

Ronald Leslie Melville, 11th Earl of Leven
Broken Lilies (1871)

Collodion
$8\frac{5}{16} \times 11\frac{3}{16}$ *in*   *21.2 × 28.4 cm*
In a Private Scottish Collection

Tennyson re-told in *Idylls of the King*
Malory's story of Elaine's fatal love for
Lancelot. Straightaway she became a
popular symbol of selfless virgin love.
Elaines sprouted on canvas, in stone and in
photography. Like much 'art' photography
of the time, Melville's image emerged from
the tradition of the country-house *tableau
vivant*, which at this time was turning
increasingly to 'medieval' and Pre-
Raphaelite themes. Elaine is lying on her
bier holding two items made much of in
Tennyson's version: lilies for purity and
death, and a letter confessing her
unrequited love. The photograph lacks the
mythic gloom which could occasionally
rescue this kind of enterprise.

fig. 162

Ronald Leslie Melville, 11th Earl of Leven
Romeo and Juliet (mid-1860s)

Collodion
In a Private Scottish Collection

One of the many objections to the
narrative photograph was that it was too
dependent on the skill of the model (the
same has been said of particularly mimetic
Victorian paintings). Very few models in
these photographs looked as if they
believed in what they were doing. This was
especially true of images that were
essentially photographed *tableaux*. It was
more than the medium could do to
transform cavorting house-party guests
into ardent characters from Shakespeare,
Tennyson and Scott. Melville's
composition here followed an earlier
tableau of Scott's *The Antiquary* by Hill and
Adamson.

that Cameron's preference for blur derived from the gauze curtain of the *tableaux* – although the makeshift character of her costume pieces points more to another country-house pastime, amateur theatricals.

As professionals and amateurs both increasingly sought to rival painters in telling a story or pointing a moral, their success in this was inevitably seen as the very index of photography's artistic status. Writers like W. D. Clark in the *Photographic News* argued that a photograph could never tell a story and that the medium was therefore debarred from art. Samuel Fry, while acknowledging that Clark was employing the right criterion to decide whether photography was art, disagreed, citing Robinson's *Bringing Home the May* as an example. 'I defy any unprejudiced person to assert that there is not in this picture the most exquisite "story" of rustic life, or to state it does not appeal to the feelings in the strongest and most forcible manner.'[3] Fry implied here that there was a distinction between telling a story and 'appealing to the feelings', but to most people they were one and the same. As painter or photographer one appealed to the feelings by articulating the narrative. The audience was satisfied as long as the details were accurately adhered to and errors of taste avoided.

Even at this time there were, however, some purists who felt that photographers should concentrate on recording fact and that the attempt to illustrate fiction was misconceived. The Pre-Raphaelite type of subject became caught up in the ensuing debate. 'Can you fancy Tennyson turned photographer?' Thomas Sutton asked with rhetorical indignation, 'and illustrating his "Lady of Shallott" (sic) by a photograph?'[4] Sutton could not imagine it, but when Tennyson (who had never enthused about artists' attempts to illustrate his poems) *asked* Cameron to illustrate the *Idylls*, he did indeed 'turn photographer' in spirit. Sutton's polemics are a footnote in photographic history, but the fanciful productions he detested also drew the fire of more distinguished critics. Baudelaire disliked all photography, particularly 'male and female clowns, got up like butchers and laundry-maids in a carnival' in imitation of legendary scenes.[5] George Bernard Shaw was, on the other hand, a photographic enthusiast. But he was equally sure that photography's 'terrible truthfulness' ruled out forays into literature. A painter could get away with depicting an attractive model as Juliet: 'The photographer finds the same pretty girl, he dresses her up and photographs her, and calls her Juliet, but somehow it is no good – it is still Miss Wilkins the model. It is too true to be Juliet.'[6]

Shaw wrote this later when photographic Juliets were more or less a thing of the past, but he identified the main problem with the genre: dependence on the model. Even those who had no objections to the narrative photograph *per se* acknowledged that it was crucial to get Miss Wilkins to forget she was Miss Wilkins. Robinson's *Ophelia* (1859) was said to be a failure 'being dependent for its effect upon the expression of the model' – which was inadequately tragic.[7] But perhaps only very accomplished actresses could succeed in a business where they were asked at one moment to impersonate an 'innocent northern peasant preparing for market' and at another 'a sentimental inmate of an Eastern harem'.[8] Cameron was at least aware of the problem. In her finest pictorial work – her more boldly composed Madonnas, angels and Tennysonian heroines – (though not of course in her portraiture) she distracts from physiognomy. The use of profile, highlighting of accidentals, soft focus and bold abstract composition make Shaw's criticism redundant. We do *not* think of the models – and the difficulty scholars have had in identifying some of them is a measure of her success. There were many lapses though. The *Photographic Journal* commented that in her two depictions of the *Wise and Foolish Virgins* (1864) it was difficult to tell the Wise from the Foolish since the same girls were used for both and looked equally foolish in both.[9] It is hard to dissent from this.

The photographers' themes were often Pre-Raphaelite but this disproportionate influence of the model on the final result, the overturning of the normal equilibrium between creator and subject, also echoes the Movement. From the first the Pre-Raphaelites had been so concerned that their models should believe in their conceptions that they had dispensed with professionals (although this was also sometimes due to lack of finance). Only friends could really be relied on. Stephen Spender has argued that 'in Pre-Raphaelite paintings ... just when the painter should be endowed with transcendent imagination, the model is expected to supply it by assuming the expression which the painter then imitates.' This criticism perhaps does not take account of the variety of ways in which a painter's imagination can operate (for instance by 'permeating' rather than 'transcending'), but it is true as far as it goes: F. G. Stephens could think himself into the role of Shakespeare's Ferdinand, and Millais could copy him just as he looked. Even Annie Miller could assume the expression of one whose Conscience had been Awakened, the lineaments of which Hunt then transcribed with as much care as he was giving to the carpet and the cat's whiskers.

Influenced, as ever, by Pre-Raphaelitism, the photographic critic Alfred Wall recommended photographers to follow the Movement's practice in the choice of models. Choose them, he advised, 'from among men and women whose minds are imbued by nature, or cultivation, with poetical conceptions'.[10] Given the right model, indeed, photographers did not have to go to a lot of trouble to bring about the realization of history or myth. Ronald Melville prevailed on Miss Compton to drape a shawl over her head, put a cross around her neck, and hold some white flowers: and there was St Agnes, waiting to be summoned to meet the Heavenly Bridegroom (fig. 163), Cameron found that with a woman of Marie Spartali's exotic beauty, it was even simpler: a trail of ivy (for memory) at the waist and in the hair, and she is Mnemosyne, goddess of Memory. This elementary device, the addition of flower or frond, was often used by Cameron: a way of assisting 'Modern Beauty' to lend 'her lips and eyes/To tell an Ancient Story!'[11]

Here too the Pre-Raphaelites had contributed much by fostering a willingness to read a great deal into symbols, especially botanical ones. In a short 'Song' written in 1849, Christina Rossetti had invested in plants the entirety of human experience:

fig. 163

Ronald Leslie Melville, 11th Earl of Leven
St Agnes (1860s)

Collodion
In a Private Scottish Collection

St Agnes, like a lot of legendary figures, took on new life in the Victorian era once she had been made the subject of a poem by Tennyson. She was depicted by Millais in a fine 1854 drawing; Cameron tackled her more than once. The convention was to show her waiting in ardent expectation of the summons to heaven. Given the right model, apt but unobtrusive accessories, and careful lighting, such subjects were manageable photographically, but it must be said that compared with his mentor, Cameron, Melville here failed on all three counts.

fig. 164

Julia Margaret Cameron
Mnemosyne (1868)

Collodion
$11\frac{13}{16} \times 12\frac{11}{16}$ *in* 30×32.2 *cm*
Sotheby's, London

The model is Marie Spartali. She sat for Rossetti, Madox Brown and Burne-Jones, and was herself an artist. Her husband was the American Pre-Raphaelite and photographer, W. J. Stillman. Mnemosyne was a female Titan, the pre-Olympian goddess of memory: hence the ivy trimmings. Comparison with Melville's *St Agnes* shows Cameron's true portrait photographer's eye for the disposition of costume and adornment.

fig. 165

Henry Peach Robinson
Elaine Watching the Shield of Lancelot (1859)

Collodion
$9\frac{7}{8} \times 7\frac{15}{16}$ in   *25.2 × 20.3 cm*
*From the collection of the the Royal Photographic
Society*

In 1862 the *Photographic News* claimed that
Robinson had 'beyond a doubt' come
under the Pre-Raphaelites' 'spell' [*PN*, 6,
20 June 1862, p. 293]. This was no
exaggeration: he portrayed one by one the
afflicted heroines of Pre-Raphaelitism:
Mariana, Elaine, the Lady of Shalott and
Ophelia. This photograph illustrates the
beginning of Tennyson's 'Lancelot and
Elaine'. Placing Lancelot's shield so that
the reflected gleam of the sun woke her
each morning, Elaine would arise to a day
of gazing: '. . . so she lived in fantasy'.

> Oh roses for the flush of youth
>   And laurel for the perfect prime;
> But pluck an ivy branch for me
>   Grown old before my time.
> Oh violets for the grave of youth
>   And bay for those dead in their prime . . .

Her brother Gabriel was especially persistent in his use of symbols, from the
esoteric Christian bric-a-brac of his first major painting, *The Girlhood of Mary
Virgin* (1848–9), to the fatal pomegranate on which Proserpine feeds as she
wanders in the corridors of Dis. William Michael summarized the precise
rendering of Pre-Raphaelite symbolism as 'The intimate intertexture of a
spiritual sense with a material form; small actualities made vocal by lofty
meanings.' Cameron also attributed lofty meanings to small (floral)
actualities. 'I always think,' she wrote to Tennyson, 'that flowers tell as much

fig. 166

Julia Margaret Cameron
Elaine the Lily-maid of Astolat (1874)

Collodion
$9\frac{11}{16} \times 11\frac{1}{4}\,in$ $24.6 \times 28.6\,cm$
From the collection of the Royal Photographic Society

Static and ecstatic, Elaine was an inevitable
choice for Cameron when she illustrated
the *Idylls* of Tennyson. Like the evolved
Pre-Raphaelitism of Rossetti and his
followers, Cameron's imaginative
photography is vague and dream-like, but
with recourse also to passages of literalism.
Here, the shield and its embroidered case,
carefully described by Tennyson in the
opening section of 'Lancelot and Elaine',
vie for attention with the 'Lily-maid'
herself.

of the bounty of God's love as the Firmament shows of His handiwork.'[12]

There were pitfalls for photographers who wished to imply extra-pictorial
meaning by the simple addition of a few properties, floral or otherwise. The
spectator might miss the point and take the image as a product of a mere
vague fancy. Melville photographed a girl lying, eyes closed, lilies on her
breast with another girl kneeling beside her in an apparent display of grief. Given
the universal reverence for Tennyson and the number of painted, sculpted
and photographed Elaines of the 1860s and 1870s the subject should have been
clear, but at least one reviewer was baffled. 'We are left in some doubt as to
the story .... Of course it is a tale of woe, although we have not discovered
the point'. Was the girl dead, sleeping or 'merely studying botany'?[13]

H. P. Robinson had photographed *Elaine Watching the Shield of Lancelot* (1859;
fig. 165), and had got into critical hot water of another sort: from the
literalism to which photography critics, no less than writers on art, were

especially prone. Lancelot's shield was not battered enough, said one commentator: 'the shield which awakens Elaine's fantasies would, we think, show more dints and bulges, traces of heavy usage'.[14] No wonder, when Cameron broached this subject (fig. 166), she went to bizarre lengths to adhere to the text: sticking a cut-out bird on to the shield case (Elaine was envisaged by the poet embroidering a bird); working on the negative to comply with Tennyson's phrase, 'all the devices blazon'd on the shield'.

This literalism is not a predominant feature of Cameron's art, since she of all photographers was most aware of the danger of the intrusion of the facts on finer feelings. 'Beauties impalpable', 'spaces unfathomable': this (in Frederick Myers's later assessment) was the territory of the 'novel symbolism' that came in with Pre-Raphaelitism, and in which Cameron was thoroughly versed. Rossetti could depict the pomegranate with Ruskinian fidelity and yet convey the idea that it was an unearthly pomegranate. What happened in photography if the symbols were too palpable and fathomable is clear in Cameron's *Elaine*: and even more so in the work of her imitator, Melville. In *St Agnes* (1860s), the rough texture of Miss Compton's garment, even the string around the flower stems, distracts. St Agnes is earthbound: we have little faith in her powers of ascension. Photography is by its nature hamstrung with this kind of subject. Many believed, and still believe, that it was a mistake even to try. Nevertheless, part of Cameron's originality lay in her attempt to mitigate the difficulties by exploring all the possibilities of vagueness. This courted another danger, though: that of losing control of the spectator's response. Cameron's intentions were often purely devotional – though not too soberly so: hers was the kind of exuberant faith that led her in youth to 'wander forth (with her sister, Sarah) and kneel and pray on the country roadsides'.[15] Images like *The Shadow of the Cross* (1865), *The Angel at the Sepulchre* (1869) and *The Kiss of Peace* (1869; fig. 167) were seriously intended as Christian icons: a spiritual ideal embodied by means of the seductive blurring of already beautiful models. (It is odd incidentally, that P. H. Emerson should have associated her with the clear, pure 'sentiment of the Old Florentines',[16] since her work followed more sepulchral Counter-Reformation traditions.)

But that very blurring, the soft-focus sensuality of her images undermined their religious intention. There is little to distinguish her Madonnas from her *Beatrice Cenci* (1870) or a Tennyson subject like *The Gardener's Daughter* (1867). They are all attractive young women photographed in the most flattering possible way, whether they happen to be holding a lily for purity or not. Writing of the poetry of the troubadours and William Morris, Walter Pater argued that an artist may employ religious symbols yet undermine them by infusing too much pagan sensuality. It would be overstating the case to say this is what Cameron did. Yet a comparison between Cameron's *The Kiss of Peace* and Rossetti's *Paulo and Francesca da Rimini* (1855) (or Alexander Munro's sculpture of the same subject), shows that the boundary between sacred and profane yearning can be fragile. As Pater said apropos of 'aesthetic poetry', there is a kind of loveliness, mingled as often as not with morbidity, that, despite an aura of religion, gives 'new seduction' to 'the bloom of the world'.

fig. 167

Julia Margaret Cameron
The Kiss of Peace (1869)

Collodion
$13\frac{1}{2} \times 11$ in   34.3 × 28 cm
From the collection of the Royal Photographic Society

This is one of the finest of many photographs in which Cameron attempted to follow the tradition of the Old Masters, combining, as she hoped, the pure feeling of the Italian Primitives and the chiaroscurist drama of later Counter-Reformation artists. By suppressing detail, she believed that she could reveal the divine within the human. She convinced many of her contemporaries, though not the photographic fraternity. William Michael Rossetti compared her work, somewhat quixotically, to Ruskin's art criticism: Cameron's photography and Ruskin's writing alike transfigured the subject 'and the reproducing process itself, into something almost higher than we knew them to be' [William Michael Rossetti, *Fine Art, Chiefly Contemporary* (London and Cambridge 1867), pp. 333–4].

Unnatural Combinations

The greater number of models photographers massed in front of their lens, the greater the difficulty in making the scene convincing. In many stereoscopic productions or in Cameron's *Wise and Foolish Virgins*, for example, one or two models hold on to the photographer's conception; the rest, fatally distracted, seem about to 'crease'. Rejlander described the problems with this kind of work as 'a feeling of stiffness, a want of action and purpose, and an absence of unity'.[17] His solution was the combination photograph.

With this medium, a print was produced from the combination of images from a number of negatives. In *The Two Ways of Life*, Rejlander printed from thirty negatives on one large piece of photographic paper. H. P. Robinson, on the other hand, championed photomontage, a technique inaugurated with his morbid *Fading Away*. Here, various portions of prints were cut out and pasted on board. The joints were retouched and the whole re-photographed. Rejlander and Robinson were warned not to trespass on the domain of High Art. 'The hand of man,' cautioned the *Art-Journal*, 'guided by the heaven-born mind, can alone achieve greatness in this direction.'[18] Only the painter could combine numerous impressions to form a pleasing whole; photographers would do better to stick to what they excelled in (and what painters should not attempt): the 'perfect transcript'.

Rejlander and Robinson disagreed. Their defence was precisely that they were following the painters by securing separate studies and grouping them according to an Idea. Robinson exhaustively searched the traditional authorities for vindication. He referred to the Ancient Greek, Zeuxis, who had allegedly assembled a painting of Helen from impressions of five different women. He admitted that photography could not pretend to the Sublime, but it could represent the Beautiful, while the third standard category, the Picturesque, 'has never had so perfect an interpreter'. When more than one negative was used, the conditions of the Picturesque were admirably fulfilled: objects in different planes were in focus; true atmospheric and linear perspective were assured. Robinson also appealed to a modern authority: 'A Hunt, inspired by a Ruskin,' he wrote, 'can make a picture from an oystershell'. There was nothing in nature too low to be excluded from selection by the combination photographer. The medium confirmed the Ruskinian tenet that 'Art can be extracted out of almost anything'.[19]

Despite Robinson's nod in this direction, his theories, with at their core the principle of selection, were plainly more conservative and Academic than Ruskinian or Pre-Raphaelite. Conversely, Pre-Raphaelite circles repudiated composition photography in so far as they were aware of it. William Michael Rossetti dismissed it as 'bad invention and futile photography'.[20] This was just a remark in passing. W. J. Stillman, American Pre-Raphaelite, and husband of the exotic Marie Spartali, became more involved with the question. He was one of those whose youthful attachment to Ruskin's ideas had led him to despair. A painting, *Bed of Ferns* brought all the way from America in 1859, had gone into the fire after Ruskin had indulged his habit of criticizing work even when it had been carried out according to his own principles. As a result, Stillman reverted to a conventional theory of art while the part of him that had been inculcated with a Ruskinian regard for the facts was diverted into photography. He took some magnificent Frith-like views of Greek ruins and in 1872 engaged in a polemic with Robinson. Having persuaded himself that the facts – so precious to him – were not art's province, he wanted to preserve one medium, photography, in which they could remain supreme. He charged Robinson with letting photography's glory go by default. Robinson reiterated his old argument: that though combination photography was not the highest form of art, it was the nearest photography could come to making the facts comply with artistic conceptions. Whatever the theoretical objections, he concluded, the effect was often beautiful.[21]

Robinson, and those nurtured in Pre-Raphaelitism, like W. M. Rossetti and Stillman, were thus theoretically in opposite camps. That Robinson's composition photographs have a structural affinity with certain Pre-Raphaelite works therefore comes as a surprise – until we recall the photographer, H. L. Keens's remark (referred to earlier) that, in Pre-Raphaelite paintings, objects seemed 'cut out of pasteboard and pasted on the canvas'. It was academic practice in painting to build up a picture evenly from monochromatic material. The Pre-Raphaelites had broken with this tradition and constructed piecemeal. Details were often garnered from different locations. For his early picture on the subject of Rienzi, Hunt had copied a fig tree from a friend's garden in Lambeth; a patch of grass, dandelions and a bee from nearby; pebbles from another place; a row of saplings from Hampstead. The figures were added indoors. Hunt's industry was such that we never see what a painting looked like half way through this process: he always finished. Not so Rossetti. His oil painting, *Found* (1854–c.1859; fig. 168), carried out in the orthodox, 'niggling' Pre-Raphaelite manner and then abandoned in despair, is a living demonstration of the piecemeal approach. A meticulous wall, a woman's head and a farmer's cart stand flat against blank canvas resembling a Robinson composition with one or two prints in place awaiting the addition of the rest (e.g. fig. 169)

The finished results were not dissimilar either. The figures in Pre-Raphaelite paintings, no less than in Robinson's combination works, have an air of not partaking of their surroundings. Painted separately in deep colours, they often seem encased in a hard outline. These people neither breathe the air around them, nor rest their feet on the ground. Defective scale often emphasizes a problem deriving essentially from tonal inconsistencies. Millais's Ruskin, standing shadowless on the Glenfinlas rock, and Hughes's sailor boy (in *Home from Sea*) all askew on his mother's grave, are particularly glaring examples. Both seem cut out and pasted down *à la* Robinson.

When several figures are involved the bond between Robinson and the Pre-Raphaelites is even more apparent. Effie Millais's notebook reveals the trouble her husband had with *Apple Blossoms* (fig. 171): one lot of blossom had to come from one garden, one from another; some figures one year, others

fig. 168

Dante Gabriel Rossetti
Found (1854–c.1859)

Oil on panel
$16\frac{1}{2} \times 18\frac{1}{2}$ *in*   *41.9 × 47 cm*
Carlisle Museum and Art Gallery

fig. 169

Henry Peach Robinson
Study for a Composition Picture (c.1860)

Collodion, with pencil
*Gernsheim Collection, Harry Ransom
Humanities Research Center, University of
Texas*

This first version of *Found* is rare
evidence of the Pre-Raphaelites'
piecemeal methods. The brick wall
was painted at Chiswick, the calf
and part of the cart at Finchley, the
woman's head (modelled by Fanny
Cornforth) several years later at
Chelsea. Robinson's *Study* allows us
to ponder the similarities with
composition photography. Here
too space was gradually filled up
with 'perfect' but disconcertingly
autonomous units.

the next. To amass the details took four years (1856–9). Relative to his intrinsically less demanding medium, Robinson went to similar lengths with his *Bringing Home the May*. Models, costumes, accessories were carefully selected and photographed. For nine days a pony cart laden with blossoms came to Robinson's house, only to be turned away because of bad weather. As it happened, Millais's painting and Robinson's photograph were exhibited in London simultaneously. The following appeared in the *Photographic News*:

Mr Robinson has beyond a doubt come under (the Pre-Raphaelites') spell, and to their influence and example some of the faults in this picture are attributable, as anyone examining Millais's painting in the Picture Gallery in the Exhibition, especially the 'Apple Orchard', may readily see.[22]

The comparison was inescapable. With an effect somewhere between scissors-and-paste and bas-relief, Millais and Robinson had assembled a line of young girls in floral surroundings. The embellishments were symbolically appropriate, but visually girls and blossoms were merely 'attached' to each other. Equally unsurprising was the *Photographic News*'s criticism of Robinson. Despite his theories, he had offended against the pictorial conventions as blatantly as the Pre-Raphaelites themselves.

For his part, Millais was by this time making use of photography, which helped him with his *Apple Blossoms* montage: he had one of the models photographed and, in various stages of completion, the painting itself. This was a foretaste of what was to be his regular practice. In the 1870s he became friends with Beatrix Potter's father, Rupert, a keen amateur photographer, who supplied him regularly with landscape backgrounds, photographs of sitters and of his work in its various stages – to help him 'see where the drawing's wrong', as he told Potter.[23] It is not recorded whether Millais saw his use of photography as a way of aiding his escape from the irksome letter of Pre-Raphaelite doctrine, or, on the contrary, as a way of being less of a renegade from his original principles by staying that much truer to nature. Like many painters, he kept quiet on the subject of photography.

Robinson's engagement with Pre-Raphaelitism was on the other hand open and deliberate. Besides employing similar techniques, he plundered the medieval dreamworld. In a mood of remorse he later explained:

At that time pre-Raphaelite painters were as plentiful as impressionists now. Their art, unlike impressionism, was not merely a smile at the public, but quite serious, and I tried to make a pre-Raphaelite picture in photography. Truth was fortunately not necessary, nor six months study. All that was wanted was a weird effect, with some awkward lines in it, for the P. R. Brotherhood did not believe in composition. I made the barge, crimped the model's long hair, P. R. fashion, laid her on the boat in the river among the water lilies, and gave her a background of weeping willows, taken in the rain that they might look dreary; and really they were very expressive. It may be remembered that the Lady of Shalott, unlike Elaine, floated down the river, alive and singing, and

'Singing in her song she died'

This gave me the opportunity for a little more freedom, and I nearly wrecked the whole thing by making the model try different positions. I think I succeeded in

making the picture very pre-Raphaelite, very weird, and very untrue to nature – I mean imaginative; but it was a ghastly mistake in our realistic art, and, with the exception of an Ophelia done in a moment of aberration, I never afterwards went for themes beyond the limits of the life of our day.[24]

Robinson came to see this Tennysonian effort (1861) as a 'ghastly mistake'. Others believed from the start that it was one, but by and large it caught the mood of the times, as shown in the *Photographic News*'s response. By adopting 'the quaint poetic manner of the Pre-Raphaelites', Robinson had capably suggested the poem's 'weird feeling and subtle spirit of gloom'. He had advanced the pictorial range of photography. 'We have seen many paintings illustrating the same poem,' the review concluded, 'but none comparable in artistic power and poetic expression to this photograph.'[25]

fig. 170

Henry Peach Robinson
Bringing Home the May (1862)

Collodion, combination print
$39\frac{5}{16} \times 15\frac{1}{4}$ in 99.8×38.7
From the collection of the Royal Photographic Society

fig. 171

John Everett Millais
Spring (Apple Blossoms) (1856–9)

Oil on canvas
$43\frac{1}{2} \times 68$ in 110.5×172.7 cm
The Right Hon. The Viscount Leverhulme

The *Photographic News* held that 'some of the faults' of *Bringing Home the May* (admirable though it was technically) were 'attributable' to works like Millais's *Spring* [*PN*, 6, 20 June 1862, p. 293]: in neither case did the protagonists 'belong' to each other or partake of their surroundings. Assembling separate truths, Pre-Raphaelitism and composition photography alike undermined the convention of pictorial unity and hence the perception of a coherent world.

Robinson need not have been so harsh on himself. If his Pre-Raphaelite subjects were a mistake, they were no more so than the rest of his output. He believed that *The Lady of Shalott* had been absurdly untrue to nature. Truer to life, he believed, were the scrubbed peasant girls, cooing in picture-postcard scenery, to which he devoted himself after recanting the Pre-Raphaelite heresy. But this was an illusion. Though ingeniously crafted, they were no more real than the sugary Birket Foster watercolours from which they in part derived. The problem with Robinson's Pre-Raphaelite subjects was different – he was irredeemably a photographer of the old 'sharp' school of the 1850s.

On the face of it, it should have been a viable enterprise to translate the aesthetic of hard-edge Pre-Raphaelitism into a medium which could (and Robinson believed should) revel in detail; to reproduce a poetic narrative with archeological accuracy and fidelity to appearance. This had been the Brotherhood's early achievement. Details such as the moth in *The Hireling Shepherd* and Ophelia's pansies and forget-me-nots, had come laden with symbolic power by the intensity of the painters' involvement. The photographer, however, neither had colour for emotional range nor could he invest objects with the aura of loving labour. The shield in Robinson's *Elaine* picture or the potted plant on the window-sill in *Sleep* have merely been 'arranged' as if by a competent stage manager. The more the incidentals are thrust in sharp focus in front of our noses, the more we become aware of the artificiality of the whole. With the disappointment of the opera-lover who finds that a pedestrian production fails to conjure the Venusberg or the Egypt of the Pharaohs, we stay outside the dream.

Other photographic conjurors of the Pre-Raphaelite dream tried to avoid the problems Robinson made for himself by adhering to sharpness. Melville's *St Agnes* was as we saw too sharp for the poetry of sainthood, but when, like Charles Collins in *The Good Harvest of 1854*, he addressed himself to gathered corn (fig. 174), he avoided the enumeration of strands for which the painting is remarkable. The result is a sultry mood piece suggesting that his poetically-dressed gleaners are sheltering from summer storm. Similarly the patterned dresses and leafy surroundings in a Melville study of 'rustic charity' and in Cameron's *Adam Bede* illustration (1874; fig. 173) are charmingly atmospheric rather than intrusive. Nevertheless, the balance between inner and outer – summarized in the Rossettian nostrum, '... to embody and symbolise without interfering with the subject *as a subject*' – was elusive in photography. It was all too easy for the quest for authenticity to result in ludicrous embellishment. A suit of chain mail, visually fussy and with clear historical associations, was inevitably destructive of the desired mood of timelessness, however softly focused. In Cameron's *The Parting of Lancelot and Queen Guinevere* (1874; fig. 175) the chain mail is mere fancy dress, sabotaging the authentic tenderness conveyed by the models. By contrast the heraldic devices in Rossetti's similarly composed *The Wedding of St George and Princess Sabra* (1857; fig. 155) are mesmeric patterns, metaphors for states of mind, *contributing* to the mood of trance-like mutual absorption.

fig. 172
Arthur Hughes
The Long Engagement (c.1854–9)

Oil on canvas
41½ × 20½ in   105.4 × 52.1 cm
By courtesy of Birmingham Museums and Art Gallery

fig. 173
Julia Margaret Cameron
The Twilight Hour (1874)

Collodion
13½ × 11 in   34.4 × 28 cm
From the collection of the Royal Photographic Society

Cameron was trying here to illustrate the 'little airs' with which the flirtatious Hetty Sorrel enticed Adam Bede 'back into the

net'; but the camera could at this time no more capture little airs than fluttering leaves or skimming clouds. She might have done better to follow Hughes (an artist she admired) in depicting a scene of statuesque resignation.

fig. 174

Ronald Leslie Melville, 11th Earl of Leven
Gleaners (1860s)

Collodion
In a Private Scottish Collection

This photographic Pre-Raphaelitism is Cameronesque, no longer crisply enumerating strands of hair or corn in the manner of the 1850s, but rejoicing in sultry evocation.

The problem of how to prevent reality intruding on the dream was only solved with the development of a thoroughgoing pictorialism in photography towards the end of the century. The Linked Ring and the Photo-Secession possessed both the technical means and the consciously artistic ends that could bring this about. Inviting the wrath of their purist successors, they used special papers with distinct surfaces, tints, and textures and subjected the negative or print, to any amount of treatment to make the image resemble an engraving or drawing as much as a photograph.

All this came about as the Pre-Raphaelite dream was in eclipse. Yet in 1897 one of the founder members of the Linked Ring, James Craig Annan, published a photograph of a woman standing forlornly in a wood with a ghostly ruin in the background (fig. 178). She had all the attributes of the Pre-Raphaelite goddess, the hair, the long diaphanous gown. She was Tennyson's *Eleänore* of the 'large eyes imperial'. Able to photograph in a wood at a gloomy time of day and then to work what magic he would with the negative, Craig Annan injected a sense of mystery into the scene that had eluded Cameron in her larger-scale efforts, and Robinson with his disjointed mock-ups.

fig. 175
Julia Margaret Cameron
The Parting of Lancelot and Queen Guinevere
(1874)

Collodion
13½ × 11⁵⁄₁₆ in   34.4 × 28.7 cm
From the collection of the Royal Photographic Society

This portrayal of the anguish of the
adulterous queen and her lover was
among the more successful of the *Idylls*
series. It was the photograph with which
Cameron took the most trouble (she made
forty-two attempts) and which finally
pleased her most. The intense communion
is emphasized by a light which seems to
radiate outwards; but chain mail and
photography do not go well together.
Such trappings have to be transformed (as
in Rossetti's watercolours of the 1850s) into
metaphors for states of mind, or risk
suggesting mere fancy-dress antics.

fig. 176
Dante Gabriel Rossetti
Arthur's Tomb (1855)

Watercolour with gum arabic, pencil and pen
9¼ × 14⁷⁄₈ in   23.5 × 37.8 cm
British Museum

fig. 177
Julia Margaret Cameron
Gareth and Lynette (1874)

Collodion
13³⁄₁₆ × 10⁷⁄₁₆ in   33.5 × 26.5 cm
National Portrait Gallery, London

Cameron's *Idylls* series draws on Rossetti's
early watercolours in its depiction, in
otherworldly, 'medieval' settings, of
moments of rapped communication
between lovers. Rossetti's drawing shows
Guinevere's renunciation of Lancelot
before her husband's tomb; Cameron
depicts Lynette's upsurge of feeling for the
sleeping Gareth:

 Sir Gareth drank and ate, and all his life
 Past into sleep; on whom the maiden
  gazed
 '. . . Seem I not as tender to him
 As any mother?'

fig. 178

James Craig Annan
Eleänore (1897)

Reproduced in Vol. 8 of The Practical
Photographer
$4\frac{3}{4} \times 3\frac{3}{4}$ in   12.1 × 9.6 cm
The British Library

By 1892 H. P. Robinson had come to believe
that 'the histories and mysteries of the
past' were an absurd subject for a 'realistic'
medium like photography: King Arthur
may never have existed 'and you cannot
photograph a doubt' [*Photographic Quarterly*,
3 October 1891–July 1892–, pp. 96–105]. He
believed that British photographers had
now finally turned their backs on legend.
But as Annan's *Eleanore* makes clear he was
premature. There was a fashion at the time
for dim, atmospheric landscapes and
though doomed Pre-Raphaelite damsels
were hackneyed they looked at home in
such places. 'Eleänore' (1832) is one of
Tennyson's early poems to female fantasy
figures, referred to by Edward FitzGerald as
'that stupid Gallery of Beauties':

> ... Thought seems to come and go
> In thy large eyes, imperial Eleänore

The soft focus Pre-Raphaelitism, which Cameron had inaugurated but
lacked the means to develop, finally culminated, as far as can be imagined
from mid-Victorian Freshwater, in the creation (for this is surely the word)
in 1900 of an *Arthur and Guinevere* (fig. 179) by the New York photographer, Frank
Eugene. Of all the Photo-Secessionists, Eugene was the most graphic and
most painterly. Like Cameron, but with infinitely more sophistication, he
would scratch and draw on the negative. He achieved what she had never
quite managed, an Arthurian photograph that transports us away from the
time and place of its making. Here the armour is no Victorian folly but an
eloquent motif, enhancing the male figure and gleaming out of the shadows

fig. 179
Frank Eugene
Arthur and Guinevere (1900)

Platinotype on Japan tissue
4½ × 3½ in   11.4 × 8.8 cm
Albright-Knox Art Gallery, Buffalo, New York

The Pre-Raphaelite dream in photography had always suffered from the intrusion of reality. With the determination of many photographers at the end of the century to cut the tie with reality – to experiment with focus, manipulate the negative, employ textured papers and so on – the dream was finally free to materialize. Eugene all but obscured his costume protagonists in Dark Age murk and painted in the landscape. The work succeeded where Cameron's Arthurian photographs had never quite: the imagination had wide spaces in which to wander. This faculty was now all but exhausted by Pre-Raphaelite fantasy, however – and was this in any case truly a photograph?

as if painted by Giorgione. The models are perhaps theatrical but this is hardly noticeable so enveloped are they in mythic gloom. They are all but believable Dark-Age heroes stranded in a symbolic landscape of dim-dark woods and storm skies. It is ironic that the Arthurian myth so appealing to the 1850s was only fully brought to life by the camera when photography was at the furthest extreme from the clear, direct vision of that era.

There are Victorian photographs that look more like paintings than this or other kinds of 'Pre-Raphaelite' photography: Rembrandtesque Hill and Adamson portraits, Rejlander genre scenes, Emerson landscapes. There are also Victorian paintings that resemble photographs more than the Pre-Raphaelites' works do. Some authorities have even argued that the directness and informality of the photographic vision appeared in painting *before* the invention of photography in the landscapes of Girtin, Constable, Friedrich, Corot, and others.[26] Certainly by the mid-1860s the look of photographs had been universally assimilated. Intentionally or not, photographic tonality appeared in the work of a variety of Academic painters from the social realist Frank Holl to an exotic like Alma-Tadema. (We recall that 1864 was the year of Atkinson Grimshaw's more 'photographic' than 'Pre-Raphaelite' *Nab Scar*.) The subsequent development of the snapshot had a less pervasive but more instantly recognizable influence on paintings. A portrait of Robert Louis Stevenson by Sargent (1885) catches the writer walking past a casually opened door, twisting his moustache. He is on his way out of the picture while his wife, lolling in a chair opposite, is already half out, cropped by the edge. These examples are more truly photographic than Millais's Glenfinlas rocks or Hunt's view of Nazareth: although the Pre-Raphaelites imitated the action of the camera in 'passively recording', their vision was affected neither by the consistent tonality nor by the increasing informality of actual photographs.

The bond between photography and Pre-Raphaelitism lies therefore not in identical results, but in a pursuit of common ends by different means. Photographers and Pre-Raphaelites together ploughed the seas between the opposing shorelines of the Real and the Ideal: to begin with, enchanted with nature; and then, overcome by the desire to beautify and to mythologize. Riding the waves together, they sometimes raced, sometimes skirmished, sometimes lost their separate identities in the fog. This confusion of identity in particular prompts us to view Victorian photography in the light of Pre-Raphaelitism.

Susan Sontag has rightly pointed out that the language of photographic criticism is 'too often parasitical on the vocabulary of painting'.[27] Photography has certainly *become* a very different thing from painting. To evaluate Weegee's Mean Streets, Bill Brandt's nudes or Don McCullin's reportage by the norms of the older art is often to resort to irrelevance for want of knowing how else to respond. With more personal photography – the image of someone we love or miss – there is no meaning in any kind of 'evaluation'. What sense can it make to say that a photograph of a loved-one ravaged by illness is a 'good' or 'bad' photograph? We then realize that most photographs, not just those of people we know, are spheres for the operation of human sympathy rather than of critical judgment. But with Victorian photography – technically hampered, moving only hesitantly towards its quintessential piquancy, looking over its shoulder at painting, even resorting to painterly techniques – with this infant photography certain parallels with painting are inescapable. Many Victorian photographers, like Henry White and Cameron, were indeed pioneers in their different ways of a true photographic vision – yet how is it possible to look at a Henry White cornfield without thinking of Madox Brown, or at photographic Elaines and Marianas without recalling their Pre-Raphaelite sisters?

The Photographers - Biographical Notes

Brief biographies of the photographers whose works are reproduced here

Robert Adamson 1821–48
(*see also* Hill)

fig. 152 *Sophia Finlay and Harriet Farnie*
   (*c*.1848) p. 152

Adamson was intended for the career of engineering, but delicate health lead him to the gentler profession of portrait photography. In 1843 he opened a calotype studio in Edinburgh and, after an introduction by Sir David Brewster, embarked on the famous partnership with D. O. Hill.

James Craig Annan 1864–1946

fig. 178 *Eleänore* (1897) p. 178

Annan was Scottish, the son of the Glasgow professional portrait photographer, Thomas Annan. He was a fine portrait photographer in his own right but his chief importance lies in his role in the late nineteenth-century pictorial movement. He was a member of the Linked Ring and in 1904 became the first President of the International Society of Pictorial Photographers. His work was published in the influential journal *Camera Work* edited by Alfred Stieglitz. He also contributed to the revival of interest in Hill and Adamson, making high-quality gravure prints from their work.

H. Mark Anthony 1817–86

fig. 148 *Wild Flowers* (1856) p. 148

Anthony was a landscape painter born in Manchester. Between 1834 and 1840 he lived in Paris and Fontainebleau and was influenced by Corot and Dupré. Back in England he became acquainted with the Pre-Raphaelites through his friendship with Ford Madox Brown. In April 1851 he travelled to the Isle of Wight with Brown and Holman Hunt. He was a regular contributor at the Royal Academy between 1837 and 1854. Collections of his paintings, which reflect a mixture of French and Pre-Raphaelite influences, can be found in the Museum of Cardiff and the Walker Art Gallery, Liverpool. Anthony, who was also a part-time dealer in violins, became involved in photography in the mid-1840s. Madox Brown's diary entry for 12 November 1847 reads: 'went to see Mark Anthony about a Daguerotipe (sic) think of having some struck off for the figures in the picture (*Chaucer at the Court of Edward III*) to save time.' (*The Diary of Ford Madox Brown*, ed. Virginia Surtees, New Haven and London, 1981, p. 14.) Around 1853 Anthony took the first extant photograph of Rossetti, holding the arm of his brother, William Michael. During the mid-1850s Anthony became a member of the Photographic Society. He was never prolific as a photographer but contributed one image, *Wild Flowers*, to the *Photographic Album for the Year 1857*.

Frederick Scott Archer 1813–57

fig. 20 *Kenilworth: Caesar's Tower from the Inner Court* (1851) p. 25

A key figure in the history of photography, Archer was born in Bishop's Stortford, Hertfordshire, the son of a butcher. He lost both his parents in childhood. Apprenticed at first to a bullion and silver dealer in London, he became interested in numismatics and eventually set up as a sculptor. He was taught the calotype process in November 1847 by Dr Hugh Diamond, an important photographic pioneer. The intention was to obtain true likenesses of his sitters, but Archer gradually neglected sculpture for photography. He published his revolutionary wet collodion process in *The Chemist* in March 1851 and then in a *Manual of the Collodion Photographic Process* a year later. The process involved coating a glass plate with a solution of cellulose nitrate mixed with alcohol and ether in which potassium iodide had been dissolved. Just before exposure the plate was immersed in a solution of silver nitrate to form silver iodide, which is light sensitive. The glass negative was developed and fixed immediately after exposure. The difficulties of the process were compensated for by speed of exposure and quality. Gentle and unassuming by nature, Archer was uninterested in patenting his invention and lost the chance to make a fortune. He died in poverty remembered for his 'poor health ... somewhat sorrowful look and angel wife' (*Practical Photographer*, 4, January 1893, p. 1).

Francis Bedford 1816–94

fig. 21 *Rock on the Seashore* (1862) pp. 28–9

fig. 56 *Bettws-y-Coed. Ffos Noddyn (The Fairy Glen), No. 1* (c.1860) p.69

fig. 97 *The Village of Siloam, in the valley of Jehoshaphat, with the Hill of Evil Counsel, and the valley of Hinnom* (1862) p. 101

Bedford came from a prominent family of lawyers, admirals and architects. He was the son of Francis Octavius Bedford, an important figure in the early nineteenth-century Greek revival. He joined the family architectural practice and exhibited architectural drawings at the Royal Academy between 1833 and 1849. He also executed 158 coloured lithographs for Sir Matthew Digby Wyatt's *The Industrial Arts of the Nineteenth Century at the Great Exhibition*. Having taken up photography in 1853, he was quick to attain both commercial success and royal patronage, though he remained unambitious, as he had sufficient private means to withstand commercial pressures. He travelled throughout Britain photographing landscape and architecture. His views often, though by no means always, fit into the conventions of landscape painting with the placing of the figures and the 'correct' viewpoint. Overall he was the most proficient topographical photographer of the Victorian period. He was active in the Photographic Society from 1857 and was elected vice-president in 1861. The culmination of his career was the invitation to document the educational tour of the Prince of Wales to the Near East in 1862. The 148 prints were published in 1863 and won Bedford a silver medal at the 1867 Paris Exposition Universelle. An unusual feature of the photographs was the inclusion of clouds which Bedford achieved not, as many thought, by painting on the negatives but by overlaying a second negative. Bedford's work was included in William and Mary Howitt's *Ruined Abbeys and Castles of Great Britain and Ireland* (1862) and in the following years Bedford's publishers, Catherall and Pritchard of Chester, were very active on his behalf, distributing views of north Wales, Tenby, Exeter, Torquay, Warwickshire and Stratford-on-Avon, as well as a stereoscopic series, *English Scenery*. Towards the end of his career Bedford handed over much of his business to his son William whom, nevertheless, he outlived by a few months.

John Brett 1831–1902

fig. 67 *The Lion Rock from Asparagus Island* (1870) p. 79

A painter who incorporated photography into an essentially Pre-Raphaelite sensibility, Brett was born in Surrey, the son of an army officer. Having studied in Dublin where his father was stationed, he entered the Royal Academy Schools at the age of twenty-three. In 1856 he exhibited three portraits at the Academy. The same year saw his momentous meeting with the Ruskin disciple, J. W. Inchbold, in Switzerland after which he was drawn into the orbit of the influential critic. Three works, *The Glacier of Rosenlaui* (1856), *The Stonebreaker* (1856–8) and *Val d'Aosta* (1858) show his newfound dedication to the principle of minute observation. Praised only equivocally by Ruskin, Brett attempted a more lyrical vein in works like *Morant's Court in May* (1864) and then gradually restricted himself to large sea-coast pictures for annual exhibitions at the Academy. Brett's interest in photography can be associated in particular with this latter phase, where preliminary photographic studies were an integral part of his procedures.

Julia Margaret Cameron 1815–79

front cover *Pre-Raphaelite Study* (1870)

fig. 88 *Holman Hunt in Eastern Dress* (1864) p. 96

fig. 117 *A Dantesque Vision* (1865) p. 123

The most original Victorian photographic portraitist, Cameron was the third daughter of James Pattle, a civil servant posted in Bengal. In 1834 she married Charles Hay Cameron, Benthamite philosopher and jurist, an important figure in the society of Calcutta. Moving to England in 1848 the Camerons became involved with the social life of Little Holland House, Kensington, where another Pattle sister, Sarah Prinsep, regularly entertained such luminaries as Sir John Herschel, Thackeray and Tennyson. In 1860 the Camerons moved to Freshwater, Isle of Wight, mainly to be near the Tennysons. In 1863 Cameron was given a camera and wet collodion kit by her daughter and son-in-law and immediately applied herself to photography with the energy for which she was already renowned among her friends. She learned the rudiments from David Wilkie Wynfield and after concentrating initially on religious and allegorical themes turned to the portraits for which she is still most admired. Prevailing on even her most august contemporaries to sit stock still for up to seven minutes in the converted chicken house that served as her studio, she photographed in unorthodox close-up on large (10 × 12 in or 12 × 15 in) plates. These required long lenses that were often difficult to use so that the focus often lacked clear definition. Cameron was also slipshod about thumbmarks, spots, and scratches — her main concern was with the 'immortal' essence of her sitters. At their best her portraits do indeed possess a profound strength and pathos. The approval of her artistic friends and of non-specialist critics like Coventry Patmore compensated Cameron for the hostility of orthodox photographic circles. Her private exhibitions at the Colnaghi Gallery in 1866 and the German Gallery in 1868 were not a success, but she obtained a following on the Continent after showing in Berlin in 1866 and Paris in 1867. In the early 1870s she concentrated on poetic illustration, producing two series for *Idylls of the King* at Tennyson's request (1874). Her husband's ill-health necessitated return to the sub-continent in 1875. Settling in Ceylon she executed only a few more photographs before her death four years later.

Lewis Carroll (Charles Lutwidge Dodgson) 1832–98

Charles Lutwidge Dodgson adopted the pseudonym Lewis Carroll in 1856, the year he took up photography. Born in Cheshire, the son of a clergyman, he was educated at Rugby and then spent the rest of his life at Christ Church, Oxford, first as a student, later as clergyman and professor of mathematics. His principal fame rests on the classic *Alice* books, written for the daughter of his friend Dean Liddell. Alice Liddell was also the subject of one of his first successful photographs and was often to sit for him (she also sat later for Julia Margaret Cameron). Though he was especially fond of her, she was only one of many such children with whom he was at once emotionally and photographically involved. He had been introduced to the calotype by his uncle Skeffington Lutwidge in 1855, but it was the Photographic Society's exhibition which fully converted him to photography. He bought wet collodion apparatus and, either using his rooms in college or hiring a studio, soon became obsessed with this medium.

He undertook a wide range of portraiture: artists and literary people were often responsive to his invitations. In 1857 he photographed the Tennyson family in the Lake District. In October 1863 he moved his apparatus among the Pre-Raphaelite circle, photographing the Hughes, Munro, and Rossetti families. He subjected his hobby to ironic literary treatment in the Longfellow parody, 'Hiawatha Photographing', and in a number of short prose pieces including 'A Photographer's Day Out'. With sound understanding of lighting, flair for the telling incidental and above all his ability to get his sitters to relax, Carroll, though essentially an amateur, was an important pioneer of naturalism in photographic portraiture. He gave up photography in 1880 probably in order to give himself more time for writing.

Joseph Cundall 1818–95

(*see also* Delamotte)

Cundall was a leading photographer and photographic publisher of the 1850s. His interest in photography began as early as 1844 when he published an article on the calotype process in *The Philosophical Magazine*. He was a member of the Calotype Society, a precursor of the Photographic Society. He engaged in a succession of partnerships. With Robert Howlett at the Photographic Institution, he was commissioned by Queen Victoria in 1856 to produce portraits of Crimean War heroes. He contributed to *The Sunbeam*, edited by Delamotte, with whom he had earlier collaborated on *A Photographic Tour among the Abbeys of Yorkshire*.

Francis Edmond Currey 1814–96

fig. 18 *Foxglove* (1869) p. 22

Currey succeeded his father as agent for the Duke of Devonshire's estate at Lismore, County Waterford in 1839. He became interested in photography in the early 1850s. He joined the Photographic Society and contributed to the exchange of prints within the Society and to the Photographic Exchange Club in 1855. He was one of the few early amateurs to continue photographing after the 1850s. During the 1860s he became involved with the Amateur Photographic Association. His interest in photography continued, with that of other members of his family, till later in the century.

Philip Henry Delamotte 1821–89

(*see also* **Cundall**)

fig. 75 *Bolton Priory* (1856) p. 86

Son of the landscape artist, William Delamotte (one of the John Varley circle), P. H. Delamotte had a successful career as an art teacher. He eventually became Professor of Drawing at King's College Cambridge. His interest in photography began in the late 1840s when he started experimenting with the calotype and waxed paper processes before later moving to collodion. His most original contribution to photography came from his commission to document the reconstruction of the Crystal Palace at Sydenham in 1854. The images, at once a celebration of manual labour, technical ingenuity, and geometry and light, were published in *The Progress of the Crystal Palace* (1855) and in a portfolio brought out by the Crystal Palace Art Union (1858). Delamotte's work was often used as book illustration, for example in *A Photographic Tour among the Abbeys of Yorkshire*, a joint collaboration with Joseph Cundall (1856), and *The Sunbeam* (1859). Before his interest in photography waned in the 1860s he taught at the Photographic Institution in New Bond Street, London, and published a photographic manual, *The Practise of Photography* (1855).

W & D Downey

fig. 142 *Fanny Cornforth* (1863) p. 144

Downey's was a reputable firm of portrait photographers with premises in Ebury Street, Chelsea, and Newcastle-on-Tyne. William Downey became something of an official photographer to the Pre-Raphaelite circle, photographing Arthur Hughes, D. G. Rossetti, Fanny Cornforth, William Bell Scott and Ruskin. Ruskin was so upset that a photograph of him with Rossetti and Scott, taken on 29 June 1863 in Chelsea, had been made public that he reproached Rossetti for introducing him to Downey, 'a mere blackguard' (Oswald Doughty, *A Victorian Romantic*, 2nd ed., London 1960, p. 327). Downey won the praise of a later celebrity however: Sarah Bernhardt wrote in the firm's autograph book 'vous êtes le plus aimable des hommes, et le roi des photographs . . . je crie, Vive le roi Downey' (Jeremy Maas, *The Victorian Art World in Photographs*, London 1984, p. 153).

Ernest Edwards 1837–1903

fig. 10 *Cleft in the Rock. Anchor Church. Derby* (1860s) p. 16

fig. 61 *Upper Ice-Fall of the Ober Grindelwald Glacier* (1866) p.73

Edwards was educated at Cambridge University and joined the Photographic Society in 1866. He was a well-qualified and inventive photographer. In the early 1860s he manufactured one of the first pocket-sized folding camera with a walking-stick tripod. In 1869 he introduced the heliotype, a photo-mechanical printing process which was a variation on the better-known collotype. He took many portraits of prominent people but he is best-known for the twenty-eight photographs he contributed to H. B. George's *The Oberland and its Glaciers* (1866). In the 'Notes by the Photographer' appended to George's text, Edwards pointed out that the advantage to photography of colourless glacier scenery was almost lost in the problems caused by the violent contrasts of light and shade.

James Elliott (active 1850s–70s)

fig. 160 *Broken Vows* (c.1856) p. 158

Elliott, who began his photographic career as a daguerreotypist operating from Piccadilly, London, was one of the most prolific producers of stereographic photographs. He specialized in fictional, historical and comical scenes. His *Sacking of the Jew's House* (1858) staged in four scenes, was one of the first attempts to present a picture story in stereo. He sought advice from antiquarians to attain authenticity in his two *English History* series. He published stereos by other photographers such as William Grundy and Victor Prout.

William England (d.1896)

fig. 59 *Study of a Waterfall* (mid-1860s) p. 72

As chief photographer for the London Stereoscopic and Photographic Company, England travelled widely. He was one of the photographers to make a stereograph of Blondin crossing the Niagara Falls in 1859 and brought back the first stereo-views of American scenery to be seen in Europe. In 1862 his firm was commissioned to photograph the International Exhibition in London. England's pictures recorded the ceremonies, huge layout, and exhibits individually and in groups. Leaving his employers in 1863, England toured the Alps soon afterwards under the patronage of the Alpine Club. His views were published as stereo slides.

Frank Eugene 1865–1936

fig. 179 *Arthur and Guinevere* (1900) p. 179

Born in New York, Eugene studied art in that city and in Munich. He was Alfred Stieglitz's collaborator and a founder member of the Photo-Secession. He contributed to *Camera Work*. He moved to Germany in 1906 and painted in the *art nouveau* style. He was appointed Professor of Art Photography at the Kunstakademie, Leipzig in 1913, by which time a reaction had set in against his style of painterly, manipulative photography.

Roger Fenton 1819–69

fig. 50 *North Wales: Hillside Study* (1858) p. 60

fig. 52 *Falls of the Ogwen: North Wales* (1858) p. 65

fig. 79 *Raglan Castle, the Watergate* (1856) p. 90

fig. 109 *Nubian Model Reclining* (late 1850s) p. 116

fig. 120 *Interior of Tintern Abbey* (late 1850s) p. 128

One of the most prominent figures in the photography of the 1850s, Fenton came from a prosperous Lancashire banking family. Having obtaining a B.A. from University College, London, he studied art and moved to Paris in 1841 where he was taught by Paul Delaroche. He exhibited three times at the Royal Academy and then gave up art for the law. He qualified as a solicitor in 1847 and was in practice until 1864. He was however increasingly taken up with his new interest, photography. On a trip to Russia in 1852 he took some fine photographs using Gustave Le Gray's waxed paper process. He was appointed by the Trustees of the British Museum to photograph exhibits and became active in promoting organized photography, helping in 1853 to found the Photographic Society, later the Royal Photographic Society. His position was so well established that he was invited to photograph the Royal Family and was sent in a semi-official capacity to the Crimean War. He acquired enduring fame as one of the world's first war photographers. After the Crimea he became the chief photographer for the Photo-Galvanographic Company, which employed the photo-engraving system of the Viennese printmaker, Paul Pretsch, and worked extensively for the London publisher Lovell Reeve, producing stereos principally of architectural and landscape subjects, subsequently of still lifes of fruit and flowers. For the latter he won a medal at the International Exhibition of 1862. In the same year, apparently disillusioned with the lowering of standards in photography, Fenton retired and sold off his photographic materials.

Francis Frith 1822–98

fig. 72 *Hastings from the Beach (Low Tide)* (1864) p. 83

fig. 93 *The Sphynx, and the Great Pyramid, Gizeh* (1857) p. 98

fig. 98 *Self-portrait, Turkish Summer Costume* (1857) p. 103

fig. 99 *Jerusalem, The Pool of Siloam* (late 1850s) p. 104

fig. 101 *Philae: the Approach* (late 1850s) p. 109

fig. 103 *Crocodile on a Sandbank* (1857) p. 111

fig. 104 *The North Shore of the Dead Sea* (1857) p. 111

Frith came from a Devon Quaker family and, after apprenticeship to a cutler in Sheffield, and a number of business ventures, took up photography in the 1850s. He was to become one of the most proficient and adventurous masters of the collodion era. His reputation rests mainly on the photographs he took on three journeys to the Near East between 1856 and 1860. Using a wicker carriage as studio and living quarters he overcame the difficulties added by dust and heat to the already delicate manipulations of the collodion process. Besides a set of one hundred stereos from the first trip, he produced a large number of flawless, aesthetically ravishing albumen prints which were published in a variety of spectacular publications between 1858 and 1862. *Egypt and Palestine* published between 1858 and 1860 by J. S. Virtue contained a lively descriptive text by the photographer. Frith's contemporaries were awestruck by his achievement in bringing to life the ancient monuments. In 1859 Frith set up a printing establishment in Reigate, Surrey and, employing other photographers, began to mount what was in effect a massive topographical survey of the British Isles, later extended to the Continent. Francis Frith and Co. also published the work of photographers who had been active in the 1850s, like Roger Fenton, and marketed postcards on a large scale. The business was solidly enough based to last until 1971. Frith's own later photography was somewhat anonymous in character, though the illustrations to *The Gossiping Photographer at Hastings* (1864) and Longfellow's *Hyperion* (1865), rival some of the Near Eastern work.

Frank Mason Good (active late 1850s to 1880s)

fig. 41 *A Study of Trees* (1870) p. 48

fig. 78 *A Cotswold Farm* (late 1850s) p. 88

fig. 91 *Interior of a Workshop* (late 1860s) p. 97

Good lived in Hartley Wintney, Hampshire and joined the Photographic Society in 1864. His contributions to J. Redding Ware's *The Isle of Wight* (1869) – a very popular and, for Good, geographically convenient subject – are notable for directness. This was the hallmark of a style that evolved under the influence of Bedford and Frith. Good assisted Frith at one point in his photographic career and traced his own path to the Near East in the late-1860s. This trip resulted in the publication of stereo slides (issued by Léon & Levy of Paris), lantern slides, and a book of photographs, *Glimpses of the Holy Land* (1880). Photographs by Good also appeared in *Photo-Pictures from the Land of the Bible*, among other publications. Good was one of the judges in the Photographic Society's 1880 exhibition.

James Graham (active 1850s)

fig. 95 *Kedron Valley* (mid-1850s) p. 99

fig. 100 *General View from Mount of Olives* (1855) p. 106

fig. 106 *Meeting point of Valleys of Hinnom and Kedron with En Rogel in foreground* (mid-1850s) p. 112

fig. 108 *Nazareth. General view from north* (Oct. 27 1855) p. 114

A Scotsman, Graham was active as a photographer while working in Jerusalem as lay Secretary of the London Society for the Promotion of Christianity among the Jews. He resigned his post in 1856 amid controversy over the running of the Diocesan school. Graham's negatives are usually dated 1854 or 1855 while his prints are signed and dated on the mount 1856 or 1857 which suggests that he kept a store of negatives for printing on his return home. His most impressive photographic achievements were two panoramas of Jerusalem, one of six parts, one of ten parts. His work was exhibited in 1859 at the Exhibition of Fine Arts at the Palais de l'Industrie, Paris. Chromolithographs made after his photographs illustrate H. B. Tristram's *Scenes in the East* (1870). Graham's more or less total obscurity would have been guaranteed had he not struck up a friendship with Holman Hunt and Thomas Seddon when the two Pre-Raphaelites were staying in Jerusalem. He supplied the artists with *aides-memoir* and makes a lively appearance in Hunt's memoirs. Hunt also wrote a pamphlet in defence of Graham's professional activities in Jerusalem (*Jerusalem Bishop Gobat in re Hanna Hadoub*, London, 1858). The principal collection of Graham's photographs is held by the Palestine Exploration Fund, London.

Clementina, Lady Hawarden 1822–65

fig. 137 *Study of Two Girls* (c.1860) p. 141

fig. 141 *Girl in Fancy Dress* (c.1860) p. 143

Lady Hawarden was born near Glasgow the daughter of the M.P. for Stirlingshire, Charles Elphinstone-Fleming. She married Cornwallis Maude, 4th Viscount Hawarden, in 1845. Many of her photographs were taken at the family house, Dundrum, at Cashel, County Tipperary, but she is best known for numerous photographs of her four daughters taken in their London residence in Prince's Gate, Kensington. Her work was well-regarded by her contemporaries. In 1863 she won the medal at the Photographic Society's exhibition for the best amateur and the following year for the best composition from a single negative. One reviewer wrote of 'graceful arrangement, and unusual and extremely artistic lighting, great transparency, and much tenderness and delicacy of treatment'. (*PN*, 8, 24 June 1864, p. 303). Another amateur who had broken with the stiff conventions of studio portraiture, Lewis Carroll, also admired her work, while Rejlander, mourning her premature death, observed that there was in her work 'nothing of mysticism nor Flemish Pre-Raphaellistic conceit' (*BJP*, 12, 27 January 1865, p. 38). (This was a typical way at the time of saluting naturalism and absence of obtrusive detail.) Modern commentators on Lady Hawarden have been intrigued by her subtle treatment of light and ambiguous eroticism.

David Octavius Hill 1802–70
see also **Adamson**

fig. 134 *Prayer* (1850s) p. 140

fig. 152 *Sophia Finlay and Harriet Farnie* (c.1848) p. 152

Hill was a mediocre landscape painter and Secretary of the Scottish Royal Academy. He would probably never have become involved in photography if he had not been commissioned to paint the 474 members of the Scottish Free Church in 1843. It was probably Sir David Brewster, a friend of Talbot who had introduced the calotype into Scotland, who suggested to Hill that photography might help him with his daunting task. Hill embarked on a partnership with Robert Adamson which resulted finally in the production of some 1500 negatives, chiefly portraits of prominent Scots but also including architectural, landscape, and genre work. The unaffected dignity and chiaroscuro of the portraits did much to enhance photography's claims to art (comparisons with Rembrandt were frequent) and the Hill and Adamson oeuvre has always been recognized as photographic portraiture's first monument. The painting of the 'Disruption', not finished by Hill until 1866, has found few admirers. Hill was the moving spirit behind the partnership with Adamson, arranging the poses and composition, but he achieved little of note after Adamson's untimely death in 1848. He returned to photography for a short time in the 1850s and then again in partnership with Andrew MacGlashon in the early 1860s. MacGlashon's sharp focus was unsuited to Hill's talents. Their work appeared in *Some contributions towards the use of photography as art* (1862), but in this respect Hill had long ago 'contributed' his utmost.

Henry Holiday 1839–1927

fig. 147 *Phoebe ('Effie') Newall* (1871) p. 147

Photography was only one of Holiday's interests, which included astronomy, music, travel, socialism and dress reform (he was for a while President of The Healthy and Artistic Dress Union). He entered the Royal Academy Schools in 1855 and was one of the progressive-minded artists who at that time followed the example of the Pre-Raphaelites to the despair of older Academicians. He had a promising start as an illustrator and then became very successful as a stained-glass designer, having been taken on by the firm of Messrs Powell & Co. in 1862. He also sculpted and painted, exhibiting at the Royal Academy and the Grosvenor Gallery. He tried his hand at photography after getting to know Lewis Carroll in 1869. In later years he was a vituperative foe of new movements in art such as Cubism and Futurism.

Thomas Keith 1827–95

fig. 25 *Foliage on a tombstone, Greyfriars (Tomb of John Byres of Coates)* (c.1852) p. 34

The Rev. Alexander Keith was the author of *Evidence of the Truth of the Christian Religion* (1837) whose later editions contained engravings from daguerreotypes by his son, George Skene Keith. Another of his seven sons was Thomas Keith, one of early photography's perfectionists. Thomas was a doctor and ovarian surgeon who was to reach a position of eminence in Scottish medicine. His photographic activities lasted only from 1852 to 1857. He favoured the waxed paper process which combined ease of use with a high-quality image. He had a particular eye for the way light redistributes architectural form. Though photographing mainly in Edinburgh, he also made photographic excursions to rural Scotland with his fellow-photographer and relative-by-marriage, John Forbes White. Keith and White were both instrumental in setting up the Photographic Society of Scotland in 1856. Keith's most powerful photographs were of the ruins of Iona Cathedral, taken shortly before he gave up photography due to pressure of medical commitments.

John Dillwyn Llewelyn 1810–82

fig. 15 *Botanical Study with Bird* (early to mid-1850s) p. 18

fig. 24 *Lastrea Filix Mas* (c.1854) p. 33

fig. 31 *Rabbit* (early to mid-1850s) p. 40

fig. 33 *Piscator No. 2* (1856) p. 41

fig. 43 *View of Rocks* (c.1854) p. 50

fig. 69 *Thereza with a Telescope* (c.1854) p. 81

fig. 73 *Two Girls on the rocks at Dunraven* (c.1854) pp. 84–5

Llewelyn's background embraced Quakerism, Liberal politics, ancestral affluence and science. He was the son of the botanist and South Wales M.P. Lewis Weston Dillwyn and the heiress Mary Llewelyn. After finishing his education at Oxford and marrying Emma Thomasina Talbot, a cousin of Henry Fox Talbot, he was drawn into a circle whose scientific and artistic interests led naturally to photography, including Henry Collen (the Queen's drawing master), the Reverend and Mrs Calvert Jones, and Sir David Brewster. Llewelyn's breadth of interests was typical of this group. He painted watercolours, wrote poetry, toured the Continent, had a strong social conscience and built a church in the neighbourhood of his home at Penllegare, near Swansea. His daughter Thereza knew Darwin. He was elected to the Royal Society of Arts in 1837. As soon as Talbot had published his prescriptions for 'photogenic drawing' in 1839 Llewelyn was experimenting with this technique. In the early 1840s he took up the daguerreotype and the calotype and corresponded with Talbot on the results. He continued with the calotype until well into the 1850s but also started to use the collodion process after its introduction in 1851. He was the first photographer to tackle botanical and geological subjects systematically, chiefly in the vicinity of his home but also on tours to the Cornish peninsula and the North. He arranged settings for his photographs in a studio equipped with running water, often including stuffed animals from his large collection. He was a pioneer of 'instantaneous photography'. Four photographs incorporating breaking waves won the silver medal at the 1855 Paris Exposition Universelle. In 1853 he was elected to the council of the newly formed Photographic Society and three years later he published his Oxymel process, a method of preserving collodion plates with a mixture of honey and acetic acid. He contributed to P. H. Delamotte's *The Sunbeam* (1859). Llewelyn is perhaps the most complete embodiment of the leisurely, cultivated scientific spirit that informed photography in early Victorian Britain.

Thomas Lukis Mansell 1809–79

fig. 40 *Lane Guernsey* (1855) p. 47

Mansell was from Guernsey and trained as a doctor at Trinity College Dublin. He was typical of many amateur photographers in his wide interests. He was a member of Guernsey's governing body. He pursued meteorology and horticulture, being responsible for much of the public planting in St Peter's Port, the capital of Guernsey. His earliest photographs were produced with the calotype process. He was a regular subscriber and correspondent to *Notes and Queries*, writing an article in February 1854 on 'The Calotype and the Sea-Shore'. This described Mansell's method of preparing paper suitable for coping with the problem of reflected light from the sea and large expanses of sky. He was a member of the Photographic Society and contributed to the Photographic Albums. Like J. D. Llewelyn with the Oxymel process, he developed a method for keeping a collodion plate wet and light sensitive. This Syruped Collodion process was published in the *Photographic Journal* in February 1855. Several of Dr Mansell's Exchange Club prints were made by this process.

Ronald Leslie Melville, 11th Earl of Leven 1835–1906

fig. 2 *Mrs Godfrey Clarke* (1860s) p. 2

fig. 161 *Broken Lilies* (1871) p. 159

fig. 162 *Romeo and Juliet* (mid-1860s) p. 159

fig. 163 *Saint Agnes* (1860s) p. 162

fig. 174 *Gleaners* (1860s) p. 175

Melville was typical of the aristocratic amateurs who formed the membership of the Amateur Photographic Association, to which he was elected in 1866. He was the son of the 9th Earl of Leven by his second marriage, succeeding his half-brother Alexander, 10th Earl of Leven in 1889. Educated at Eton and Christ Church, Oxford, he became a well-known figure in the City of London, the head of an Anglo-American banking house and a director of the Bank of England. Photography was a private pursuit, of which he was a versatile though perhaps never an outstanding practitioner. His range of subjects included topographical and tree studies, portraiture (both straightforward and symbolic) *tableaux* and genre. His most original contribution was a handful of images relating to the British campaign in Abyssinia of 1868. When Melville exhibited at the International Exhibition of 1871 he was compared favourably with Julia Margaret Cameron. Melville was sustained in photography by challenges which technical advance and commercialization in due course undermined, and like many amateurs he lost interest in the 1870s. He resumed photography again in the 1890s but did not produce anything of special interest.

John H. Morgan (active late 1850s)

fig. 39 *Trees* (late 1850s) p. 46

Morgan lived in Bristol and formed links with the South Wales group of photographers of Llewelyn and the Calvert Jones's. He specialized in river and tree scenery. Though the *Literary Gazette* longed for 'some leaves on the naked trees, and a little more sunshine glancing along the water' it commended Morgan's work 'to the careful study of our younger landscape painters'. (Quoted: *PJ*, 5, 1858–9, 21 January 1859, p. 147.)

Eveleen Myers (active c.1890)

fig. 112 *Rebecca* (c.1891) p. 119

Myers was the youngest daughter of Charles Tennant of Cadoxton Lodge, Neath. She married Lord Stanley and later the poet and essayist, Frederick Myers. She lived with her second husband in Cambridge from 1881. With her sister Dorothy she often sat for G. F. Watts. She began to study photography at the end of 1888 in order to take photographs of her children and quickly became a perfectionist in portraiture and subject pictures. With their clean lines and classical drapery her photographs are somewhat Greek in feeling though the soulfulness of her models marks her as a Cameron successor. Her work was published in *Sun Artists* (1891) edited by W. Arthur Boord. The critic John Addington Symonds contributed the text on Myers. The subjects were portraits of Gladstone and Browning, *Rebecca*, and *The Summer Garden* in which as Symonds wrote, 'The figures of the two children are beautifully combined and brought into harmony with a leafy background' (p. 53).

Thomas Ogle (active 1850s–60s)

fig. 53 *Nab Scar Rydal Water — Hartley Coleridge's Cottage home (c.1860)* p. 67

Ogle was a topographical and landscape photographer, and partner in the stereoscopic firm of Ogle and Edge which operated from Preston, Lancashire. His work was much used for book illustration. He contributed to William and Mary Howitt's *Ruined Castles and Abbeys of Great Britain and Ireland*. His work was used for an 1863 edition of Sir Walter Scott's *The Lady of the Lake* and for *Our English Lakes, Mountains and Waterfalls, as seen by William Wordsworth* (1864). He lived in Penrith in the Lake District and was a member of the Photographic Society from 1866.

John R. Parsons

fig. 129 *Jane Morris* (1865) p. 136

fig. 131 *Jane Morris* (1865) p. 137

fig. 133 *Jane Morris* (1865) p. 137

Before selling his works Dante Gabriel Rossetti used to have them photographed. One of the photographers he employed for this purpose was Parsons, who practised in addition as a picture-dealer in association with Rossetti's agent, Charles Augustus Howell. Parsons had premises off Portman Square and later in Wigmore Street.

John Percy 1817–89
(*see also* Spiller)

fig. 16 *The New Mill, Near Lynton, North Devon* (1856) p. 21

Percy was a man of wide scientific interests. He trained as a doctor, became interested in photography in the 1840s and achieved eminence as a metallurgist. In his 1853 survey of the iron ores of Britain, carried out for the Royal School of Mines, he was assisted by John Spiller with whom he also collaborated photographically.

Oscar Gustave Rejlander 1813–75

fig. 116 *Group Portrait of Sophia Pattle, Lady Dalrymple and G. F. Watts* (c.1860) p. 123

fig. 136 *Grief* (1864) p. 141

Rejlander was a Swede who trained in Rome as a portrait painter and settled in England in 1840 on marrying an Englishwoman. He at first used the camera as an aid to painting but went over to photography entirely in 1853. He set up in business in Wolverhampton. His genre themes, often with a strongly theatrical element, mirrored his previous work as a painter. In 1857 he achieved notoriety with his ambitious combination photograph, *The Two Ways of Life*. Due to nudity, the work was shown half-covered in Scotland, but Rejlander's reputation was salvaged when the Queen bought a copy of the photograph for Albert. Critical opinion remained divided on combination printing but Rejlander's genre studies were very widely admired for their balance of 'truth' and 'sentiment'. Many of his images, for instance *Poor Jo* (1861) showing a pauper child weeping on a doorstep, drew attention to social problems. In 1862 Rejlander moved to London and concentrated on portraiture. He collaborated with Charles Darwin for *The Expression of the Emotions in Man and Animals* (1872). Rejlander's photograph of a child howling, signifying 'mental distress' sold over 60,000 copies. Incapacitated by diabetes, he had by this time over-extended his photographic business and he died in poverty. Nevertheless he had a considerable following in the London artistic community and his funeral was attended by the fashionable founder of the Grosvenor Gallery, Sir Coutts Lindsay. There is an offbeat quality about Rejlander's work that reflects an eccentric (it has even been claimed, schizophrenic) personality.

Henry Peach Robinson 1830–1901

fig. 5 *The Lady of Shalott* (1861) p. 9

fig. 158 *Sleep* (1867) p. 157

fig. 165 *Elaine Watching the Shield of Lancelot* (1859) p. 164

fig. 169 *Study for a Composition Picture* (c.1860) p. 170

One of the principal defenders of photography's claims to art in the Victorian period, Robinson was born in Ludlow, Shropshire. He was apprenticed to a print publisher and also received training in drawing and painting. He exhibited at the Royal Academy in 1852. In the same year, having become friendly with the influential photographer, Dr Hugh Diamond, he started taking photographs concentrating on landscape and architecture. In 1857 he opened a studio in Leamington Spa. Well versed in art authorities from the French seventeenth-century Academicians to the more recent John Burnet and Ruskin, Robinson was determined to divert photography from its preoccupation with technicalities. His vehicle was the combination print, a technique he learned from Rejlander for producing an image from several negatives. Robinson was astute at gauging popular taste and earned

fig. 170 *Bringing Home the May* (1862)
pp. 172–3

success with his first attempt, *Fading Away* (1858). In the following decade he wooed the public with a mixture of literary, genre and Pre-Raphaelite themes. Whatever the ultimate status of his work, Robinson certainly brought photography closer to what his contemporaries regarded as art. He offended photographic purists in the process. Coinciding with his departure from the Photographic Society (of which he had become vice-president in 1887) to form the Secessionist Linked Ring in 1892, he graduated to pictorial landscapes with figures. He had by this time written voluminously on photography. The most complete statement of his views is found in *Pictorial Effect in Photography* (1869). His influence extended until well into the present century. *Picture Making by Photography* (1884) was reprinted as late as 1925.

James Robinson

fig. 157 *The Death of Chatterton* (1859) p. 156

Robinson was a photographer with premises in Grafton Street, Dublin. His decision to conclude a stereographic series on the poet Chatterton with a scene staged in precise imitation of Henry Wallis's painting, *Chatterton*, had important consequences for the relationship in law of photography and painting. A successful injunction was brought by the owner of the engraving rights, Robert Turner, in 1859. The judgment established that a photographic mock-up of a painting (easily enough achieved at a time when artists painted photographically) was equivalent in copyright terms to an engraving (or indeed a photograph) of the painting itself.

Alfred Rosling 1802–80s

fig. 13 *Young Emeus (sic) and Eggs, bred at Brackham Lodge* (late 1850s) p. 17

Rosling was a successful Hackney timber merchant and early photographic enthusiast. In 1846 his calotypes of inanimate objects for Wheatstone's reflecting stereoscope were on sale in James Newman's shop in Soho Square, London. After the arrival of the collodion process he specialized in the micro-photograph. At London's first full-scale photographic exhibition at the Society of Arts in 1852 he exhibited four 'tiny' prints, each showing two pages of the *Illustrated London News* which, when seen through a magnifying glass, could be read clearly. He illustrated *80 of the Kings and Queens of England* by the same method. In January 1854 more Rosling work, 'Specimens of exceedingly minute copies of Prints and Papers', was on show at the Society of Arts. He also took landscape photographs and was well-known in photographic circles. He was first treasurer of the Photographic Society. He knew J. D. Llewelyn (one of his photographic excursions was to the Swansea area). In 1859 he moved to Reigate and lived near the printing establishment of Francis Frith, who published a number of Rosling photographs in the 1860s.

John Ruskin 1819–1900

fig. 29 *A Courtyard in Abbeville* (1858) p. 37

fig. 44 *Rock Study* (late 1840s to mid-1850s) pp. 52–3

fig. 62 *Mountain Study* (1854) pp. 74–5

fig. 63 *State of Mer de Glace in 1874* p. 75

fig. 83 *The Towers of Fribourg* (1856) p. 92

fig. 84 *The St Jean d'Acre Columns and the south side of St Mark's* (c.1850) p.93

Highly influential writer on art, and social critic, Ruskin was the son of a wealthy sherry importer. The roots of his theories, and perhaps the source of perpetually unresolved contradictions in his work, lay in his stern evangelical upbringing and in his instinctive feeling for nature. The first volume of *Modern Painters* (1843) exalted Turner above the accepted seventeenth-century masters; the second volume (1846) praised early Italian painters at the expense of their more worldly successors. When he turned to architecture Ruskin further assaulted conventional taste. *The Seven Lamps of Architecture* (1849) and *The Stones of Venice* (1851–3) argued that medieval Gothic, as the expression of a healthy society, was superior to the Renaissance styles. With his commanding eloquence he influenced the direction of the Pre-Raphaelite movement and the Gothic Revival. The climax of his public recognition came with his appointment in 1869 as Slade Professor of Fine Art at Oxford. By this time however the emphasis in his writings had shifted to the condition of society. In a series of lectures and pamphlets he attacked not merely the abuses of *laissez-faire* economics but its underlying competitive ethos. His later years were overshadowed by mental instability though this is nowhere apparent in his finely written late autobiography, *Praeterita* (1885–9). As befitted one with a voracious eye for the beauty of the world, Ruskin was, despite reservations, a lifelong photographer. He was assisted at first by his manservant John Hobbs who enjoyed this aspect of his duties even though, when they were in the Alps, it meant entire evenings spent processing daguerreotypes and return trips up the mountain when failure had occurred.

Frederick Crawley, who succeeded Hobbs in 1854, was equally proficient with the daguerreotype. The Ruskin Galleries at Bembridge School, Isle of Wight, contain a catalogue of 233 daguerreotypes. They are of mountain and architectural subjects, ninety-five relating to Venice. For his later pedagogical work Ruskin would commission commercial photographers.

John Spiller 1833–1921
see also **Percy**

fig. 16 *The New Mill, Near Lynton, North Devon* (1856) p. 21

Spiller was one of those whose interest in photography grew out of the profession of chemist. A Londoner, he studied and later lectured at the Royal College of Chemistry. In 1856 he was appointed assistant chemist at the Woolwich Arsenal where in 1861 he founded a photographic department. At this time he was in demand as a lecturer on photography to the military. In 1868 he became chief chemist of the dye-making firm, Brookes, Simpson & Spiller. Elected to the Photographic Society in 1867 he held the unique record of filling every office in turn, including editorship of the *Journal*. He was President in 1874–5. Throughout his life he was interested in the experimental side of photography. Like many in the 1850s he tried to find a way of preserving collodion plates. His method, worked out with Sir William Crookes, kept the plate damp with a solution of deliquescent salt.

William Henry Fox Talbot 1800–77

fig. 9 *Leaf of a Plant* (1845) p. 14

Ensured immortality as the inventor of the first photographic negative/positive process, Talbot was born in Melbury, Dorset and educated at Harrow and Trinity College, Cambridge. One of the best scientific minds of his generation, he was elected to the Royal Society in 1831. Among other subjects, he was interested in archeology, mathematics, botany, and chemistry. His photographic experiments evolved out of the latter, specifically from the desire to fix the image formed by the *camera lucida* (a drawing aid descended from the *camera obscura*). He tried paper coated first with nitrate of silver then with chloride of silver. He found that, when waxed, the paper could be used as a negative and the image printed onto another piece of paper. Talbot announced this 'photogenic drawing' process in 1839. Further improvements resulted from the discovery that silver iodide formed a latent image capable of being developed in gallic acid. This Talbotype or Calotype process was demonstrated in his six-part *The Pencil of Nature* (1844–6) and *Sun Pictures of Scotland* (1844–5) a portfolio of twenty-three images. Meanwhile Talbot had opened a printing works in Reading and a studio, the Sun Picture Rooms, in Regent Street, London. The calotype was never as popular as the sharper daguerreotype partly because Talbot was (some have said irrationally) jealous of his patent. (Hill and Adamson were fortunate that it did not extend to Scotland.) In Talbot v. Laroche (1854) it was laid down that Scott Archer's collodion process was not covered by Talbot's patent, a decision that did much to release photographic energies in England. Though resented by some photographers for the brake he had applied to his own invention, Talbot was awarded the Grand Medal of Honour at the 1855 Paris Exposition Universelle and was made an honorary member of the Photographic Society in 1873. By this time he had, however, long given up photography for mathematics.

Stephen Thompson (active 1850s–80)

fig. 76 *General View of Kenilworth* (1864) p. 87

Thompson, a Londoner, was mainly an architectural and landscape photographer. He published a series of stereos of Venice in 1858 and contributed to William and Mary Howitt's *Ruined Abbeys and Castles of Great Britain and Ireland*. He also photographed works of art for *Masterpieces of Antique Art* (1878).

John Whistler 1830–97

fig. 151 *Sleep* (c.1855) p. 152

Whistler was a prosperous builder and decorator from the village of Sherborne St John, near Basingstoke in Hampshire. He took up photography in the 1850s. His only extant works are salt prints dating from this period, mainly cottage and rural scenes. Later he photographed buildings under construction and in 1885 documented his own firm's restoration of the village church. He was the grandfather of the artists, Rex and Laurence Whistler.

Henry White 1819–1903

fig. 34 *Wheat* (1856) p. 42

fig. 37 *Oats* (1856) p. 45

fig. 58 *The Lledr Bridge, near Bettws-y-Coed* (1855–60) p. 70

White lived in Surrey and was a solicitor by profession. He joined the Photographic Society in 1855 and was active in its affairs, being treasurer for some years. His work won international acclaim at the Paris Exposition Universelle of 1855, and at the Brussels international photography exhibition of 1856, where his photographs were said to 'have elicited from connoisseurs an admiration without bounds' (*PJ*, 3, 1856–7, 21 October 1856, p. 147). He visited Bettws-y-Coed in North Wales which had long been a haunt of artists in search of picturesque subject matter, but his speciality was the intricate but boldly composed image of cornfield or hedgerow. His photographs invariably have high quality printed mounts which reflect no intention to distribute or sell but the affluence typical of the amateur photographer of this period.

George Washington Wilson 1823–93

fig. 47 *Fingal's Cave, Staffa* (1856–8) p. 55

The son of a crofter, Wilson epitomized the Victorian self-made man. After apprenticeship as a carpenter he trained as an artist in Edinburgh. He set up as a portrait painter and art teacher in Aberdeen having married in 1849. He decided to move into photography at the point where the medium, through Scott Archer's collodion process, was overcoming the coarseness that had prevented commercial rivalry with painting. However successful Wilson was to become as a photographer he always saw himself primarily as an artist and in fact his artistic training did much to ensure his supremacy. By 1857 he was firmly established as the leading portrait photographer in Aberdeen, much assisted by the prestige resulting from a commission from Prince Albert to photograph the rebuilding of Balmoral Castle. His success in landscape photography came from his feeling for the literary and historical associations of the Scottish terrain. He knew how to select and present the scenes tourists would wish to take away as mementoes. He received critical acclaim with his 'instantaneous' images of the later 1850s. He was the first photographer in Britain to combine figures and water evocatively and to show populated streets. By 1860 Wilson had become a considerable local employer with a huge printing works selling thousands of prints a year. He enlarged his catalogue to include the rest of Britain and foreign countries. Artistic standards declined, but the business continued to expand as he bought works from foreign photographers and exploited every format from stereos and *cartes* to lantern slides and finally postcards. With his wealth Wilson built a luxurious house in Aberdeen, but his final years were clouded with illness, probably from chemical poisoning, one of the hazards of photography's pioneering days.

David Wilkie Wynfield 1837–87

fig. I *John Everett Millais* (1862) p. I

fig. III *Simeon Solomon* (c.1870) p. 117

Born into an army family in India, Wynfield was the great-nephew of the Scottish artist David Wilkie. Abandoning for painting an early desire to become a priest, Wynfield specialized in historical genre. He founded the St John's Wood Clique, a loose artistic grouping whose chief shared joys were punning and practical jokes. Wynfield's liking for historical costume spilled over into his photography. He photographed numerous Royal Academicians in costumes chosen to express their personalities. These images were exhibited in the early 1860s and some of them were also published by Herring of Regent Street under the title of *The Studio*. Julia Margaret Cameron came to Wynfield as a photographic pupil in 1864. Her rejection of contemporary costume and use of soft focus both derived from Wynfield to whom she was always ready to acknowledge her debt. In 1867 the Wynfields and the Camerons rented Hever Castle together, Wynfield intending to photograph the ghost of Anne Boleyn. Many critics disliked both Wynfield's fancydress subjects and his approach to focus, but to others he was the Titian or Van Dyck of photography, whose work represented 'the greatest step forward in the direction of good photographic portraiture since the time of D. O. Hill' (*PN*, 8, 4 March 1864, p. 115).

List of Paintings and Drawings

Notes

INTRODUCTION

1 *Ath*, 29, 12 January 1856, p. 46.
2 For Fry's views on Cameron, *see* Virginia Woolf and Roger Fry, *Victorian Photographs of Famous Men and Fair Women* (London 1926).
3 J. M. Cameron, 'Annals of My Glass House' (1874). Reprinted: Mike Weaver, *Julia Margaret Cameron 1815–1879* (Southampton 1984), pp. 154–7.
4 *see* Helmut Gernsheim, *Julia Margaret Cameron*, 2nd ed. (London 1975), p. 35.

CHAPTER I

1 G. H. Lewes, *Sea-Side Studies* (Edinburgh and London 1858), pp. 54–5; John Tyndall, *The Glaciers of the Alps* (London 1860), p. 130.
2 'Particularity' was analysed by Carol T. Christ in *The Finer Optic. The Aesthetic of Particularity in Victorian Poetry* (New Haven and London 1975).
3 *PJ*, 3 (1856–7), 21 January 1857, p. 192.
4 *Ath*, 27, 7 October 1854, p. 1200.
5 *Ath*, 29, 12 January 1856, p. 47.
6 *PJ*, 3 (1856–7), 21 February 1857, p. 217. Helmut Gernsheim in *Creative Photography* (London 1962) attributes these remarks to Joseph Durham ARA, Member of the Photographic Society.
7 W. B. Scott, *Autobiographical Notes* (London 1892), I, p.251.
8 *PN*, 5, 22 March 1861, p. 134.
9 *The Life and Letters of Frederic Shields*, ed. Ernestine Mills (London 1912), p. 182.
10 Appendix: *The Diaries of George Price Boyce*, ed. Virginia Surtees (Norwich 1980), p. 120.
11 *Ath*, 27, 7 October 1854, p. 1200.

12 *PN*, 3 (1859–60), 17 February 1860, pp. 281–2.
13 *PJ*, 6 (1859–60), 15 November 1859, pp. 77–9.
14 *PN*, 6, 28 November 1862, p. 565.
15 *PJ*, 7 (1860–1), 15 February 1861, p. 112.

CHAPTER II

1 This refers not to Holman Hunt, but to William Henry 'Birds Nest' Hunt.
2 *QR*, 101 (January–April 1857), pp. 442–68.
3 *The Works of John Ruskin*, ed. E. T. Cook and Alexander Wedderburn (London 1903–12), III, p. 210n, VI, p. 82, XIX, p. 150, XXII, p. 377. For a thorough review of Ruskin's changing attitudes to photography, see R. N. Watson, 'Art, Photography and John Ruskin', *BJP*, 91 (1944), pp. 82–3, 100–1, 118–19.
4 *Ath*, 31, 29 May 1858, p. 692.
5 Ruskin, *Works*, XIV, p. 247–8.
6 Unpublished letter quoted: *John Dillwyn Llewelyn 1810–1882*, Catalogue of Welsh Arts Council Exhibition (1980), p. 15.
7 William Henry Fox Talbot, *The Pencil of Nature* (London 1844–6), pl. X.
8 5 September 1854, 21 July 1855. *The Diary of Ford Madox Brown*, ed. Virginia Surtees (New Haven and London 1981), pp. 90, 145.
9 *PJ*, 4 (1857–8), 21 September 1857, p. 45.
10 *PJ*, 3 (1856–7), 21 May 1856, p. 54.
11 Ernest Lacan, editor of the early French photographic magazine, *La Lumière*, as stated in Helmut and Alison Gernsheim, *The History of Photography*, revised ed. (London 1969), p. 280.
12 *PJ*, 3 (1856–7), 21 February 1857, p. 216.
13 *AJ*, n.s.3 (1857), p. 65.
14 Edward Weston, *My Camera on Point Lobos* (New York 1968), p. 78.

15 *PN*, 3 (1859–60), 3 February 1860, p. 254.
16 Lewes, *Sea-Side Studies*, p. 190.
17 Tyndall, *Glaciers of the Alps*, pp. 438–9.
18 Private Llewelyn MS.
19 Quoted: *PJ*, 5 (1858–9), 21 January 1859, p. 149.
20 *Ath*, 31, 20 February 1858, p. 246.
21 Note appended to a Forrester photograph in the *Photographic Album for the Year 1855* at the Royal Photographic Society, Bath.
22 *Ath*, 30, 24 January 1857, p. 120.
23 *Ath*, 31, 20 February 1858, p. 246.
24 Ruskin, *Works*, XI, pp. 201–3.
25 Ruskin, *Works*, XXII, p. 220.
26 Roland Barthes, 'Rhetoric of the Image', *Communications*, 4 (1964), p. 44.

CHAPTER III

1 *BJP*, II, 16 September 1864, p. 375.
2 *PN*, 5, 18 January 1861, p. 28.
3 *Photographic Notes*, 2, 15 April 1857, p. 141.
4 *PN*, 6, 3 January 1862, p. 1.
5 *PN*, 5, 18 January 1861, p. 28.
6 *PJ*, 6 (1859–60), 15 November 1859, p. 73.
7 *PJ*, 6 (1859–60), 15 May 1860, p. 236.
8 *PJ*, I (1853–4), 21 June 1853, p. 77.
9 C. R. Leslie, *A Handbook for Young Painters* (London 1855), pp. 256–8.
10 *Letters of James Smetham*, ed. Sarah Smetham and William Davies (London and New York 1891) pp. 57–8.
11 *Letters of Smetham*, p. 41.
12 *Diary of Madox Brown*, p. 92.
13 Letter to R. D. Cory, 20 October 1860. Quoted: Marcia Pointon, *William Dyce 1806–1864* (Oxford 1979), p. 173.
14 Quoted: John Hannavy, *Roger Fenton* (London 1975), p. 52.
15 Leslie Stephen, *Essays on Freethinking and*

Plainspeaking (London 1873), pp. 155–97.

16 Quoted: Robert Hershkowitz, *The British Photographer Abroad* (London 1980), p. 82.

17 Ruskin, *Works*, VI, pp. 232–3.

18 J. G. Millais, *The Life and Letters of Sir John Everett Millais* (London 1899), I, p. 342.

19 Ruskin, *Works*, XIV, p. 238n.

20 21 December 1883. *The Journal of Beatrix Potter*, transcribed from code by Leslie Linder etc. (London and New York 1966), p. 65, quoted in 'The Life of John Brett' a 1982 unpublished University of Sussex Ph.D thesis by David Cordingly, to whom I am indebted for information on the artist's use of photography.

21 John Brett, 'Landscape at the National Gallery', *Fortnightly Review*, n.s. 57 (January–June 1895), pp. 623–39.

22 John Brett, 'The Relation of Photography to the Pictorial Art', *BJP*, 36, 5 April 1889, pp. 235–7.

23 *AJ*, n.s. 6 (1860), p. 256.

24 *BJP*, II, 14 October 1864, p. 407. I am indebted to Roger Taylor for drawing my attention to Wilson's letter.

25 *PJ*, 4 (1857–8) 21 September 1857, p. 47.

26 Lewes, *Sea-Side Studies*, pp. 30–1, 190.

27 William and Mary Howitt, *Ruined Abbeys and Castles of Great Britain and Ireland*, Second Series (London 1864), p. 1.

28 *AJ*, n.s.2 (1856), p. 49.

29 *Ath*, 29, 21 June 1856, p. 783.

30 William and Mary Howitt, *Ruined Abbeys and Castles of Great Britain and Ireland* (London 1862), Preface, n.p.

31 *PN*, 5, 13 September 1861, p.434.

32 *PN*, 8, 27 May 1864, p. 255.

33 Ruskin, *Works*, VI, pp. 46–7.

CHAPTER IV

1 Ruskin, *Works*, XIV, p. 465n.

2 Quoted: *Egypt and the Holy Land In Historic Photographs 77 Views by Francis Frith*, ed. Julia Van Haaften and Jon E. Manchip White (New York 1980), p. xvii.

3 W. M. Thompson, *The Holy Land* (London 1866), pp. 3–4.

4 Quoted: *PN*, 5, 17 May 1861, p. 240.

5 *AJ*, n.s.4 (1858), p. 30.

6 H. B. Tristram, *The Land of Israel* (London 1865), p. viii.

7 Alexander Keith, *Evidence of the Truth of the Christian Religion*, 36th ed. (Edinburgh 1848), pp. iii–iv.

8 Letter to Graham from Maria Gobat, 6 June 1856. *The Fifth Annual Report of the Jerusalem Diocesan Missionary Fund* (London 1858), p. 43.

9 For Graham and Hunt's friendship, *see* W. Holman Hunt, *Pre-Raphaelitism and the Pre-Raphaelite Brotherhood* (London 1905), I, pp. 403–4, 425–44; II, pp. 3–51.

10 *Jerusalem Missionary Fund Report*, pp. 49–51.

11 Francis Frith, 'The Art of Photography', in *Photography: Essays and Images*, ed. Beaumont Newhall (London 1980), pp. 115–19. Reprinted from *AJ*, n.s. 5 (1859), pp. 71–2.

12 This and remaining Frith quotations are taken from the unpaginated text of Francis Frith, *Egypt and Palestine* (London 1858–60).

13 John Cramb, 'Palestine in 1860, or a Photographer's Journal of a Visit to Jerusalem', a series of 12 articles in *BJP*, 7 (1860), 8 (1861).

14 *BJP*, 8, 2 December 1861, p. 425.

15 John Pollard Seddon, *Memoir and Letters of the Late Thomas Seddon* (London 1858), p. 111.

16 *Ath*, 29, 10 May 1856, p. 589.

17 Hunt, *Pre-Raphaelitism*, II, p. 40; Hunt diary, John Rylands Library, Manchester, Rylands Eng. MS. 1211, ff. 69–70.

18 Rev. Albert Augustus Isaacs, *The Dead Sea* (London 1857), p. 31.

19 Seddon, *Memoir*, p. 111.

20 Charles Baudelaire, 'Photography', reprinted in *Photography*, ed. Newhall, pp. 112–13.

21 P. G. Hamerton, *A Painter's Camp in the Highlands and Thoughts about Art* (London 1862), II, pp. 200–42.

22 *AJ*, n.s.5 (1859), p. 46.

23 Quoted: *PJ*, 5 (1858–9), 21 January 1859, p. 145.

CHAPTER V

1 *PN*, 8, 4 March 1864, p. 110.

2 Hamerton, *Painter's Camp and Thoughts*, II, p. 228.

3 *PJ*, 5 (1858–9) 21 September 1858, pp. 19, 33.

4 *PJ*, 7 (1860–1) 15 October 1861, p. 287.

5 *PJ*, 7 (1860–1) 15 August 1861, p. 243.

6 Reprinted: *PN*, 5, 25 January 1861, pp. 41–2.

7 *The Young George Du Maurier*, ed. Daphne Du Maurier (London 1951), p. 14. The

episode was illustrated in Du Maurier's first cartoon for *Punch* (6 October 1860).

8 *PN*, 9, 16 June 1865, p. 283.

9 *PN*, 12, 27 March 1868, p. 276.

10 *PN*, 16, 23 August 1872, p. 399.

11 *QR*, 116 (July–October 1864), pp. 514–15.

12 *PJ*, 5 (1858–9), 21 October 1858, pp. 46–7.

13 *Ath*, 31 (January–June 1858), 29 May 1858, p. 693.

14 *PJ*, 8 (1862–3), 16 February 1863, pp. 232–4.

15 *PJ*, 8 (1862–3), 16 February 1863, p. 234.

16 *PN*, 9, 17 February 1865, p. 75.

17 J. M. Cameron, 'Annals', Weaver, *Cameron*, p. 157.

18 *PN*, 8, 4 March 1865, p. 109.

19 For the history of this debate, see James Borcoman, 'Purism versus pictorialism: the 135 years war. Some Notes on Photographic Aesthetics', *Artscanada*, Issue 192–5 (December 1974), pp. 69–82.

20 *QR*, 116 (July–October 1864), pp. 507–8.

21 Letter to Sir John Herschel, 31 December 1864. Gernsheim, *Cameron*, p. 14.

22 P. G. Hamerton, *Thoughts About Art* (London 1875), pp. 64–5.

23 Lowes Dickinson, 'Modern Portrait Painting and Photography', excerpt from *The Contemporary Review*. *PN*, 10, 9 March 1866, pp. 111–2.

CHAPTER VI

1 Quoted: Michael Harvey, 'Ruskin the Pre-Raphaelites and Photography (Part 3) *BJP*, 120, 6 April 1973, p. 312.

2 Helmut Gernsheim, *Lewis Carroll Photographer*, revised ed. (New York 1969), p. 45.

3 *All the Year Round*, 14 (1865–6), 12 August 1865, pp. 60–2.

4 Charles H. Cameron, *Two Essays* (London 1835), pp. 28–9.

5 Henry Holiday, *Reminiscences of My Life* (London 1914), pp. 49, 165, 171–5, 244.

6 Gernsheim, *Carroll*, pp. 21, 60, 64–5, 79.

7 Roland Barthes, *Camera Lucida*, trans. Richard Howard (London 1982), p. 117.

CHAPTER VII

1 *PN*, 6, 20 June 1862, p. 293.

2 *PJ*, 4 (1857–8), 21 May 1858, p. 208.

3 *PN*, 7, 5 June 1863, p. 272.

4 *PJ*, 8 (1862–3), 15 January 1863, p. 203.

5 Baudelaire, reprinted in *Photography*, ed. Newhall, p. 112.
6 G. B. Shaw writing in *Wilson's Photographic Magazine* in 1909. Quoted: John Szarkowski, *The Photographer's Eye* (New York 1966), p. 23.
7 *PN*, 5, 7 June 1861, p. 269.
8 *Literary Gazette*. Quoted: *PJ*, 5 (1858–9), 21 January 1859, p. 147.
9 *PJ*, 10 (1865–6), 15 August 1865, p. 126.
10 *PJ*, 6 (1859–60), 16 January 1860, p. 143.
11 Rev. Charles Tennyson-Turner, brother of the poet. Gernsheim, *Cameron*, p. 48.
12 Letter to Tennyson, 1855. Gernsheim, *Cameron*, p. 22.
13 *BJP*, 18, 12 May 1871, p. 216.
14 *PN*, 5, 13 September 1861, p. 434.
15 As told to Anne Thackeray. Gernsheim, *Cameron*, p. 16.
16 P. H. Emerson in *Sun Artists*, ed. W. Arthur Boord (London 1891), p. 40.
17 *PJ*, 10 (1866–7), 15 January 1867, p. 193.
18 *AJ*, n.s.4 (1858), p. 121.
19 PJ, 6 (1859-60), pp. 201–3; H. P. Robinson, *Pictorial Effect in Photography* (London 1869), pp. 15, 192. (Like George Eliot *see* note 1 chapter II, Robinson is referring to 'Birds Nest' Hunt.)
20 W. M. Rossetti, *Fine Art, Chiefly Contemporary* (London and Cambridge 1867), p. 15.
21 *PN*, 16 (1872), pp. 80, 94, 105, 117 etc. For Stillman and photography, *see* Elizabeth Lindquist-Cock, 'Stillman, Ruskin & Rossetti: The Struggle Between Nature and Art', *History of Photography*, 3 (1979), pp. 1–14.
22 *PN*, 6, 20 June 1862, p. 293.
23 For Millais and Potter, *see* Harvey, 'Ruskin the Pre-Raphaelites and Photography', *BJP*, 120, pp. 313–14.
24 *Photographic Quarterly*, 3 (October 1891–July 1892), pp. 104–5.
25 *PN*, 9, 5 May 1865, pp. 205–6.
26 See Charles Rosen and Henri Zerner, *Romanticism and Realism* (London 1984), pp. 95–110.
27 Susan Sontag, *On Photography* (London 1978), p. 138.

Bibliography

Bennett, Mary, *Merseyside: Painters, People & Places*, 2 vols (Merseyside 1978)

Bloore, Carolyn, and Seiberling, Grace, *A Vision Exchanged* (London 1985).

Boord, W. Arthur (ed.), *Sun Artists* (London 1891).

Buckland, Gail, and Vaczek, Louis, *Travellers in Ancient Lands* (Boston 1981).

Cook, E. T., and Wedderburn, Alexander, *The Works of John Ruskin*, 39 vols (London 1903–12).

Darrah, William C., *The World of Stereographs* (Gettysburg, Penn. 1977).

Davis, William, and Smetham, Sarah (ed.), *Letters of James Smetham* (London and New York 1891).

Delamotte, Philip H. (ed.), *The Sunbeam: A Book of Photographs from Nature* (London 1859).

Fredeman, William E., *Pre-Raphaelitism: A Bibliocritical Study* (Cambridge, Mass. 1965).

Frith, Francis, *Egypt and Palestine* (London 1858–60).

George, H. B., *The Oberland and its Glaciers* (London 1866).

Gernsheim, Helmut, *Julia Margaret Cameron*, 2nd ed. (London 1975).

— *Lewis Carroll Photographer*, 2nd ed. (New York 1969).

Greenhill, Gillian B., 'The Death of Chatterton, or Photography and the Law', *History of Photography*, 5 (1981), pp. 199–205.

Hamerton, Philip Gilbert, *A Painters Camp in the Highlands, and Thoughts About Art*, 2 vols (London 1862).

Hannavy, John, *Roger Fenton* (London and Bedford 1975).

— *Thomas Keith's Scotland* (Edinburgh 1981).

Hanson, Brian, 'Ruskin's architectural drawing and the daguerreotype: Carrying off the Grand Canal', *The Architectural Review*, 169 (1981), pp. 104–9.

Harker, Margaret, *The Linked Ring* (London 1979).

Harvey, Michael, 'Ruskin the Pre-Raphaelites and Photography', *BJP*, 120 (1973), pp. 234–7, 268–72, 298–301, 312–15.

Hewison, Robert, *Ruskin and Venice* (London 1978).

Howitt, William and Mary, *Ruined Abbeys and Castles of Great Britain and Ireland*, 2 vols (London 1862, 1864).

Hunt, William Holman, *Pre-Raphaelitism and the Pre-Raphaelite Brotherhood*, 2 vols (London 1905).

Jay, Bill, 'Francis Bedford 1816–1894', *The Bulletin of the University of New Mexico*, 7 (1973), pp. 16–21.

Jones, Edgar Yoxall, *Father of Art Photography: O. G. Rejlander 1813–1875* (Newton Abbott 1973).

Knoepflmacher, U. C., and Tennyson G. B., *Nature and the Victorian Imagination* (Berkeley and Los Angeles 1977).

Leeds City Art Gallery, *Atkinson Grimshaw 1836–1893* (1979).

Lindquist-Cock, Elizabeth, 'Stillman, Ruskin & Rossetti: The Struggle Between Nature and Art', *History of Photography*, 3 (1979), pp. 1–14.

Maas, Jeremy, *The Victorian Art World in Photographs* (London 1984).

McCauley, Elizabeth Anne, 'Evasion in Victorian Landscape Photography: the Amateur Photographic Association Album', *Bulletin the University of New Mexico Art Museum*, 12 (1978–9), pp. 3–13.

Millais, John Guille, *The Life and Letters of Sir John Everett Millais*, 2 vols (London 1899).

Millard, Charles W., 'Julia Margaret Cameron and Tennyson's *Idylls of the King*', *Harvard Library Bulletin*, 21 (1973), pp. 187–201.

Mills, Ernestine (ed.), *The Life and Letters of Frederic Shields* (London 1912).

Onne, Eyal, *Photographic Heritage of the Holy Land* (Manchester 1980).

Pointon, Marcia, *William Dyce 1806–1864* (Oxford 1979).

Robinson, Henry Peach, *Pictorial Effect in Photography* (London 1869).

Rose, Andrea, *Pre-Raphaelite Portraits* (Oxford 1981).

Rossetti, William Michael, *Fine Art, Chiefly Contemporary* (London 1867).

— *The P. R. B. Journal* (Oxford 1975).

— *Ruskin: Rossetti: Pre-Raphaelitism* (London 1899).

Scharf, Aaron, *Art and Photography* (London 1968).

Seddon, John Pollard, *Memoir and Letters of the Late Thomas Seddon* (London 1858).

Smailes, Helen, 'A gentleman's exercise: Ronald Leslie Melville, 11th Earl of Leven, and the Amateur Photographic Association', *The Photographic Collector*, 3 (1982), pp. 262–93.

Spender, Stephen, 'The Pre-Raphaelite Literary Painters', *New Writing and Daylight*, 6 (1945), pp. 123–31.

Staley, Allen, *The Pre-Raphaelite Landscape* (Oxford 1973).

Stern, Jeffrey, 'Lewis Carroll, the Pre-Raphaelite: "Fainting in Coils"', in *Lewis Carroll Observed*, ed. Edward Guiliano (New York 1976).

Stevenson, Sara, 'Tableaux, Attitudes and Photography', in *Van Dyck in Check Trousers*, Scottish National Portrait Gallery (1978).

Surtees, Virginia, *The Paintings and Drawings of Dante Gabriel Rossetti 1828–1882*, 2 vols. (Oxford 1971).

— (ed.), *The Diaries of George Price Boyce* (Norwich 1980).

— (ed.), *The Diary of Ford Madox Brown* (New Haven and London 1981).

Tate Gallery, *The Pre-Raphaelites* (1984).

Taylor, John, 'Henry Peach Robinson and Victorian Theory', *History of Photography*, 3 (1979), pp. 295–303.

Taylor, Roger, *George Washington Wilson* (Aberdeen 1981).

Thompson, W. M., *The Holy Land* (London 1866).

Van Haaften, Julia, and White, Jon E. Manchip (ed.), *Egypt and the Holy Land in Historic Photographs: 77 Views by Francis Frith* (New York 1980).

Victoria and Albert Museum, *The Golden Age of British Photography 1839–1900* (1984).

Walton, Paul H., *The Drawings of John Ruskin* (Oxford 1972).

Watson, R. N., 'Art, Photography and John Ruskin', *BJP*, 91 (1944), pp. 82–3, 100–1, 118–19.

Weaver, Mike, *Julia Margaret Cameron 1815–1879* (Southampton 1984).

Welsh Arts Council, *John Dillwyn Llewelyn 1810–1882* (1980).

Index

Page numbers in *italic* type indicate caption pages.

Oscar Gustave Rejlander

John Dillwyn Llewelyn

Ronald Leslie Melville

John Brett

Roger Fenton